ALASKA

ALSO BY SPIKE WALKER

Working on the Edge

Nights of Ice

Coming Back Alive

ALASKA

TALES OF ADVENTURE
FROM THE LAST FRONTIER

Edited and with an Introduction by

SPIKE WALKER

ST. MARTIN'S GRIFFIN NEW YORK

*This book is dedicated to all the people who have come to Alaska
and been awed by it, from those first hardy humans
who ventured across the ice so long ago to the newest cheechako.*

ALASKA: TALES OF ADVENTURE FROM THE LAST FRONTIER.
Copyright © 2002 by Tekno Books, Spike Walker and Denise Little. All rights reserved.
Printed in the United States of America.
No part of this book may be used or reproduced in any manner whatsoever
without written permission except in the case of brief quotations
embodied in critical articles or reviews.
For information, address St. Martin's Press,
175 Fifth Avenue, New York, N.Y. 10010.

www.stmartins.com

Library of Congress Cataloging-in-Publication Data

Alaska : tales of adventure from the last frontier / edited and with an introduction by Spike
Walker.—1st ed.
    p. cm.
    ISBN 0-312-27562-5
1. Alaska—Description and travel—Anecdotes. 2. Alaska—History, Local—Anecdotes. 3.
Frontier and pioneer life—Alaska—Anecdotes. 4. Outdoor life—Alaska—Anecdotes. 5.
Pioneers—Alaska—Biography—Anecdotes. 6. Adventure and adventurers—Alaska—Biography—
Anecdotes. 7. Alaska—Biography—Anecdotes. I.
Walker, Spike.

F904.6 .A43 2002
979.8—dc21

2001048662

3   5   7   9   10   8   6   4   2

CONTENTS

Gold Rush

Natural Wonders

Black Gold

Modern Adventurers

Alaskan Voices

Don't Laugh . . . It's Not Funny!

PREFACE

Denise Little

Breathtakingly beautiful, harsh and unforgiving, Alaska is both a treasure and a testing ground; a tourist magnet and America's last great frontier. For those seeking the ultimate challenge, its vast frozen wastes in the depths of winter provide it. For those seeking unspoiled wilderness, the Denali mountain range, the open tundra, and the glaciers are magnificent retreats. For those seeking their fortunes, the lure of gold and oil and immense untouched reserves of nature's bounty call irresistibly. All of these people have compelling stories to tell of their adventures in Alaska.

From the day that men first set foot there, the region has inspired awe and terror in the hearts of those who measured themselves against the vastness. Nobody comes to the region and is untouched by it. Perhaps that is the reason that some of the most stirring nonfiction works put on paper in the last two hundred years have been about Alaska. The journals of the early explorers who first ventured into the Yukon resonate with the wonder they felt, just as the stories of those who test themselves against the wilderness today have the power to thrill us. This collection of writings about Alaska brings together the best of these works, from John Muir's first glimpse of Glacier Bay to tales from the recent runnings of the Iditarod. Together, they provide a portrait of a land bigger than life itself, the last great adventure: Alaska!

Introduction

Spike Walker

It's hard to know what to say about Alaska—the state is so big and beautiful, so diverse and wild, it's difficult to know where to begin. If I remain blind to her faults, it is because I'm in love with the place, having spent a good part of my life exploring her mountains and shores, her rivers, and back waters. Alaska is a remarkable place, and has something to offer everyone. I've been lucky enough to enjoy my share of its riches. At the outset, let me tell you about something I once witnessed in the southeast corner of the state. I think it goes a long way toward explaining Alaska's magic.

I had gone hiking along the shore of a pristine bay, packboard on my back, and was pausing to rest when a bald eagle swung in low over the platinum blue water. Ahead of it, I could see the back of a salmon that had risen recklessly to the surface. Bolting suddenly, the fish darted across the flat and otherwise undisturbed surface of the bay in quick, convoluted spasms. On it raced, driven, I suspected, by the mad, primal nature of the last days of its spawning cycle.

Unaware of the eagle's approach, the salmon dove, then rose again, leaping in a high, glittering arch out across the water. Twisting in mid-air, it flashed pink and silver in the warm September sun. Landing on its side, it slapped against the surface of the water with a resounding "Whack!" Then, as unpredictably as it had begun, the salmon paused, idling there on the surface with just the tip of its dorsal fin showing.

Guided by the keenest eyesight of any living creature, the eagle continued to close in on its prey. With its broad black wings outspread, it made several minute adjustments as it descended. The salmon was wallowing complacently on the surface when the eagle struck.

The instant the eagle's needle-sharp talons buried themselves into the flesh of the salmon's back, ten million years worth of evolution and instinct must have erupted in the predator's consciousness, all screaming that a serious error in judgment had been made. For just as the eagle came to play against the surprisingly unmanageable weight of the salmon, he crashed headlong into the salty bay water.

As its snowy head toppled forward, suddenly torn from the glory of flight into precarious balance on the back of a fish, it uttered a terrified, shrieking cackle, almost gull-like in tone. The salmon, weighing in at least ten pounds, bolted once again.

Unable to free its talons and release the fish until it reached dry land, the eagle found itself being carried on a wild side-saddle ride across the bay, all the while desperately and vainly trying to release the fish and fly free. The eagle's wings stretched nearly six feet wide when fully extended in the fight for its life, and the sound of the giant bird's struggle for freedom filled the air with a thick and furious flapping—one that resembled the noise of an umbrella being rapidly opened and closed.

If I could have reached the embattled pair, I would have killed the salmon and saved the eagle. For the salmon would only survive a few more days, regardless of who proved victorious. As soon as it finished its spawning run, it would die, and, likely as not, have its bones picked clean by a roving bear, while the beautiful bird of prey, now tiring so quickly before my eyes, might have survived another decade or more, wild and free. But the fish and the eagle were too far out on the bay, and I was alone, afoot, and ashore.

With each beat of its wings, the eagle became more waterlogged, heavier, and less able to escape from its fate. In the end, with its white crown of feathers matted against its head and neck, it looked forlorn and beaten, like a chicken caught in a rainstorm.

Suddenly, the salmon dove, dragging the frantically struggling bird beneath the surface with it. Then I caught sight of the eagle's white head streaking through the depths, and the churning trail of the surface currents as the salmon carried the eagle into deeper waters. It was clear that, even submerged, the eagle was still attempting to fly.

Perhaps it was nature's way of showing her impartiality, but in only seconds the patch of water where the salmon and the eagle had crossed paths grew motionless once again, so calm that the spruce trees lining the shoreline reflected off the water's mirror-like surface with perfect clarity.

In the distance, I could hear the irregular impacts of countless other salmon reveling in their last brief moments of glory before they departed from this world. Looking far out across the water, I caught the silvery, wet glints of light reflecting off other salmon as they leaped and turned in the afternoon sun.

I happened upon this scene in my first summer in Alaska, back in 1977, in a place called Rowan Bay on Kuiu (you pronounce that "Q-E-U") Island in the southeastern panhandle of the state. I'd found work in a logging camp there, and after twenty-six straight days of hard labor, had taken some time off to backpack into the head of the bay for several days to fish, read, and spend some time alone. That night, as I sat by my campfire and studied the brilliant spread of stars overhead, the image of the fateful encounter between eagle and salmon, in which both the predator and the prey had perished, lingered on in my mind.

Alaska has changed a bit since then, though not as much as some would tell you. The majority of logging camps are long gone, the clear-cut scars they left behind replanted and often invisible without close inspection. The eagles and fish, as well as wolves and bears, still roam the wilderness. Today, 100 million acres of land (an area roughly the size of California) in Alaska have been set aside in the form of parks, national monuments, and wilderness preserves. The 200 miles of shoreline in Prince William Sound that was once awash in Exxon crude oil once again supports a normal population of bears and bald eagles. Men have made their mark on the wilderness here, but Alaska has proven itself to be both big enough and vital enough to fight back.

For example, the southeast Alaskan panhandle where the eagle and salmon battled is an archipelago of islands and sea four hundred miles long and a hundred miles wide. Though small by Alaska's standards, it contains America's largest national forest, the 20 million acre Tongass National Forest, a place rich in natural beauty and wildlife. This one section in Alaska is home to no less than 35,000 bald eagles, while the sea that wanders among its thousands of islands supports the largest concentration of humpback whales on earth. During the summer of 2000, when some 350 million salmon returned to streams throughout Alaska to spawn, roughly 150 million of them came back to southeast Alaska.

But statistics don't even begin to convey the vast untouched beauty and spiritual essence of Alaska. To understand that, you need to experience the land and its wonder firsthand. And not just the cities and the tourist haunts. Visitors can best discover the real Alaska by venturing into its vast, uncharted wilderness. For it is to those who venture off the beaten path that Alaska will most often reveal her true self. Whether it's a mountain climber scaling the 20,000-foot-high Mount McKinley, the backpacker hiking north through the Brooks range and on to the edge of the Arctic Ocean, the canoeist paddling down one of the state's mighty rivers—the fabled Yukon, the Kuskokwim, or the Stikine—or the kayaker picking a way along some tiny portion of the state's 33,000 miles of wilderness shoreline, those who venture forth often have unforgettable experiences and return home with memories that will forever remain their own.

For the young at heart (and fit of body), I can personally attest that the forty-mile-long four-day hike over the Chilkoot Pass is a worthy challenge, one that carries the hiker along the very footsteps of those gold-crazed fortune hunters of 1897. The trail begins at the edge of the sea, just outside of Skagway, and ends where the Yukon River begins, at Lake Bennett. The river travels on for 2,000 miles, growing steadily in size, twisting its way through the heart of the Klondike gold fields near Dawson in Canada's Yukon Territory, before reaching Alaska.

Roughly a thousand miles downstream from Lake Bennett, the Yukon's silt-laden waters flow through Alaska's interior, winding back and forth much the way the Mississippi does, snaking lazily along in a broad swath of muddy brown water. Near Fort Yukon, the river flows briefly north of the Arctic Circle, meandering through a broad floodplain of islands occupied by bears, and a seemingly endless maze of channels teeming with beaver, martin, moose, and every imaginable kind of waterfowl. This swampland, known as the Yukon Flats, is no less than 190 miles long and is more than 10 miles wide in places.

Once, during a month-long solo canoe trip I made down the Yukon, I took what looked to be a clever shortcut, veering into a new channel that had managed to force its way inside a forested point of land in that wild place. I'd only just entered the inviting detour when I felt the belly of my canoe begin rubbing bottom. At that moment, on the river bank a few feet away from me, a large brown bear rose up out of the brush, nearly close enough for me to reach out and touch him. Balanced on its hind legs, the bear was a good eight feet tall. And, standing on the five-foot-high embankment, it towered over me, peering curiously down at me and my fiberglass canoe, its nostrils flaring as wide as shotgun barrels, moving in and out as it sifted the air for the scent of me. Poised there on the riverbank, its head fully twelve feet above me, the bear looked as wide as a dump truck and as tall as a totem pole.

With my heart beating like a jackhammer, I pulled on the paddle so hard that I could hear its sturdy wood composition crack under the strain. Seconds later, I passed out into the main branch of the river unscathed, cursing my cleverness, and swearing off all future short cuts absolutely, completely, and once-and-for-all-forever. But in retrospect, it's a fabulous memory.

Happily, most natural encounters in Alaska are far less harrowing. Long-time residents I've met are more likely to relate memories of the simple things that life in Alaska has given them, like gardens that produce vegetables that grow like nowhere else in the world in the twenty-two hours of summer sunlight every day, of freezers full of halibut, salmon, and trout, along with the memories of the fishing trips that secured them, of the sight of moose grazing through their back yards, of traveling to and from work each day on everything from canoes to snowmobiles to snowshoes. In the rarified air of the northern sky, they enjoy watching the night sky brilliant with the light of millions of stars, and can often see the transcendent light show of the Aurora Borealis, the Northern Lights, dancing across the heavens in rich iridescent colors, like rainbows shattering in space.

Alaskans have a proud tradition of hard work and self-sufficiency. And yet they also share a common bond, a kind of unwritten code—the commitment to look after their neighbors. Even in largely homogenized Anchorage, where roughly half of the state's 600,000 people reside, the pioneer spirit remains strong. Several winters ago, when my loaner car broke down on the outskirts of the city, the first four cars that passed me all stopped and their occupants immediately offered their help. No doubt they all knew the basic fact of life in the Big Bear State—that even in these modern times, frostbite and death from hypothermia are still the most common ways to be injured or killed in Alaska. Standing together in the arctic cold, the steam from our breath trailing off into the frigid wind, they made my problem theirs.

Like the colorful and mysterious Aurora Borealis, Alaska offers those who venture there many seasonal wonders. For instance, each spring in Sitka Sound, herring fish arrive in such numbers that they turn the waters there white with the business of spawning. Recently, during just such an event, I went for a night hike south (more or less) from town there, walking along the winding waterfront, past the Sheldon Jackson College and the picturesque monument to James A. Michener, who'd lived and worked in Sitka for several years as he researched and wrote his epic novel *Alaska*.

The night was crisp and cool, bright with the light from a moon that was nearly full, the landscape around me pleasantly gleaming in the silvery light. As I walked along the water's edge, I noticed the curious appearance of the surf washing against the beach. The waves spilling ashore were milk white and glowing, lit from within by tiny phosphorescent specks of algae. The overall effect was at once beautiful and surreal—in the silvery white waves, the tumbling particles left tracer-trails of light in their wake, like fireflies tumbling in the surf. It was a perfect Alaskan moment.

Less than a hundred miles away, situated on the banks of the Wrangell Narrows, is the Norwegian-built fishing port of Petersburg, a place that has captured my heart. A more lovely or captivating seaport you will not find. From the deck of a ship coming or going from there, one can see a magnificent rock in the distance—the Devil's Thumb—and the cleanly painted canneries mounted over the tidelands on stilt-like pilings nearby.

Over the years, my travels always seem to draw me back, for it is here, in winter, that the icebergs from the La Conte Glacier sometimes drift into the narrows and along the waterfront, and black bears wander into town and have to be driven off before they help themselves to the contents of the nearest kitchen, and where snowflakes as big as silver dollars fall from the sky.

Each summer, as the salmon season gets underway, the town's main street, which skirts "cannery row," echoes with the robust sounds of trucks carrying loads of crewmen, gear, and foodstuffs to wherever they are needed; the growl of seine boats maneuvering for dock space; the raucous sound of laughter and music spilling from the bars; the pleading cry of seagulls; and the shrill toot of whistles marking yet another shift change at one of the local canneries.

This is also the season when the seabirds arrive, pausing long enough in their migratory odyssey to feed and play in the tidelands across the channel. I can remember watching them swarming across the bright green marsh grasses and kelp of those tidelands in countless numbers, their flashing white forms banking sharply against the dark backdrop of the spruce forest, thousands and thousands of seabirds in fight, all changing directions as one, navigating in lovely, swirling patterns of in-flight precision.

I remember the blue skies and the bold unblemished green of the forest clinging to the steep sides of Petersburg Mountain, and my satisfying life laboring, once again, as a deckhand (during the summers of 1995 and 1996) living and working aboard the one-hundred-foot salmon packer *Theresa Marie.*

The incredible beauty I've tried to share with you in these passages is not at all uncommon in Alaska. And as you read the selections in this book—from Jack London's fact-based story of a miner struggling against the cold, to the careful wilderness descriptions written by naturalist John Muir, to the stories of Iditarod sled dog racers who have endured the brutal 1,100 mile run to commemorate the men who once carried urgently needed medical supplies from Anchorage to Nome and saved the city, to the tales of today's commercial fishermen and the modern-day settlers who still come to Alaska to carve out new beginnings—you'll get a sense of the kinds of authentic adventures you can find here. It is my hope, therefore, that you might draw near to these vignettes of Alaskan life, both past and present, and savor for yourselves a portion of the banquet that is Alaska.

LIVING ON THE EDGE

ONE OF ALASKA'S greatest draws is also one of its most treacherous drawbacks. Alaska is a place where people come to test their courage and stamina against something dangerous, even deadly. They live on the edge, pushing themselves to the limit, whether it's to find their fortunes or merely to see if they are strong enough to take what nature can dish out. In these harrowing true tales of survival, Alaska proves that while people may challenge her, they can never tame her.

Excerpt from *Nights of Ice*

SPIKE WALKER

LOST AND ADRIFT

W hite, with green trim, the fishing vessel *Cloverleaf* stretched just sixty-three feet from bow to stern. Built originally in Astoria, Oregon, she was small by Alaskan standards—"just an old wooden whore" of a scow, Rick Laws recalled, when he and a friend, Dan Nelson (affectionately known as "Slippery Dan"), went to work rebuilding her. The overhaul quickly became a love-hate affair but with a tremendous amount of time, effort, and money, they were eventually able to restore her.

Having rejuvenated her into a first-class little shrimp boat, they fished the *Cloverleaf* hard. And in the years to come she proved to be a dependable and productive vessel, a midsized highliner of sorts.

Each winter, before the shrimp season began, Laws and his crew would use their trawl net to drag up tons of cod and other fish from the bottom and sell them as bait to tanner crab fishermen who worked the shores all along Kodiak Island. He and his two-man crew had managed to carve out a pretty good living for themselves.

Depending upon the season, those journeys took them over on the Alaska mainland, and even as far west as Dutch Harbor in the Aleutians. The Alaskan mainland had always been a vast wilderness country, and it was while traversing the hundreds and hundreds of miles of wilderness shores between Kodiak and Dutch Harbor that the *Cloverleaf* was occasionally pushed to the limits of her capacity. Many of the bays in which the *Cloverleaf* rendezvoused with the crab boats and delivered her fresh hold of hanging bait were uncharted, and remain uncharted to this day.

The *Cloverleaf* had a radar that worked "most of the time," and a good compass. But she had no loran, no running lights, and no auxiliary engine. In favorable weather, she topped out at six knots.

During the winter, travel along the Alaskan mainland often includes cruel and extended blasts of arctic weather. Heavy icing conditions are common. And then, with so little modern electronic navigational equipment on board, piloting the *Cloverleaf* often became a matter of guesswork, improvisation, and fly-by-the-seat-of-one's-pants navigation.

During the winter of 1980, Rick Laws faced just such a situation. He had received word that a fleet of crab boats was fishing for tanner crab in the waters around Sutwik Island, down off the Alaskan mainland. Normally, Laws knew, they wouldn't run that far. But there were a lot of crab boats fishing in the area, and they'd probably welcome his business. Once there, he knew they could anchor up on the lee side of the island and ride out even the worst of weather. The *Cloverleaf* had a nice load of bottom fish on board, so he thought, Well, let's take it to market. It would be a fine payday if everything went as planned.

It was dark when Laws motored past Cape Alitak on the south end of Kodiak Island and out onto the unpredictable waters of Shelikof Strait. The waves were moderate, the winds steady.

It was not until they had moved into that huge triangular body of sea stretching from Cape Alitak to the Semidid Islands and west to Sutwik Island that the situation grew extreme. In no time, it seemed, the wind stiffened sharply and tall seas arose. The *Cloverleaf* began to leap and roll. As they drew closer to the Alaskan mainland, the temperature dropped abruptly. And in the late-evening light, a heavy snowfall rolled in over them, shutting down visibility and leaving them in whiteout conditions. Now forty-knot winds blew a blizzard of snow in blinding slants across the heaving gray face of the sea.

When Rick Laws awoke to relieve Crewman Kim Handland, one of his two deckhands, from his watch, it was pitch black outside and the seas were "sloppy as all hell." There was no way to illuminate the darkness, as the *Cloverleaf* had no running lights. "Basically she just had a hull and one old screaming Jimmy," Laws recalls, referring to the vessel's diesel engine.

With darkness closing all around, Rick Laws considered the building sea and the blizzard of wind-whipped snow. Outside, the tall figures of the ocean waves, some fifteen feet high and more, began lumbering out of the gray-black night like mammoth shadows. They crashed repeatedly across the *Cloverleaf*'s back deck, flooding around the wheelhouse itself and spilling over the side.

Laws came awake fast now. He gulped coffee and began mentally updating his position. He had a good depth finder in working order and a complete array of marine maps of the area, so in theory he'd be able to use both in order to help him find his position. In addition, the boat's travel time, compass reading, and estimated speed could all be used to help fix the *Cloverleaf*'s position.

With the help of a good meter, a chart, a compass, and the moody output of a very old Decca radar system, Laws had always been able to find his way. He often dryly referred to it as his own style of "dead reckoning."

Laws remained alone at the helm through the long, battering night. Then at about dawn, he looked out on the back deck and noticed that part of a pile of net stored there was beginning to work itself loose.

"Hey, guys," he called to his crew in their bunks below. "You need to get up and tie down the net that came loose on the back deck."

As always, crewmen Wink Cissel and Kim Handland rose without complaint. When they had dressed, Laws slowed the *Cloverleaf* and turned her bow into the oncoming seas.

It was then that Laws sensed danger. Idling into the dark green slopes of the approaching waves the crew noticed it, too. Normally quick to respond, the *Cloverleaf* now felt slow and cumbersome. As he stood at the controls, Laws noticed with growing concern that each time he turned the wheel, the ship would respond only after a lengthy delay.

Her sluggish feel wasn't the only thing that concerned Laws and his crew. The *Cloverleaf* was squatting heavily in the water. And each time a wave broke onto her deck, the deck remained awash far too long. It was not draining at the rate it always had. The *Cloverleaf* moved now in slow side-to-side motions. It was clear that she was having trouble recovering.

Off and on all night, Laws had been chatting over the marine radio set with Bert Parker, owner and skipper of the ninety-one-foot crab boat *Amber Dawn*. Laws now made a hurried call.

"Bert, I don't know," he said in a worried voice. "This thing's feeling awful heavy and the decks aren't clearing very fast." He paused. "You better stay on the air, because this just doesn't feel right. The seas are breaking over my decks."

Bert Parker knew Laws was in trouble. He could hear the tone of alarm building in his voice, and he agreed to stand by on his radio.

Then, as Laws studied his radar screen, he thought he could make out land in the distance. A quick calculation told him he was looking at the tip of Sutwik Island. Believing that he was nearing the island, Laws once again called his friend.

"Bert, where's a good place around the island there to get out of this blow?"

Bert Parker was quick to respond. "Yah, just go ahead and come on in," he said encouragingly. "Stay about a mile off the tip of Sutwik and come on around and get in the lee of the island here. But I'd get your survival suits out and put them someplace where you can get to them quickly," he warned. "I'll be standing by here."

Laws turned and yelled to one of his crew members. "Wink! Run down in the engine room and check it out! See if there's any water in there!"

Wink Cissel leapt to the task and soon returned with good news. "Nope, engine room's dry! Everything's fine!"

Still Rick Laws didn't like what he saw outside. He rushed to call Parker back. "Bert, she just doesn't seem to be able to shake the water," he radioed. "I can't get her to come up. The deck won't clear and she feels real sluggish."

"Shit! You guys better get into your survival suits," warned Parker.

Turning to his crew, Laws yelled, "Everybody get your survival suits out and put them on!"

The suits were stowed close by in the galley for easy access. Laws remained at the wheel. In only the few seconds it took to shake the suits out of their bags, Laws felt himself losing control of the *Cloverleaf*. He grabbed the engine throttle and opened up the main engine, but the *Cloverleaf* refused to respond.

"Holy shit!" yelled Laws.

He grabbed the radio mike and called Bert Parker. "We're in trouble here! I believe we're about thirteen miles off the northern tip of Sutwik Island," he announced, yet even as he spoke, he knew this was only guesswork. The *Cloverleaf*'s pitiful radar system could not reach over to the Alaskan mainland. He couldn't even be sure it was Sutwik Island he was heading for. Perhaps it was the Semidis. But without another reference point, Laws had no way to get a triangulation and pinpoint his exact position.

"Yah, but where?" shot back Parker in frustration.

"I don't know!" shouted Laws as he struggled to pull on his survival suit. Just then, he felt the *Cloverleaf* begin to roll. Wink Cissel stuck his head in the back door and screamed, "Rick! Get out of there!"

Looking out the back door of the vessel he had come to depend upon for so long, Rick Laws took in what seemed an impossible vision. The stern of the *Cloverleaf* had sunk out of sight. Not a single deck plank remained visible. Her entire stern deck was submerged. And now a sprawling body of heaving seawater stretched out in every direction before lost to the slanting, gray-white oblivion of a blizzard snow.

Damn! thought Laws, fighting the urge to run. I've got to let someone know where we are!

Suddenly, the *Cloverleaf* rolled completely on her starboard side. As the vessel went over, Laws yelled into the mike; "Mayday! Mayday! Mayday! Hey, Bert! You guys better get out here, 'cause she's going down!"

In the next instant, Laws found himself tossed across the room. He landed on top of the radar set. In the inverted space of the wheelhouse, the port-side door hung above him. He still couldn't believe what was happening.

Holy shit! he said to himself. I gotta get the hell out of here!

He dropped the mike and began climbing up the face of the instrument panel. He ascended toward the rectangular space of gray light overhead. Once there, he pushed open the horizontal form of the wheelhouse door. Then he placed his hands on either side of the doorway, hoisting himself up through the rectangular space and out onto the side of the wheelhouse cabin, as if he were climbing into an attic space.

Back aboard the *Amber Dawn*, skipper Bert Parker could feel his blood pressure soar.

"Hold on! And stay together!" he shouted into his mike. "I'm coming full bore toward yah, Rick!"

When he received no reply, Parker rushed to notify the U.S. Coast Guard base in Kodiak.

"Mayday! Mayday!" he called over the far-reaching marine-band radio for the entire Alaskan fleet to hear. "This is the fishing vessel *Amber Dawn*, WTP-three nine zero five. I just got a Mayday from the fishing vessel *Cloverleaf!*" Then, locating the *Cloverleaf*'s last tentative position on his map, Parker quickly gave the Coast Guard his current loran readings and told them the area from which the *Cloverleaf* was believed to have last transmitted.

Rick Laws found himself standing on the side of the *Cloverleaf*'s wheelhouse. The circumstances he and his crew faced now seemed unreal, even fantastic. As he struggled to keep his balance, the ship he had rebuilt, piloted, and trusted for so long foundered beneath his feet.

And with nearly three-quarters of the vessel already under water, Laws rushed to finish pulling on his survival suit. Even as he zipped the final chin flap in place, seawater rose above his waist. Not five seconds later, he felt himself float free of the hull as the *Cloverleaf* sank out from under him.

The ship went down in an eerie silence. Small pockets of air boiled silently on the surface. For a space of time, Laws could see clearly into the depths. He could look directly down at the *Cloverleaf*. He would remember forever the vision of her sinking. As the boat descended farther into the deepwater currents below, she remained frozen in the exact horizontal position she had assumed on the surface: on her starboard side, her bow raised slightly.

The *Cloverleaf* descended with her interior lights on. Laws could see the entire boat at once now. And as she sank, he took in the strangeness of the image below. Her wheelhouse was still illuminated, and he could see directly into its submerged and flooded interior through her square-framed windows—windows that were now blazing with a warm, golden light.

Laws was amazed at how quickly her sixty-three-foot body sank and how minuscule she eventually became, free-falling into the depths far below. Long after he lost sight of the vessel itself, he could make out the tiny and yet distinct yellow squares of light still glowing against the greenish black back-drop of sea space.

"Hey, Laws!" shouted someone close by in the water. It was Kim Handland, the youngest crewman on board; his voice sounded shaky and disheartened. "I forgot my suit!"

The skipper's heart fell. The young deckhand had panicked and left his only hope for survival behind inside the boat.

"Hold on!" Laws hollered back.

Though only minutes had passed, he could see that Kim was already having difficulty staying afloat. The young man couldn't seem to catch his breath.

Laws swam over to Kim and grabbed him. "I've got you, man! I'll hold you," he assured his friend.

Yet secretly, Laws held out little hope. *There's no way,* he thought as he held on to the cold-ravaged crewman. *There's no way I'm going to be able to get him out of this alive.*

Laws knew there was an inflatable collar pillow built into the vest of his survival suit somewhere. But the two men were struggling mightily just to remain afloat, and Laws decided against trying to inflate it.

In but a few short minutes, Kim grew so numb in the 38°F seas that he could no longer move his legs or his arms. And a howling wind of approximately fifty knots drenched the two with an icy, stinging spray.

Locked rigidly in his skipper's arms, Kim could only try to remain afloat as long as possible. He stared into Laws's face as they drifted down through the deep wave valleys and then over the tall wind-whipped crests.

Rick Laws's arms ached from the life-and-death effort to carry his friend. The aching in his upper body gradually went beyond fatigue, passing into a kind of pain-racked numbness. Now it took everything he had to hold on to his helpless companion and keep them both afloat. It amazed Laws how quickly immersion in the cold water had rendered the young man completely immobile. The wintery Gulf of Alaska water had "sucked the strength right out of him."

The last words Kim spoke were calm and matter-of-fact. "I can't move. I can't feel," he said with resignation.

Rick Laws looked into his face. "Don't worry, Kim. I'll hold you" he said.

But even as he spoke, Laws felt his grip beginning to fail him. He knew then he wouldn't be able to hold on to Kim much longer. "Oh dear God," he prayed. Kim Handland had worked for Laws since he had gotten out of the Coast Guard. He was a hard worker, a nice, quiet, and dependable youngster with as fine a combination of personality traits as one could hope to find in any man.

Near the end, Kim did not seem to be breathing. He uttered no words. His body drifted alongside Laws apparently void of feeling. And as they passed together through the icy flood of sea and spray, he grew completely rigid.

Laws could feel himself gasping for air as he struggled against exhaustion. He could see no sign of life coming from Kim—not a word, not a sound, not a movement. Nothing except, that is, for the young man's eyes. They remained wide open, fixed on Laws through the entire ordeal.

When an exceptionally large wave broke over the two, Kim's rigid body was torn from Rick Laws's weary grasp, and he immediately began to sink. Laws knew it would be impossible to dive in the survival suit he was wearing. Besides, he was far too fatigued even to attempt it. Laws could only watch as the body of his friend drifted toward the bottom, a thousand feet below. But the image that would remain forever etched in the skipper's mind was that of Kim's frozen gaze staring back at him as the young man slipped into the dark green depths below.

Now, as Rick Laws drifted over the steep and building storm waves, he was struck by a wrenching sense of loneliness. He'd fought hard to save the man's life, and the sudden loss left him dazed and confused.

Winded from the effort, stunned by the outcome, and chilled by the cold pressing in on him, Laws knew he had to rest. He squinted against the blinding sea spray and managed to locate the black inflator hose attached to his vest. He placed the hose end against his lips and blew. The vest billowed around his neck in the shape of a circular pillow. Even as he blew, he could feel his need to struggle easing as the buoyant force of the air bag began to lift and carry him.

Laws felt a degree of satisfaction at the result. He tightened the seal cap down over the end of the inflator hose. All right, he said to himself with renewed hope. This thing just may work. But no sooner had he leaned back to relax and gather himself than the entire inflator hose unit exploded from his vest. With a hiss, the defective unit launched itself into the air like a missile. The vest around his neck deflated suddenly and completely.

Laws realized angrily that now all he had left was his own power: He would have to keep treading water if he was to remain afloat—and alive.

In launching his search from aboard the *Amber Dawn*, skipper Bert Parker went over and over his final conversations with Rick Laws. When Laws had last called him, he had reported that he could see a landmass he believed to be Sutwik Island. Laws had sounded "reasonably close" to Sutwik, Parker figured, but there was no way to know for sure.

Five crab boats immediately joined Parker in his search effort, which would continue throughout that first day and on into the night. "It was blowing sixty out, with big running seas," Parker recalls. "There were five or six boats involved in the search. And, oh, man, did we ever get our butts kicked!"

Parker felt emptied by the news of his missing friend and crew, and he stood at the wheel through the long hours ahead, refusing all offers to spell him. Crowded into the wheelhouse of the *Amber Dawn*, every crewman on board scanned the sea for signs of wreckage or life. But throughout the long day and well into the night, a blinding curtain of blizzard snow swirled across the watery landscape of broad, rugged waves, making visibility all but impossible and diminishing the chances of locating anyone still afloat.

That night, the outdoor temperatures fell well below freezing and ice began to coat the deck and superstructure of the *Amber Dawn* and the other crab boats involved in the search. But Parker and his fellow skippers continued their efforts.

Parker pounded his way over and through the unrelenting storm waves for more than twenty-four hours. His weary eyes scrutinized the face of each new wave as it appeared out of the gray-black depth of blizzard storm. He searched the offshore waters around Sutwik Island for a distance of more than fifteen miles, then hunted downwind from the nearest edge of the island for another twenty miles. But he found nothing.

Now as he drifted and struggled to remain afloat, Rick Laws found himself replaying the last few hours in his mind. He could recall no major mistake, nothing he had done wrong that could have led to this. In prep for running, the crew of the *Cloverleaf* had battened down her hatches, thrown a tarp over her back tank, tied and retied everything that could move in place, and lashed it all down for traveling. Then they began taking turns at the wheel. As always, Laws rotated the men: Too long alone at the helm and any deckhand might fall asleep on duty. (On the other hand, too short a wheel watch would mean that neither of the other two crewmen could get any sleep.)

Rick Laws was six one, weighed a solid 190 pounds, and sported a full black beard and a head of curly black hair. A natural athlete, he had competed as a long-distance runner.

Laws and crewman Wink Cissel had attended rival high schools down in the Sonoma wine country of northern California. At six four and 175 pounds, Wink Cissel was tall and lanky and as lean as iron. Laws both loved and respected the man. "He could work forever at his own pace," recalls Laws. "And he was no complainer." Some guys have a natural talent for telling a story. Sit old Wink down on the waterfront sipping a couple of brewskies, and pretty soon there'd be six or eight guys standing around listening to him spin a yarn. "He was a natural for that. He could hold court just about anywhere."

Rick Laws had originally come to Alaska in 1975 to photograph Wink Cissel's wedding, then ended up staying in Kodiak when he got a job sharpening J-hooks aboard an old halibut schooner.

Laws built a small cabin on a corner of Wink Cissel's property and lived there while he worked with Cissel building a house overlooking Monaska Bay. Each morning before the work began, Rick Laws would hike up the hill to have coffee and breakfast with Cissel and his wife, Janet, and their family. And Wink's kids always greeted him as part of the family, calling out, "Uncle Rick! It's Uncle Rick!" whenever he appeared.

After the *Cloverleaf* sank, Laws had briefly caught sight of Wink "three or four wave sets" in the distance. Laws had tried to scream, "Are you okay?" But the waves were tall and the wave valleys wide "and the wind was just howling." Then Laws caught sight of Cissel again as he drifted over the top of a wave. He had his hood up and his flotation device inflated. "He was lying back in the water like a man riding an easy chair," Laws recalls.

Rick waved. Then, as Wink drifted over the top of another large wave, he signaled Laws back with an encouraging "thumbs-up" sign. Rick Laws never saw his friend alive again.

Up until that time, Laws had been concerned only with the welfare of his friend. He hadn't had much time to worry about himself. He'd been safely locked in that focus, and he had found comfort there. But Kim had died. And his good friend Wink had drifted away into the blizzard and seas. And when his own inflatable survival suit vest failed him, Law's mind raced to deal with a new and monstrous reality.

Holy God, I'm totally alone out here! he thought. It was a sickening and frightful aloneness, the "most alone" he could ever imagine one could be. He was plagued by bouts of sadness over his friends, by worry and thoughts of doom. He was forced to admit to himself, Hey, I may not get out of this damned situation alive!

The thought of never seeing his mother and father again wore at him. His mind flashed to his father. He could picture him sitting on the back deck on a hot and sunny California afternoon with his shirt off, holding a cold bottle of Michelob in his hand and spouting funny stories to the men working in the stables.

Then, in the darkness, Laws somehow managed to spy the shadow of a log drifting past. New life shot through him. If I can get on that, I'll make it, he thought. Though exhausted, he "swam and swam and struggled like hell to get over the seas" to the log. But when he caught up with it, he was discouraged to find it was almost no help at all. Every time he tried to lean on the log or climb atop it, the log rolled. He had to keep treading water even to hold on to one end of it.

So engrossed was Rick Laws in his minute-to-minute struggle to survive that he had lost all sense of time. The short, dull gray durations of winter had come and gone, daylight and now darkness surrounded him. It was near midnight (more than sixteen hours after the *Cloverleaf* had sunk), that Laws felt the most hopeless. And as the cold and waves continued to bombard him, he felt almost undone by the savage bouts of hunger, thirst, and exhaustion that hounded him.

At one point during the night, a sooty sheerwater bird landed on the opposite end of the log from him. You know, thought Laws, if I can just get ahold of that bugger, I'm going to rip its head off, eat its heart, and drink its blood. The dark outline of the bird resting on the log seemed to indicate it was sleeping. In the late-night darkness, with the constant commotion of water lapping over the log, Laws figured he had a good chance of sneaking up on the bird.

Carefully, Laws made his way along the back of the log. He had maneuvered only halfway down its length when the bird leapt into the air and disappeared. Laws cringed, discouraged and almost beyond hope. Oh man, he thought dejectedly, that bird might have made the difference.

Ever since Kim had died, many of the beliefs to which Rick Laws had always held fast had undergone an onslaught of change. Confronted with a life-and-death need to adapt, Laws found himself abandoning the old for the new, shedding past alliances suddenly and completely. And in the long, cold, body-numbing hours of struggle and suffering ahead, Laws would often be struck by a sense of wonder at the exceptional nature of thought and emotion that came to him.

Already, his mind had undergone several transformations. Getting through the initial denial was one: He had been unable to accept what was happening. His first thought when he had hit the water and was left to drift in that wilderness of surrounding sea was Damn, I'm sure going to miss my truck! It wasn't until he saw Kim Handland drifting toward the bottom that he came to terms with the truth. In accepting the death of his crewmate, he had also forced himself to acknowledge the possibility that he, too, might die. And in doing so, he had faced the primitive and brutal nature of his struggle.

He saw then that he was utterly alone. Fear was another stage: Finding himself adrift in the night in a haunting black chamber of shadows and sea was a frightful experience. Yet during that time, Rick Laws came to a gritty decision: He would keep himself afloat and do battle with whatever came his way. He would assume the entire responsibility for his survival.

It was fortunate that Laws came so quickly to such a conclusion. For all that night, he fought against the loss of strength as the icy seawater enveloped him and tried to sap his body heat. His belly gnawed with insidious bouts of hunger and thirst. Laws felt himself pass through entirely new thresholds: The racking pain and numbing cold were still there, but once he'd made his decision to fight they paled alongside his fresh desire to remain upright and alive.

Ideally, when a boat sank, the crewmen on board zipped up their suits, and someone passing nearby came immediately to rescue them. But Laws knew it seldom happened that way. With the huge expanse of Alaska's wilderness waters totaling well over a million square miles, there was always the possibility that no one would find him. Not ever. The older-model survival suit Laws wore wasn't designed for long periods in the water. In fact, his suit was leaking all over. Small leaks had started in the crotch area and the wrists. And he could feel icy rivelets of seawater seeping in around the rim of the hood encircling his face.

That night, Laws spotted the mast lights of numerous crab boats searching back and forth across the seas all around him. He watched them draw "closer and closer" and thought to himself, There's a chance! At least somebody knows I'm out here.

Laws could see their search lights rising and falling off in the darkness as their boats pounded their way through the lumbering seas. The boats zigzagged sharply back and forth across the water. He could tell they were working a grid pattern.

Suddenly, Laws remembered a small reflective strip sewn into the sleeve of his survival suit. And as the ships drew ever closer, he raised his arm and began to wave it wildly through the air, back and forth overhead.

"Oh man—you guys! Come on! Come on!" he pleaded, yelling into the wet night air.

Each time he drifted over one of the fifteen-foot wave crests, Laws would kick hard, rise far into the night, and wave his reflective strip.

Not long after that, he watched in utter disbelief as the entire crab fleet shut off its mast lights, turned around, and steamed away into the night.

"Oh, God! I'm not going to make it! I'm a dead man!" Laws shouted after them.

He knew now the odds of surviving his ordeal had just dropped to "near zero." Regardless, he refused to quit. The thought of breathing seawater filled him with a sickening fear, and once again he renewed his vows to himself. He resolved to fight to the end, to do everything he could to remain alive, to keep breathing air for as long as he was physically able. He would never give up!

It was perhaps 3:00 A.M. that night when Rick Laws had the vision. It came in the form of a "huge black sailing ship." The gleaming vessel sailed out of the obscurity of the night as if on a mission, and cut a direct course toward Laws. It was an eighteenth-century sailing ship. But the strangest thing about it was her color. Her hull and her billowing sails, too, were all jet black, an oily black. The ship bore down on Laws, glistening in the night as she came. And every part of her shone with the rich blue-black gleam of gunmetal.

"It's real," said Laws, astonished.

As the ship drew near, the notion struck him that if he could climb aboard the vessel, he'd know "complete comfort." Laws felt he was being given a choice. He could continue on with his painful struggle, or he could die. He viewed the crucial decision as a "crossover."

At that moment, an electrical charge shot through the length of Laws's body. The hackles on his back went up, and without hesitation, he spoke aloud to the vision. "No! Wait a minute! I haven't had my last Heineken yet! I'm not done! I may not have much hope of getting out here, but I'm not getting on your ship! And I'm not breathing seawater."

No sooner had he spoken than the phantom ghost ship turned and sailed away, vanishing into the night.

Rick Laws could feel his temperature dropping. He knew that he was dying. Now as he passed through the ever-increasing thresholds of pain, his mind took a course all its own.

His suffering brought one fact home to him: "When you're so cold you can no longer think, and you pass through all the emotions and all the pain, there's always someone still home in there—in your heart cave."

He was still paddling when the first gray light of dawn drove away the darkness. He was comforted, for a moment. But the hope he had at first felt rising was quickly overwhelmed by another harsh fact: Laws realized that all the reserve of strength he had called upon through a day, a night, and into yet another day, had finally been exhausted. Now nothing was left. His arms and legs were both failing him. He was nearing the point of complete and catatonic exhaustion. Rick Laws had no more resources left to keep himself from rolling face-down and breathing seawater. Short of a miracle, he was certain he wasn't going to make it. Unwilling to accept the terminal end to all his efforts, Laws rolled slowly over onto his back. Then, looking up at the overcast skies, he called out, "God! If you're there—really there—I need a miracle."

Within minutes, the "wind stopped, the sun came out, and the seas came down." Every hair on Laws's body stood up. At that moment, he knew his cry had been answered. He "knew in his heart" that he was going to be rescued. For the first time in his life, he believed he knew what it was to have faith.

Not more than an hour had passed when a C-130 SAR plane from the U.S. Coast Guard base in Kodiak flew onto the scene. Laws heard the plane approach in the distance, and he smiled inwardly to himself. Yep! Here it comes! I'll be damned. He's going to find me. I'm going to make it. I'm going to make it!

When he first saw the plane, it was moving low across the water, well off to the side of him. Laws lay back then and slowly began fanning his arms and legs at his sides, like a child making angel wings in freshly fallen snow.

Seated in front of a spotter's window inside the C-130 was PO Brian Blue. He was looking down and across the water at the time, and he spied the drifting hulk of a log. With the plane moving across the face of the sea at 210 miles per hour at an altitude of five hundred feet, he found he was having difficulty estimating the true dimensions of what he saw below. Almost simultaneously, however, he spotted what looked very much like an orange starfish drifting next to the log. But there was something odd about this starfish. It had only four tentacles. Not until he saw those same tentacles move did he realize he'd spotted the body of a man adrift in a survival suit. The slow-moving survivor was apparently attempting to signal him.

"Hey!" he shouted to the crew inside the plane. "I think I see one of the men down there!"

As Laws watched, the C-130 banked sharply and, with engines roaring, flew back toward him. The aircraft swung in low across the wave tops and over him. Laws could only lie back and wave tiredly. The plane swooped in repeatedly over him and continued to circle, dropping numerous colored flares and dye canisters in the area to mark his position. Once, Laws watched the C-130 until it had almost disappeared into the distance. It had only just begun to bank and return again when it suddenly veered back on course and continued out of sight. He would later learn that at that moment the pilot of the C-130 had spotted the body of Wink Cissel drifting in his brilliant orange survival suit on the surface. Though the vest of his suit had remained fully inflated, keeping him afloat, Wink had nevertheless died of hypothermia during the night.

After more than a day of fruitless searching for his missing friend, Bert Parker and his fatigued crew aboard the *Amber Dawn* were forced to conclude that Rick Laws and the men of the *Cloverleaf* had most likely perished.

Parker was certain the *Cloverleaf* had sunk. And even if those terrified and disoriented crewmen had managed to get into their survival suits, no human being in the history of Alaska had ever survived so long adrift in such icy seas. The manufacturers of these suits claimed protection from the cold and hypothermia for only three to five hours.

Parker was deeply saddened. He had just headed in to drop anchor and get some much-needed rest when something strange happened: an abrupt change in the weather. The forecast had called for gale warnings in the area, but suddenly the wind died down and the waves eased noticeably. Then the clouds parted and the sun came out. It was a dramatic and unexpected turn of events.

The U.S. Coast Guard quickly took advantage of the improved visibility. Minutes later, a C-130 SAR plane flying some forty miles from Sutwik Island (tens of miles outside the area where Bert Parker and the other crab boats had been searching) radioed that they had spotted what they believed to be a crewman floating below. And the crewman was apparently still alive! Parker and his dog-tired crew were jubilant. The crewman would turn out to be none other than Parker's good friend Rick Laws—in critical condition, but alive.

Vern Hall, skipper of the 121-foot crab boat *Rondys*, was the first to reach Laws amid the wafting clouds of flare smoke.

Despite the optimistic circumstances, Rick Laws was now nearly unconscious from the cold. Severely hypothermic, he could no longer make sense of anything. He could tell the *Rondys* crew was yelling to him; perhaps they wanted him to grab the line drifting nearby. But all his brain could think was, My God, that boat's big!

Vern Hall could see that Laws was too weak to grab hold of the line thrown to him—too disoriented, for that matter, even to locate the line directly beside him in the water. It was *Rondys* crewman Terry Sampson who quickly donned his survival suit, leapt overboard, and with rope in hand, swam out to Laws, trailing the line behind him.

Sampson wrapped the line of the buoy hook under Laws's arms, then signaled the crew to pull him in. Laws could hear the whine of the hydraulic king crab block as he was dragged through the water. In quick succession, he found himself yanked alongside the huge steel hull of the *Rondys*, craned into the air, and hoisted over the tall handrail and aboard.

"Vern Hall did a good job, I know that," Rick Laws later said appreciatively.

As he lay on the deck of the *Rondys*, Rick Laws discovered that his "body wasn't working," as he put it. Not only was he unfit to walk; he couldn't even manage to crawl. He could hear the remote voices of the *Rondys* crewmen, Terry Sampson and David Capri, as they rushed to save him.

They wasted little time. One moment, he was lying in a helpless heap on the wooden deck; the next, they were stripping his survival suit off him. Then he felt the comforting grip of many arms hoisting him from the deck. They ran carrying him into the wheelhouse, through the galley, and deposited him into the nearest stateroom, in the soft, warm, dry space of one of their own bunkbeds.

When skipper Vern Hall came into the room, he took one look at Rick Laws's blue lips and sunken eyes and knew the man was close to death. Hall asked for a volunteer to help warm Laws and stop the hypothermic fall of his body temperature. "One of you guys strip down and crawl into the bunk there with that man," he said.

Terry Sampson volunteered again. He quickly stripped, then jumped into the bunk with Laws; the *Rondys* crew immediately rolled both men in multiple layers of wool blankets.

At first, Rick Laws was embarrassed by this intimate contact with another man. He knew he was cold, but he hadn't grasped how thoroughly chilled he'd become until he felt the amazing transfer of body heat coming from Sampson.

"I could literally feel the heat from that other guy's body just pouring into me!" he recalls gratefully. "The heat coming from that man went all the way through my entire body. I believe he saved my life."

When he awoke later, his body temperature was rising. As the *Rondys* crew kept close check on his tenuous condition, Laws lay back in the soft comfort of the bunk and thought back over the incredible adventure he'd just been through. He'd survived twenty-seven hours in the deadly cold Gulf of Alaska sea—longer than any other man in history.

☞ SPIKE WALKER is the acclaimed author of *Nights of Ice, Working on the Edge*, and *Coming Back Alive*. He divides his time between Washington and Alaska.

Excerpt from *Danger Stalks the Land*

LARRY KANIUT

TOO LITTLE, TOO LATE

I can't get out. I don't want to stay here in this water.
I don't want to drown.

The GI struggled in the waist-deep muck of upper Cook Inlet not many miles north of Anchorage, Alaska. He had ventured too near the mudflats while duck hunting with friends and now expended energy in a desperate effort to free himself from the gluelike glacial silt that held him tightly in its grasp. He knew that the tide was due to change; if he failed, the inlet's cold, glacial waters would cover him within a few hours.

A short time later an airboat roared to the GI's aid. Three rescuers helped him break down his shotgun to use as a "straw" should the tide come in sooner than they could extricate him. Their efforts were futile.

The GI panicked and begged them to shoot him so that he would not suffer the death of drowning. They refused and left him in the mud as the gray-brown waters washed over his head, another victim claimed through carelessness.

That's the story the newcomer heard in 1966. He was a gung ho outdoors kid fresh from Oregon. Buoyed by visions of adventure, he gobbled up anything he could about the Last Frontier. I know because I was that kid.

After thirty-two years' embellishment it's time to chronicle the facts. In November 1988 I drove to Palmer, Alaska, to interview one of the key players in that tragic story. Lynn Puddicombe warmly welcomed me into his home and told me about his experience.

It is a sad story that serves as a warning to prospective hunters. Steer clear of the forbidden banks of the inlet; practice caution before entering that land of death.

For decades duck hunters have frequented the flats on Knik Arm north of Anchorage. A common bond connects those waterfowlers—get up early, savor the hot coffee, down some food, put on the hip waders, head for the blind, bag some birds, and go home. September 17, 1961, started out as such a day. However, it ended much differently.

A father and his sons enjoyed the day, hunting geese from their Coffee Point cabin near the hay flats. Forty-four-year-old Merle "Doc" Puddicombe enjoyed the outing with his teenaged sons Larry, Lynn, and Joe. Because there is often little water to run and an airboat has a shallow draft, the men were using the family airboat. It was a dry-run Banks Maxwell drive, fourteen-foot wood-and-fiberglass hull, with a sixty-five-horse Continental power plant.

In the midst of the hunt they heard an airplane, looked up, and saw it coming in just over the blind. The men figured it was one of many pilots they knew and didn't think much of it.

The pilot swung around, opened his door, and hollered at the men. Something about "stuck in the mud." They couldn't understand it. He made another pass. He shut down power and came in at idle. He pointed down the inlet and shouted, "Man stuck in the mud!"

Doc and the two older boys burst into action.

The low tide required some effort to work the boat free and into the water. By the time they freed the boat, the tide had started coming in. A foot bore tide was racing up the inlet, and Doc shouted over the roar of the engine, "It doesn't look good, but I still think we can save him."

The hunter was standing dead center in Wasilla Creek on the lower end of Palmer Slough, 150 to 250 yards from either shore. He was surrounded by mudflats.

They couldn't tell how deep the water was but assumed it was ankle- to knee-deep. They pulled up to him and Doc stuck a pole in. Larry and Lynn jumped out of the boat, landing in ankle-deep water. The hunter was mired crotch deep in muck, water lapping at his waist. The rescuers knew then that it was pretty bad.

The mud is soft when the tide is out. When the tide comes in and moving water hits the mud, it hardens up like cement. As long as a person keeps moving, there is no danger of getting stuck.

Larry and Lynn thought their stoutness was an advantage. Larry was twenty-one years old, six feet, and 180 pounds; Lynn was seventeen, six feet three, and approaching 200 pounds.

They learned the trapped hunter was Sp5 Roger J. Cashin, a thirty-three-year-old soldier stationed at Fort Richardson in Anchorage. He had been hunting with three fellow soldiers. At first they'd laughed at him because he was stuck. They were sitting on the shore thinking it was pretty funny.

Once they saw the water coming in and realized the seriousness of the situation, they went into action. One took off to phone the Rescue Coordination Center at Elmendorf Air Force Base in Anchorage. He had to go all the way across the hay flats at least one and a half miles.

His other two friends shouted encouragement from the bank but were afraid to venture out into the mud. A large quantity of driftwood covered the beach. If they'd known what they were doing, they could have built a trail to him and gotten him out.

Doc gave Cashin's two friends a gas can and told them to build a signal fire on the bank. One of them lit a match and dropped it onto the brush, then poured gas onto the flame! Although it blew him up the bank, at least they got a fire going.

Cashin had been stuck long enough to fire all his ammunition. He had used the three-shot signal to attract attention. Hunters in the area didn't hear his shots, and even if they had, it's not likely that they would have paid any attention because evenly spaced shotgun reports are common.

Freeing Cashin would have been easier if he'd been wearing hip boots. His choice of footgear would be a major factor in his chances of rescue. Unfortunately he wore regular army boots that lace up about halfway to the knee. Veteran hunters fear wearing ankle-tight hip waders that can't be removed.

Initially the rescuers tried to free Cashin with the boat. Doc revved the airboat while Cashin held on, but the boat pulled straight up. Next they used the boat's lift for leverage. Cashin held on to the side of the boat while Doc fired the motor a couple of times, but that also failed.

Then Larry and Lynn hung on to him, hoping to get some leverage from inside the boat to pull him out. That effort met with failure also.

Their tools were limited, consisting of a machete and two pry bars. The rescuers tried to scoop the mud from around his legs.

There was no way to break the suction on him. They slid the machete down his leg hoping to get hold of the laces and cut them. He was stuck too deep to allow the machete to reach his laces.

Larry and Lynn took turns using the machete and keeping the boat close while Doc manned the boat. The tide increased in volume.

Recalling other experiences motivated the rescuers to work frantically. They remembered shooting and wounding ducks that fell into the soft mud. The birds beat their wings and disappeared into the muck. They'd seen several moose stuck in that same area. Although moose appear strong enough to get out of anything, they couldn't escape that inlet goo.

Doc had always told his sons, "Never go out in that mud. If a moose can't get out of there, you should think about what you're going to do."

Time flashed by as the men worked feverishly. The teenagers were near convulsions from the paralyzing ice-cold, glacial water. Because the water was getting deeper, they abandoned digging.

They tried to get leverage by running an oar through Cashin's belt and over the gunwale then lifting up, trying to pry him loose. It was hopeless, but they refused to give up.

Larry and Lynn put an oar across their shoulders and Cashin held on to it. They tried to lift him out. It didn't work.

Doc stayed in the boat. He reminded the boys to keep moving, sometimes yelling at them. He'd shut down the engine. The boys kept one arm on the boat whenever they could. They kept working, trying to keep from sinking.

Larry got hung up in the mud a couple of times, and Lynn pulled him loose. They kept their hip boots on, moving enough to pop them out of the mud if they started sinking.

Cashin had a tough time standing. He'd been there so long that he must have been numb.

Next the boys bent down and put one of Cashin's arms over each of their shoulders. They bowed their necks underneath his shoulder in his armpits and tried to stand up. They could see it hurt him too badly. Their efforts were futile.

They exhausted every idea they had. There was nothing more they could do.

The water rose higher and higher. Before long the water was approaching Cashin's chest as the boys bent over him in knee-deep water.

When the Puddicombes hunted the flats, they always knew the exact size of the tides. That day they expected a small tide. Soon the water started running out.

Lynn told Larry, "This guy's gonna make it." Doc watched the tide and the boys held Cashin up.

They were overjoyed for a second as the water started receding. But all of a sudden the wind shifted, and they felt a strong wind in their faces. That's common on the mudflats. The wind picked up hard and came across the inlet. When the wind does that, it takes the tide.

The tides on upper Cook Inlet are run by the wind. Where a normal twenty-five-foot tide stops without a wind, the wind piles the water up another five or six feet, resulting in a thirty-foot tide! The wind can also bring the tide in an hour earlier. Tricky thing.

By then water was underneath Cashin's chin. The rescuers were desperate. They took apart a shotgun and told Roger, "If the tide comes over your head, pinch your nose and breathe through this barrel." But he never used the shotgun for breathing. He didn't want any part of it. It seemed he didn't think he could survive anyway.

Meanwhile a big Hercules flew up and down the river. The military was looking for Roger. When the emergency message finally reached Elmendorf, somehow the location of the stuck hunter was given as the Knik River. Two planes and two helicopters were searching the wrong area—they were flying over the Knik River instead of the duck flats!

Pandemonium reigned with the incoming tide. The ice-cold water kept surging into the area. There was a lot of noise and commotion.

One pilot flew over to the Knik trying to motion the military to come over to the duck-flat side. Another pilot flew down the inlet and found Roy Knapp. Roy arrived, parked his boat nearby, and built a huge fire.

About that time another pilot in his new Super Cub flew over. He attempted to land in the grassy, shallow water near the scene and flipped his plane over.

Roger was still alive. Doc was worried Cashin might panic and grab one of the boys. But Roger wasn't panicked.

Roger remained calm. He never got tripped up. He never panicked. He never cried. He didn't scream and ask to be shot. The boys were amazed at his reserve. He looked at Lynn and said, "I don't want to stay here. I don't want to stay in this water."

Lynn replied, "Well, I hope you don't have to either."

When it became apparent that the Puddicombes couldn't help him, Roger took his wallet out and said, "Give that to my wife. Please tell her I love her."

Reluctantly the men realized there was nothing they could do.

When the tide went over his nose, Roger tipped his head way back.

Lynn held the back of his neck. Roger didn't yell; he didn't scream. He just went limp.

He died before the water went over his nose. Maybe it was shock. The boys held Roger for a minute. They noticed his hair floating at the surface. No bubbles came up. One minute he was breathing with them; the next minute he was gone.

Doc told his boys the soldier knew there wasn't anything they could do. In spite of their failure, the rescuers felt good because they had done the best they could.

The rescuers did so much in so short a time, it seemed as though they had all day to save Roger. But when it was all said and done, they'd worked with Cashin no more than thirty minutes . . . possibly as little as fifteen.

Since Lynn had been in the water the longest and was on the verge of hypothermia, a pilot flew him to Palmer. He was met by his mother and younger brother Craig.

On the next shallow tide, officials set out to recover Cashin's body. They put ropes around him and tried to pull him out. They thought they would put a belt around him and take pressure up in the helicopter; however, the nylon rope broke when the helicopter attempted to hoist his body from the mud.

Doc Puddicombe received a letter from the U.S. Army, Alaska, a few days after the incident, commending him and his sons for their very determined effort to rescue Sp5 Roger J. Cashin.

EPILOGUE

It didn't have to happen. It was a senseless death. Had Roger Cashin's hunting buddies responded early on instead of taking the situation as a joke, Cashin would be alive. Doc Puddicombe was disturbed about that until the day he died.

People said the Puddicombes could have saved Cashin. Each skeptic had his reasons. People said, "Why didn't you remove his legs with a chain saw?" If the army was there with a doctor, the Puddicombes could probably have removed his legs and pulled him out. (How many people could survive having their legs cut off? Would a doctor ever let someone do that? Probably not.) Most people hunting geese do not carry a shovel or a chain saw!

One rumor stated that Cashin asked his rescuers to shoot him. That never happened.

Under the circumstances the military couldn't have done any more than the Puddicombes had done, even if they had arrived immediately. Their equipment was inadequate. The only thing that will get someone out of the mud is high-pressure water, and that process wasn't in use at that time.

Now rescue groups are equipped with portable compressors to deal with the problem. Helicopters can set down even if the water is deep or hover above the water.

The fire department and rescue units flush them out. The jet pump effectively blows away the muck.

Roger Cashin's death saved a lot of lives through the years. He didn't die in vain. A lot of people woke up to the dangers that mudflat country presents.

It was much worse before the 1964 earthquake. The cut banks were thirty feet high. Bore tides with six-foot heads sloshed up the slough. They rumbled into the hunting area sounding like a train in your living room. Locals joked about it: "The train's coming."

When it roared in, big slabs of mud fell from those mud banks and smacked the water. All night or all day long it sounded like cannon fire echoing up the slough.

Now water comes in and fills the whole area up, even on a small tide. A thirty-three-foot tide will sneak up on you and steal your boat. It's quiet because there are no banks anymore—just tapered, shallow shoulders. (Many people who hunt the mouth of the Little Susitna don't realize that its conditions are similar to upper Knik Arm's . . . under the right conditions a twenty-eight-foot tide will fill the area in ten minutes, completely covering the numerous tide guts.)

During the terrible ordeal and up to the very end Roger Cashin's attitude was remarkable. A rescuer stated, "It was a privilege to have known him. I wish we could have saved him."

For Roger Cashin to die, everything had to happen perfectly. And it did.

☙ LARRY KANIUT moved to Alaska in 1966, and has lived there ever since. He is the bestselling author of five books, including *Danger Stalks the Land, Alaskan Bear Tales*, and *Cheating Death: Amazing Survival Stories from Alaska.*

LEW FREEDMAN

It was in June 1986. Tejas was just completing a guided trip and was hanging out at base camp on the Kahiltna Glacier with his climbers. They were waiting their turn to be picked up by a bush pilot and flown back to Talkeetna. The next several hours, though, wouldn't involve an easy flight to Talkeetna. They would be some of the most dramatic of Tejas's life.

The code of mountaineering calls for a fit climber to stop what he is doing, wherever he is on the mountain, and come to the aid or rescue of an injured or sick climber. Sometimes this can cost the fit climber his only chance at the summit, but matters of life and death, or matters that seem to be of life and death, take precedence. After all, the summit will always be there. One can return and try again. It is the responsibility of the fit climber to respond to emergencies.

Tejas was relaxing with his group when two South Koreans stumbled into the camp. They seemed both exhausted and excited, but they didn't speak English. Their behavior didn't seem to be the simple exhilaration of having conquered the peak. Things didn't seem quite right. They were too animated and tense.

"My experience has shown me that means that something's afoot," said Tejas. "We asked them if they wanted some water. They just chugged it, so I realized they'd been moving for a long time. They each drank a quart. We asked them if they wanted food. They stuffed it in their mouths."

This communication was not accomplished through direct question and answer. The only English coming out of the Koreans mouths between inhaling the food and water was "yes" and "no," and Tejas and his companions didn't know what those affirmatives and negatives referred to.

"We were saying, 'Problem?' " said Tejas. "We were trying to ask, 'Where are you coming from?' "

Eventually, Tejas coaxed out of them the information that they had come from the Cassin Ridge, on the other side of the mountain. The Koreans drew pictures of the mountain in the snow and tried to describe their route.

"Then they made human figures up toward the top and they kept on pointing and saying stuff that I couldn't understand. I couldn't understand the words, that is, but I could understand the meaning."

Tejas took the meaning to be that there were two more climbers from the Korean group stuck high on the mountain.

What he was just learning, since he had only arrived at base camp a short while before, was what base camp manager Mary Palmer had been trying to decipher for two days. She had been monitoring garbled radio signals from near the summit. It was clear that something was wrong, but no one was able to tell exactly what. Ultimately, Palmer taped one of the radio messages and located an interpreter who spoke Korean. When he tuned in on the radio from Talkeetna, she played what was presumed to be a call for help. It turned out that the Koreans, with accents so thick no one could understand them, were actually saying "S.O.S." In English.

Immediately two Park Service rangers, Bob Seibert and Roger Robinson, began looking for volunteers to put together a team of the fittest and most able mountaineers on the mountain and in Talkeetna. They planned to rush them to the top as quickly as medically possible. Acclimatization would be everything in this kind of situation. A man could be the world's strongest climber, but that didn't mean he could just run right up to 20,000 feet. If he did, he would risk cerebral edema, the affliction that hits most climbers if they go too high too fast. The disease can strike quickly, filling the brain with fluid, and kill a climber within a day if he doesn't move to a lower altitude. What the rangers didn't need was a whole new crop of sick mountaineers. The last thing they wanted to have to do was rescue the rescuers.

Tejas's only experience with severe altitude sickness had been while skiing in California, but there is always some form of minor altitude distress if one climbs high.

"Generally, you have a headache," he said. "Loss of appetite, some shortness of breath."

Those are all symptoms, but it is the degree to which they are suffered that matters. Anyone trapped high on a mountain and not moving would clearly be showing much more severe signs of illness.

Austrians Wolfgang Wippler and Arthur Haid, Australian Gary Scott, and American Peter Downing of Denver joined the team. Tejas didn't know Wippler, but he knew that his team was a strong one on the mountain. Tejas had spoken to Scott a few days earlier.

Some of the climbers on this makeshift international team were among the strongest in the world at the time. Scott had just made a remarkable ascent of McKinley on the West Buttress route in less than a day. However, there was one problem: Wippler and some of the others had been up virtually all of the night before in Talkeetna, celebrating their ascent of the mountain. They were exhausted.

The rangers asked Tejas to join the team. Tejas's advantage was that he was the strongest climber who had been high on the mountain most recently. He would need no adjustment to altitude.

"I was free from responsibility since my group was at base camp," said Tejas. "We guides have a responsibility to our own climbers first, but we're also obligated to help the Park Service out when they have rescues."

The Park Service plan was to fly the crack team of mountaineers up to 19,000 feet in a helicopter, find the two Koreans, load them on the helicopter, and fly them to a hospital.

"The idea was to put us in as high as possible, to get 'em as quick as possible, and get the hell out," said Tejas.

The helicopter left Talkeetna about five A.M. One thing the rescuers had going for them was the long hours of daylight available at that time of year. It was near the summer solstice, and this far north the peak period of light meant nearly twenty-four hours of daylight.

One problem arose immediately. Mount McKinley was not in a cooperative mood. At 19,000 feet the wind was blasting. The helicopter couldn't come close to a set-down. Not only that, but the clouds were so thick the rescuers couldn't see anything. They didn't really have any idea where the Koreans were, except somewhere near the summit on the Cassin Ridge. They were looking for a tent, but they didn't see one.

The helicopter slowly worked its way down the mountain. The pilot looked for a place to land at 17,000 feet. No dice. Again the winds were too powerful. Finally, the copter put down at 14,000 feet, just below the headwall, and disgorged the climbers. The Koreans were somewhere in the clouds, about 6,000 vertical feet above them.

Tejas, Scott, and Wippler joined together to make an all-out push for the summit. Haid and Downing served as backup. The trio of tough climbers quickly scaled the West Buttress headwall, much faster than Tejas could ever do it with a group of clients who were amateur climbers. They advanced beyond 15,000 feet, beyond 16,000 feet, to the camp at 17,200 feet.

But the swift ascent was taking a toll. Scott felt the early warning signs of cerebral edema, or altitude sickness. He had to retreat, moving back down to 14,000 feet, or risk serious illness. If he got sick, he too might have to be rescued.

The lead group was now down to two. Tejas went to the emergency cache left by the Park Service and pulled out a 600-foot length of rope and an oxygen bottle. Tejas tossed the rope into his pack and Wippler carried the oxygen. But at Denali Pass, at 18,200 feet, the wind was ripping into the climbers, fighting them as hard as they were fighting the altitude. Wippler, who had slept only two hours the night before, craved rest.

"It was pretty nasty," said Tejas. "And I'd never gone up that fast before. Wippler felt he couldn't go on. He knew he needed some sleep and wisely chose to rest at Denali Pass."

Until that moment, there had been little time to think. The experienced mountaineers had been working fast, climbing fast, believing they could save the two stranded men.

"Up to that point I was thinking *rescue*," said Tejas. "Here we've got a group of good, qualified mountaineers. We're going to see if we can find these guys and bring them down alive."

Suddenly, Tejas was alone. Still, he didn't worry about that very much. He figured Scott was a very tough climber and would soon rejoin him and that Wippler would rest and catch up, too. What Tejas did know was that there were two men somewhere ahead who needed him. He kept climbing.

Tejas climbed to about 19,600 feet, at a spot on McKinley that climbers have nicknamed the Football Field because it is a long, flat, open area. It was there he realized that no one else was coming. He had worked hard to climb swiftly. He'd told the others, "I'm going to go ahead and I'm sure you guys will catch up to me." Now it hit him that they weren't going to make it in time.

"Little did I know that I was the most acclimated," said Tejas. "There wasn't anybody else up there, and it was approaching midnight as I was going across the Football Field."

Tejas grew emotional. Tears began streaming down his face and freezing in his beard. He didn't know what he was getting into here. He thought that at best there was a fifty-fifty chance he would find people alive. In all his years of rescue work he had never brought anyone out alive. Only people in body bags.

"Your emotions run wild," he said of the situation. "You're pushing your envelope of sanity."

The day had begun at five A.M., but by the time the helicopter dropped the rescuers off and they started climbing, it was about noon. So Tejas had been scrambling upward for twelve hours. He had packed light, carrying only emergency gear that he might need, plus the equipment necessary for his own needs. This included bottles filled with water to keep himself hydrated and food enough for a couple of meals, because there was no way of knowing how long this rescue would take—and there was always the chance the weather would turn and trap him on the mountain.

"I took a couple of lunches with me just so I knew I had plenty of food," said Tejas. "Just in case I got stranded at the summit."

After twelve hours of climbing, preceded by seven hours of preparation and flying, and that preceded by weeks on the mountain guiding a group, Tejas was tired. The weariness seeped into his muscles, and took over his mind. It had all been a rush, and now that he was slowing down, he had time to think.

"Going across the Football Field was where it hit me that I was all alone," said Tejas.

Climbing with this purpose, a rescue, and not knowing what he would find played on his thoughts. He might come upon two dead men, frozen stiff in their tent. He might come upon two desperate men, totally disoriented, beyond help.

"There could have been two bodies on the other side," said Tejas. "It was very, very emotionally tough, a tough thing to do—to just keep plugging along knowing that people weren't coming up behind me."

Three years earlier, Tejas had climbed up here carrying the ashes of his then-girlfriend, Merilee Engelke, and scattered them to the wind. Tejas and Engelke had traveled around the world together in 1984. She was with him when Tejas first thought of shaving his head. They met some Buddhist monks with shaven heads. That gave him the idea, and he thought about it for some time before clipping his hair off. It didn't hurt that he was going bald, anyway. He added his own twist by leaving the slender ponytail in back as a further statement of individuality.

"There's nothing in my life that requires me to look normal," joked Tejas.

The trip with Merilee was cut short when she became ill. They returned to Alaska. Suffering from an infection resulting from the kidney transplant medication she was taking, Engelke checked into a hospital in Seattle after a twenty-eight-hour round-the-world flight. But without warning, an aneurism burst in an artery and killed her.

Tejas had shared much with this woman, in the outdoors, in other countries. He had said good-bye to her on this mountain, not far from here; being the sole rescuer here now, worn out, fearing that he would come upon death a few steps away, turned his emotions inside out.

"I was emotionally exhausted, physically wrung out, and it was weighing on my mind that there was death all around me," said Tejas. "It was hard to keep plugging away at it and not feel that. It was coming out. I was pretty blue at that moment, thinking, 'God, I hope they're not dead.' That's why I had to keep plugging away, because if I had turned back then, I felt, they'd have been as good as dead. If I hadn't done my best, they would be dead.

"It was almost as if Merilee were right there, at the summit. It was just like I was getting a lot of . . . support. I found myself remembering my shortcomings in my relationship with her. I suppose the connection was life and death, but to fail with these guys would have been to fail with her, too. I had to go look for them. It was real important that I continue."

The fight began here. The body was tired but could go on. The mind might have been more tired still and *didn't* want to go on. So many things were working at cross-purposes with the rescue mission, including Tejas's sense of self-preservation and his normal, cautious approach to climbing.

"Here I was, solo on the mountain in a situation that I'd told people not to go solo on," he said.

The wind was blowing about twenty miles an hour, clouds were drifting in and filling up the sky. It felt like storm weather.

"It didn't look good," said Tejas. "But I said, 'Well, I'm going to go till I shouldn't go any farther, till it is no longer reasonable to keep on going. I still had reserves in my body, so I decided to go at least up to the ridge and look down."

The Cassin Ridge is just over the summit from the West Buttress side. It is a different route up the mountain, a much harder one, and the climbers who attempt it are usually more experienced than those who climb the West Buttress. The guiding groups who lead expeditions of citizen climbers up Mount McKinley don't lead groups up the Cassin Ridge.

Tejas knew, though, that from the summit, or near it from the West Buttress summit ridge, he would be able to look over the edge of the mountain down the Cassin and spot the Koreans if they were still alive, still camped nearby.

"If you can't find them from on top and you can't find them from the air, you can just assume they got blown off," he said.

From what Tejas knew, the Koreans had to be suffering from altitude sickness. He was told they had moved up the mountain in just five days—way too fast to acclimate. Regardless of how strong the climbers were, it would have been better if they had taken at least nine days. All McKinley climbing literature warns people not to go too fast.

Having fought his inner struggle and won, having rested himself a little and been rejuvenated, Tejas set out from the Football Field to the summit ridge. The ridge is about 300 yards shy of McKinley's true summit, or 100 feet of vertical gain, so Tejas was between 19,700 feet and 20,000 feet high for the rescue. He stopped short of the summit itself and peered off the ridge toward the Cassin side.

The view is generally of a bunch of rocks, and when Tejas looked down, that's what he saw—a bunch of rocks and nothing else. He didn't see anybody, so he began making noise. He mixed yelling and yodeling. Yodeling is something of a Tejas trademark in the hills. Sometimes he does it for fun. He says he would prefer to sing but rarely remembers the words to songs, so yodeling is a substitute. It is also in the tradition of the American cowboy, and that pleases him. Sometimes yodeling can be an important signature for communication. Tejas has been in snowy, cloudy conditions when visibility was limited and found that his climbing partner could pinpoint his whereabouts from a yodel, whose sound will occasionally travel well when a yell won't. Tejas tried both this time, hoping that if anyone was there, if anyone was tucked in those rocks or beneath a snowy overhang, he would be heard, and there would be a response.

He got the response he was hoping for. He heard a man yelling back, speaking Korean, or at least he guessed it was Korean. He knew it was an Asian language, anyway.

Tejas was elated. He had been feeling logy, perhaps from lack of oxygen, but the fact that people were alive, that he wasn't just going to be shipping two men out in body bags, revived him.

For the first time in a couple of hours he was anxious to talk on his radio. There had been periodic checks by the rangers earlier, flying around the mountain in a plane piloted by Lowell Thomas. They were perfunctory checks, really. "How are you doing up there, Vern?" Tejas had told them he was the only rescuer left, the only one still going. For the previous two hours, though, when he had been battling his inner feelings, determining that he could and should go on, he had refused to answer radio calls. He thought the rangers might order him back. He was shaky, but at that point he wasn't sure he was ready to abandon the attempt. He didn't want someone else to decide; he wanted to do that himself.

"They already sensed it was bad," said Tejas. "If I had told them that one guy was going up to rescue two guys . . . That doesn't make a whole lot of sense."

He had warned the rangers that he might not call back soon, but the rangers were starting to worry about Tejas anyway. It had been a long time since they'd heard his voice. There were practical reasons as well as emotional ones for that as well.

"Two reasons I wasn't talking back: it was ruining my concentration, and I was risking frostbite every time I'd get the radio out," he said. "I wanted to say, 'Okay, guys, unless it's real important, I'm just going to go. I'm not going to have the energy to stop every twenty minutes and chat. I've got to get to the top and see what's going on.' "

Once he heard the Korean's voice, though, Tejas whipped out the radio. He had something to report. This way the rangers would know the Koreans were alive and where they were. If Tejas himself slipped and fell, even died, they would know others were alive and still in need of rescue.

"They were relieved to hear from me," said Tejas. "I said, 'I'm going strong,' which was the truth of it. Emotionally, I was a little shook, but it was such an uplift to know I was not going to find bodies, that I wasn't going to go up there and open a tent full of dead guys."

He made his report brief and, renewed, began working. He tapped a couple of pickets into the snow and then tied in 600 feet of rope. Tejas hooked himself to the rope and began rappelling over the ridge slowly, hoping the voice that had called back to him was coming from a spot fairly close to the top. Tejas figured the Koreans would be packing up their gear, anxious for his arrival. But when he climbed down onto the Cassin Ridge, he once more became unsure what to expect. It turned out the Koreans' tent was more than 600 feet from the summit, so Tejas had to drop off the end of the rope and scramble down.

Tejas found two Koreans in the tent awaiting rescue. One, whose name Tejas later learned was Seoung Kwon Chung, was fairly alert. The other, Jong Kwan Lee, was not in very good shape. He was stretched out in the tent, woozy, moving slowly, clearly suffering from altitude sickness. Seoung spoke English but was in such a fog, was so weary, that Tejas couldn't understand what he was saying. And the two Koreans were debilitated enough by the altitude, exhaustion, fear, and the language barrier that they didn't understand immediately that Tejas was there to help them get off the mountain alive.

Tejas gave the men his water, the rest of his food, and a drug to combat the altitude sickness. Tejas took some medication himself, since he had just speed-climbed from 14,000 to almost 20,000 feet in half a day.

"I was a little concerned that maybe I wasn't thinking straight, and I wanted to make sure I was fit for the descent," said Tejas.

That was his next problem. He had to communicate to the Koreans not only that he was there to rescue them, but that he was it. Just him. There was no posse at the other end of the rope on the summit ridge prepared to haul them up. There were no reinforcements. It was just the three of them.

Tejas recognized this as a formidable difficulty. For one thing, the Koreans had been stuck in this spot for about five days. If they hadn't hauled themselves to the top yet, there was nothing to suggest they could do it now, even with help. And help came in the form of one man who wasn't exactly fresh.

What Tejas did have going for him was an improvement in the Koreans' morale. Just seeing him seemingly drop down from the sky, they knew that their radio calls had paid off, that there were people out there who cared and who were trying to rescue them. Plus, water and food had freshened them up some. They should have regained some of their strength and will, Tejas reasoned.

"Seeing me lifted their spirits," he said. "I figured they could get to the top. In some ways, they might not have known how close they were. The depth can be really deceptive. But having seen me just come down from there, they had an idea that yeah, indeed, it was attainable."

Tejas had already made the determination that it was safer, that there was a better chance of more help reaching them, and it was probably easier to go up over the summit and down the West Buttress, than it was to retreat along the Cassin Ridge.

There was still a communication gap, though. The Koreans just didn't believe—didn't want to believe, probably—that Tejas had come alone. That may have worked in everyone's favor. If Jong, the weaker of the two, had truly understood that Tejas was alone here, he might have become too demoralized to move. He might not have had the will to force himself to start climbing.

"They were fairly sure there were other rescuers on top," said Tejas.

Gear was packed, and Tejas and Jong began to walk, hike, and climb until they reached the end of the rope. Tejas waved it, pointed to it, made it clear Jong must clip into it with his ascender. Seoung would stay and climb after them.

Jong shakily approached the rope. His legs were wobbly, he still seemed woozy, and his fingers didn't work the way he commanded them to. He reached for the rope and tried repeatedly to tie himself into it. Tejas told him again and again not to tie himself in, to use his hand-held ascender to clip onto it.

Tejas was telling Jong he must raise himself the final 600 feet to the top; Jong was telling Tejas he couldn't do it.

"He was tying on to be pulled up," said Tejas. "He was trying to tie this knot and saying, 'Up, up, up,' and I'm saying, 'Climb, climb, climb.' He couldn't do it with his pack. I ended up dragging his pack up, but he was able to do it."

Tejas hoped that at the same time Jong had been growing weak from lack of food and water and too much time at high altitude, he had actually been acclimatizing himself enough to make his rescue possible.

Meanwhile, Seoung, left below, was actually jovial, said Tejas, happy because he was sure they were getting out of there, sure they would survive. Tejas hooked his ascender onto the line first. Finally, Jong did the same, and Tejas, moving slowly, one step at a time, worked his way up the side of the mountain. One push of the ascender, one pull on the rope. Over and over. He coaxed Jong through it, back up the same 600 feet Tejas had just quickly descended.

Tejas's instinct was right. Jong did have it in him. He made it to the top, over the ridge, to the basin adjacent to it. But once there, he seemed stunned by what he saw, because what he saw was nothing. There was no one else. There was no more help.

"When he got to the top, of course, the truth hit him," said Tejas. "This is all you got. What you see is what you got. I think that was a real letdown, because once he got up there—he was definitely fagged from the effort of getting up there—but once he looked around, feeling the way he felt, and looked out to the north summit, which is miles away, and not seeing anybody anywhere, he just lay down. That was the last time I saw him up."

That was not good at all. Tejas had needed plenty of his own strength and patience to guide Jong to the top. He was worried that Jong would give up now, would die right there before Tejas and Seoung could get him to a chopper and to a hospital.

"He stayed conscious, but he was definitely fading," said Tejas, "and since his buddy was holding the rope down below, I was just up there alone with this guy. I thought he was out. He wasn't comatose, but . . ."

Tejas felt a chill, not the usual frigidness of McKinley weather, but an internal chill, a fear that after all of his effort, after all he had tried to do, Jong would die right there anyhow.

"How am I gonna get this guy down?" Tejas asked himself.

He would have to carry him. He and Seoung would just have to carry him. It was the only way. They'd abandon his pack and carry him.

"It didn't look good."

But then, abruptly, it looked a whole lot better.

Tejas walked to the edge of the basin, to the beginning of the route that led down, and there, in the distance, just over the ridge, he could see someone. Coming fast was Wolfgang Wippler, who had revived from his nap and was climbing with oxygen and a sled borrowed from Alaska guide Gary Bocarde and his climbing party at a lower camp.

"I thought, 'Oh, man, the cavalry has arrived,' " said Tejas. "Perfect tim-ing. Any earlier and he would have just been looking at a rope hanging over the edge. Any later and we would have had to wait there while this guy got colder and colder, because I couldn't move him. I was pretty fagged at that point."

Without the timely arrival of Wippler, Tejas said later, he's not sure he could have dragged the Korean to safety.

"It was work," he said of what the two of them had to do. "We had to go uphill at Archdeacon's Tower. We were panting. Doing it alone—phew—!—Well, I would have been in trouble. There was about five hours of hard work ahead, and I thought I'd have to do the whole thing."

Tejas and Wippler took off Jong's crampons, bundled him up, loaded him into a sleeping bag, and then laid him on a sled. Then they got him going on some oxygen. As they worked on him, Seoung appeared. He had pulled him-self up the rope without help. Now he seemed wiped out.

There was no time to rest, though. It was obvious that if Jong was going to live, he had to be brought down to a lower altitude swiftly. Tejas, Wip-pler, and Seoung set out quickly, but he was strong enough to help only himself. He could walk, but he wasn't fit enough to help heft a man in a sleeping bag.

Tejas and Wippler used the same 600 feet of rope that Tejas had dropped over to the Cassin Ridge to wrap around the sleeping bag and help lower it down the West Buttress. Seoung was given the assignment of carry-ing Jong's pack. But after a short while he tied it on the end of the rescue rope.

"As we lowered our patient down on the rope, his body weight counter-balanced the weight of the pack," said Tejas, "so he was actually dragging the pack down with him. It worked great until we hit the flats."

They had reached the Football Field, the large basin at 19,600 feet, and were still a long way from home, a long way from being out of trouble. Tejas ordered Seoung to untie the pack and carry it, but just below the Football Field, where the incline is steep again, he tied it back on, and Tejas and Wip-pler dragged it behind Jong and his sleeping bag.

They carted him down to Denali Pass, just above 18,000 feet, to the camp of Bocarde's party. There they needed help. They were almost out of energy themselves and were starting to lose concentration.

"I was tired and exhausted, and so was Wolfgang," said Tejas. "I was so low on blood sugar I thought I was going to pass out. We'd drag Jong ten feet and stop and puff and cough."

Tejas and Wippler left Jong with Bocarde's party and scrambled down to the big way station, here at 17,200 feet, to rest. They spent about eight hours conked out, recovering from their effort.

Later that afternoon, Bocarde and his climbers lowered Jong in his sleeping bag to them by rope. By then the wind had subsided sufficiently for a helicopter to land, and Tejas and Wippler, resuming the rescue, helped lift Jong into the chopper. Scoung joined his friend, and the two were flown to Talkeetna.

What happened next was the most exciting part of the rescue for Tejas. After they had walked down to 14,000 feet, the chopper came back and flew Tejas and Wippler directly to Talkeetna. That meant they didn't have to climb down to Kahiltna Glacier.

"Which was great," said Tejas. "I didn't want to go all the way back to base camp. It would have been two long, slog-ass days after doing two pretty hard rescue days."

When Tejas reached Talkeetna, Jong was still there, still bundled up, about to be medivac'd to Providence Hospital in Anchorage. He was out of it, unable to communicate with Tejas.

But Seoung was wide awake and very much aware that Tejas had saved his friend, if not both of them.

He thanked Tejas over and over and then tried to force a tip on him.

"I said, 'No, no I didn't do it for money,' " said Tejas. "He said, 'From my heart.' "

Finally, Tejas accepted some money. "I said, 'Okay, from your heart, it's okay.' I didn't want to insult him. And I could tell he was very thankful that indeed somebody had showed up."

The rescue commanded tremendous attention in Alaska, in the Anchorage newspapers and on television stations. Tejas was widely praised, but he tried to downplay the achievement of sprinting up McKinley and hauling a man over the summit.

"This just turned out to be a big success," said Tejas. "A lot of things could have gone wrong, but everything went right. I don't think of myself as a hero. I was in the right place at the right time. I was acclimatized. I had a responsibility to go."

➥ LEW FREEDMAN is a reporter for the *Anchorage Daily News* and the best-selling writer of many books, including *Dangerous Steps: Vernon Tejas and the Solo Ascent of Mount McKinley; Iditarod Classics: Tales of the Trail from the Men and Women Who Race Across Alaska; Spirit of the Wind: The Story of George Attla, Alaska's Legendary Sled Dog Sprint Champ;* and *Diamonds in the Rough.*

THE IDITAROD

THE IDITAROD is far more than a sled dog race. It's a monument to human and canine endurance—an 1,100 mile odyssey through the most difficult terrain possible, often undertaken in uncertain or even impossible weather. But those who have completed it know that they are capable of anything. Here are some of the incredible stories of its winners and participants—no one with the courage to even attempt the race could possibly be called a loser.

Excerpt from *Winterdance:*
The Fine Madness of Running the Iditarod

GARY PAULSEN

Peeople, all people in Alaska, people having to do with the race, people in stores, people met on streets were all, everyone I met, wonderfully hospitable and enormously helpful. Had they not been this way I would never in my appalling ignorance have made the starting chutes, let alone the race.

It started with them not laughing at us. I cannot look back on it now without laughing, and I am amazed that they could have kept straight faces. We arrived in Wasilla, Alaska, where the race headquarters was located, with a truck literally falling apart. When we released the bungee cords holding it together the doors fell off, and yet when we went inside to sign up and tell them we had arrived one of the volunteers looked up and merely said, "Oh, yes. We heard you were coming. They say you have a bad truck but good dogs."

One thing became strikingly clear. I knew nothing, less than nothing, about running dogs long distances. Indeed, much of what I had learned in training was wrong.

First, and foremost, the race is truly about nurturing, caring for the dogs. They are everything, all of everything, and it wasn't enough to merely schlep them some food and let them rest—which was pretty much what I had been doing. Every aspect of every dog needs to be considered. Feet, teeth, conditioning, toenails, coat, wounds (from fighting—a constant problem—or trail injury). Nor is this a one-time appraisal. Feet must be examined on the half-hour while they are running, tipped up so they are in the light from the headlamp, the toes spread to look up inside them, into the web of the foot for signs of irritation, close examination beneath the nail, along the sides of the pads, up beneath the hairline on the foot. Every toe. On every foot. On every dog. Every thirty minutes. Ankles and shoulders rubbed—hands on dogs, touching dogs, feeling dogs, all the time, anytime the team is stopped, hands and eyes to dogs.

There is an old saying about sailors working in the rigging of tall sailing ships. It was so frightening up high that some of them simply clung to the rigging and the mate would cry from below: "One hand for you, one hand for the ship!"

I quickly found that with dogs, with running them, it is *no* hands for the musher and all hands, eyes, mind, soul—everything for the dogs.

After signing in and getting some of the tons of paperwork and handouts and instructions from the headquarters—much of which was almost pure Greek to me—we traveled north and camped in an area where there were many other Iditarod mushers training.

It was late December. The race did not start until the first Saturday in March, and had it not been for those two months in the bush, running dogs and seeking assistance, it would have been impossible. I begged help. A musher would come by to say hi and stop to rest his dogs and I would pump him—or her, there were several women training in the same area—for information. Anything. Everything. Tidbits. How to use booties correctly. How to feed correctly. Water them. And the one question most difficult to answer:

What was the race like?

Really like?

And always they would look at me—men, women, old and young, any who had finished it or started it and been unable to finish it (and there were many of these)—always they would look and their eyes would get what is called in the military "the thousand-yard stare" and sometimes they would smile and sometimes there would be a shot of something else (fear, perhaps, or amazement) and they would open their mouths and say:

"Well . . ."

And stop. It was not that they didn't want to help—everybody helped us, bent over backward (especially when they saw how incredibly ignorant I really was). But the race is . . . different. I did not understand it then (and indeed, am only beginning to understand it now) but it is truly different. From everything. And still now, if asked what it is like I nod and smile and get that tinge of fear/amazement in my eyes and open my mouth and say:

"Well . . ."

And stop. It is almost impossible to articulate the race as a whole. It can be broken down into sections, days, hours, horrors, joys, checkpoints, winds, nights, colds, waters, ices, deaths, tragedies, small and large courages. But as a whole, to say generally what the race is like, there are no exact words.

Outrageous, perhaps. Staggering. Insane. Altering.

All of them, and more. No one word works. But given time, given the time to stare out across nothing and think, they would start.

"It was at Rohn River. I found god there. Coming down off Rainy Pass onto Rohn River the temperature dropped from forty above to sixty-five below and I came around a corner and it hit me and my feet froze—that's where I lost my little toes—and both runners on my sled broke and I was dragged for two miles in back of the broken sled and . . ." Pause to breathe. The stare came back. "So watch it on Rohn River."

And it came then. What was described, the whole event, losing toes and being dragged and getting close to god, the whole thing took perhaps twenty minutes. In a run of eighteen or so days, of Christ knows how many twenty-minute segments, this one bit of advice that cost toes to learn took only twenty minutes to happen. *Is it all this way? Is it all jolts of suffering?*

It was then that the race, the truth about the race, began to tickle. The first thoughts, the true doubts that had to be crushed or they would end the race before it started, the first true doubts: *How the hell can I do this? How the hell can anybody do this?*

There came a time then of almost unbroken, back-breaking effort. God, it was staggering—all that had to be done.

With the realization that I knew nothing came the need to learn, and the best way to learn about running dogs—other than begging information—was to run dogs.

I ran teams constantly. At first when I met other teams I was too shy—and embarrassed about my ignorance—to talk much or ask questions. But fear quickly took over, fear that the same ignorance would lead to disaster—and I started asking.

I can remember exactly when it happened. It was in the middle of the night when I met another team head on. In the area where we were training the snow was viciously deep powder. The dog trails—hundreds of miles of them—were kept packed solid by dogs running on them, but a step off the trail could drop you armpit-deep in snow. On this night the snow off the trail was at least waist-high, and when we met I ran up to pull my team off to the side so the other musher could get past. (I was very much aware of my amateur "foreign" status—having come from "down below," or "outside"—and didn't want to inconvenience anybody.) As I approached the front of the team and reached for Cookie it brought me next to the other team's lead dog. It was a small dog, a female, and she promptly snaked in and took a chunk of my pants leg off, catching some meat along with it.

"God*damn!*" I jumped away, fell into the deep snow, and the little bitch took advantage of it by nailing me twice more, on the arm and chest, as I stumbled around in the snow. I was still clutching Cookie's harness, trying to keep her out of it. But she loved a good fight more than anything (except, perhaps, eating cats, a fact that had caused some friction between Ruth—who loves cats—and Cookie).

With a happy growl Cookie piled in, which dragged the point dogs up, and *they* jumped into it. Soon eight or nine dogs from both teams were having at it, with me on the bottom, and I wasn't all that sure I would get out of it.

"Come on, goddamnit! *Stop* this shit!" The other musher waded in, pulling dogs off me by jerking on their harnesses. "Get *out* of there, damnit!"

I rolled on my hands and knees, stood, straightened my headlamp to find myself peering at a red-bearded man with ice frozen in his beard.

"Sorry," he said. "She's bad that way—bad to start fights."

"She bit me . . ."

He nodded, his headlamp bobbing in the darkness. "Yeah, she doesn't like anybody much. I'll hold her off to the side while your team passes . . ."

He dragged the small lead dog off into the deep snow and held her in back of him with both hands while I passed. If I had felt singled out for her attention I needn't have. While he held her and I dragged my dogs past she absolutely tore his ass to pieces. It was like a meat grinder back there, shredding his clothing, spitting out bits of insulation and butt and ripping anew.

At last it was accomplished and I had passed. I stopped my sled next to his. He pulled his team out so the sleds were near each other but the dogs were heading in opposite directions and came back to his sled. His coveralls and the back of his parka hung down in shreds and his hands were dripping blood.

"I have a question," I said.

"What is it?"

"That thing is a menace. Why the hell do you keep her?"

He stared at me as if I were insane. "Christ, man, she's the best dog I've ever had. I've never seen her tug go slack . . ."

And there it was—the only absolute, the single most important thing, the be-all and end-all of running dogs on the Iditarod: a tight tug.

I did not understand it yet, did not know how important it would become; did not realize that I would live for it, die for it, fixate on it, become totally obsessed with it, eat, sleep, and dream of it.

A tight tug.

Mile after mile, hour after hour, into days and weeks and months, *thousands* of miles would pass beneath the runners while I stood on the back of the sled and stared at the tugs. And there came a time, there came in fact many times when I would gladly have taken the small bitch who tore me apart, would have paid good money for her, would have let her eat my ass off and swapped my soul for her.

Later, miles and lives later, I sat at a checkpoint and watched a man feeding his dogs. He could not get close to them without injury. They were half-wild, yellow-eyed beasts, some with hair that hung to the ground. And they hated. Not just men, not just all men—including the man who rode their sled—but all things. Other dogs, trees, the world—they simply hated. While feeding, the musher had to place the food in a bowl, then use a stick to push the bowl to where the picketed dog could reach it. In a later checkpoint these same dogs would catch a dog from another team, kill it in seconds, and start *eating* it before they could be dragged off. (In a similar story that I have not been able to verify but everybody swears is true, it is said that a woman running a team in Canada climbed into the middle of a team fight and went down and was killed and partially eaten by her dogs.) When I asked the sled driver how he harnessed them he quipped, "I had a cousin help me but he quit before the race . . ."

But they pulled.

My god, how those dogs pulled. I watched them leave a checkpoint just ahead of me, saw them churn up a small mountain like a fur-covered rocket, and would gladly have suffered injury for such a team.

Tugs, pulling, that sweet curve of power from the gangline and up over their backs became everything—more than money, love, family—more than life.

The tug.

Two things happen well before the race and they are of each other and combine to cause chaos.

First, the absolutely numbing logistical truth of the race emerges. To wit: the race, taken from a logistics standpoint, is impossible. A dog team must start in downtown Anchorage and go to downtown Nome—1,180 miles away. They must be fed a snack every hour, rested, nurtured, have booties put on their feet, fed full meals every four hours, have their harnesses replaced, and the sled they pull must be repaired. If they are injured they must be flown out and sent back to the prison in Anchorage, where the convicts will care for them until they are picked up. Food must be flown in, dropped at eighteen checkpoints across Alaska; also replacement gear, booties, spare harnesses, *different* foods for the dogs in case they get bored with the food and need a change (which happens frequently—and was the reason why I shipped sixty pounds of turkey gizzards to each checkpoint as a bonus for the team; a fact that provided some merriment when word spread around). Coupled with shipping food and gear, if by some incredible miracle a team should get to Nome, the entire team—sled, dogs, and gear—have to be crated, boxed, wrapped, taped, and flown *back* to Anchorage, as there are no roads to drive back and the thought of turning the dogs around and running back is so daunting as to be unthinkable. (There is, however, a story of an Inuit dog team that a man drove 600 miles from his village to run in a 400-mile race. He won the race, then turned around and ran his team home with the prize money.)

All of this, the enormity of the operation, the hundreds, thousands of things that needed to be done, came screaming at me at exactly the same time that a startling truth became overwhelmingly evident.

There was no more time.

Somehow it had gone. The months of training, the seemingly endless hours, the long days and longer nights had mysteriously gone and there was no time left.

And then it *all* happened. There was the thought that as the race approached things would snap into form—or at least move that way. Nothing could have been further from the truth. Indeed, everything seemed to fall apart and a frantic air dominated.

Suddenly there weren't enough booties. Six hundred had been made, sewn on an ancient Singer sewing machine. But word was the snow was bad along the trail (this meant nothing to me; I did not understand sugar snow, a granular form of crystal that is murder on dogs' feet and required constant booties). It was estimated that at least eleven hundred booties would be needed, and cloth was found in Anchorage and sewing began anew.

At the same time—and time was accelerating exponentially now—the team had to be hauled to Anchorage for the vet check. Each dog had to be checked by a veterinarian to ensure he or she was in condition to run. (One of the paradoxes of the race is that while extraordinary care is given to checking and caring for the dogs, as it should be—they are checked methodically before the race, examined by vets at each checkpoint during the race, checked for drugs or other stimulants, checked for proper feeding, checked for possible dehydration constantly—while every possible examination is made of the dogs, nothing is done about the mushers. Nobody checks the humans or the food they send for themselves—this has led in the past to such oddities as mushers running the whole race without a change of clothes, eating only Snickers candy bars for food, and thinking one set of batteries will last all the way.)

With the vet check came the need to bag supplies and ship them from the Anchorage airport and meanwhile the sled had to be virtually rebuilt, with new plastic runner shoes fastened on and every bolt or lashing examined and retightened at the same time that more booties had to be sewn and a sled bag had to be made and a dog food cooker manufactured and still *more* booties sewn and more food found and gear checked and time was gone and in a few days the dogs had to be hauled to Anchorage again for staging and the race start, and right then a man came to camp and looked at the dogs and shook his head.

"Christ, you're not going to run them like that, are you?"

A numbing fear gripped my heart. Immersed as I was in ignorance I was ready to accept anybody's opinion.

"Why—what's wrong with them?"

"They're full of it. You've got to tire them out before the race."

"Tire them—I thought it would be just the opposite. You'd want them rested."

He shook his head again. "How many dogs are you going to run?"

Rules about dogs cover many pages. You cannot add dogs—the dogs you leave Anchorage with, in harness, pulling the sled, are the dogs you must run. This is because one man had actually tried to run with two full teams—one pulling and ten spare dogs in cages on an enormous sled. It had proven disastrous—he had trouble making the first corner (something I would come to understand and sympathize with) and so came the rule about dogs having to pull. The rules state that at least seven dogs must be on a team, and not over twenty. For obvious reasons—moose attacks against teams and drivers are very common, dogfights, shoulder injuries—people try to leave with as many dogs as possible in case they have to drop some (fly them back to Anchorage). I had brought twenty dogs to Alaska but after training and running in mountains it was clear not all of them were distance-oriented dogs. I had weeded them down, found homes for those that obviously weren't going to make it, and I was going to run every dog that I thought would work out.

"Fifteen," I answered him. "I'm going to run fifteen dogs."

"No." He shook his head one more time. "You're going to run fifteen *Iditarod* dogs."

I nodded. "So?"

"They are strong, tough—hell, three of them on a sled will take you fifty miles a day. Fifteen of them, on a sled in downtown Anchorage, fresh and full of piss, is a goddamn disaster looking for a place to happen. You've got to run them, burn them down a bit so you can handle them in town."

"But the race is next week!"

"My point"—he nodded—"exactly."

Much advice is given by people who have never run, never started the race, some of it by people who have never even had dogs. It is not conceit or arrogance that causes this—simply that everybody wants so much to be *involved*. I did not know it at the time, but that was the case with this man.

Still, in a way he was right. I needed more control of the team—always, but especially in downtown Anchorage—but his method was wrong. Disastrously.

I set out to wear them down. Fifteen dogs on a sled, lightly loaded, back-to-back sixty-mile runs. To say that it didn't work would be only a half-truth.

It not only didn't work, it had the exact opposite effect. The team had become amazingly tough—bullet-proof—and the snow conditions (good, packed trail from countless teams running on them, ten-below temperatures) did nothing to tire them.

Running them on sixty-mile runs with good trail to tire them, in their condition and frame of mind, was like trying to put out a fire by pouring gasoline on it. It merely pumped them up, and by the time the clock ran out and everything came to a head and it was time to head into Anchorage for the start I had what amounted to a pack of fifteen wild dogs absolutely full of adrenalin and I knew it, could *feel* the insanity in them.

"I'm not going to get out of Anchorage alive," I told a friend.

And it proved to be just about the only time I was close to being right.

GARY PAULSEN is a prolific author of many bestselling and critically acclaimed fiction and nonfiction books, among them *Woodsong, Tracker,* The *Tucket* books, *Brian's Winter, Brian's Return, Hatchet, Nightjohn,* and *Winterdance.*

Excerpt from *Iditarod Classics: Tales of the Trail from the Men & Women Who Race Across Alaska*

LEW FREEDMAN

LIBBY RIDDLES

*A*T THE STARTING LINE *of the 1985 Iditarod no one paid much attention to Libby Riddles, then twenty-eight. She had finished far back in the pack in her two previous races, the first in 1980, and was a virtual unknown.*

Yet, Riddles opened a new era in race history that year and created one of the enduring legends of the race by driving her dogs into a severe storm that packed gusts of sixty miles per hour and whiteout conditions that obliterated the trail.

After another musher advised her that it would be impossible to go on, she plunged ahead through the storm and left Shaktoolik to cross Norton Sound. "I allowed only one thought—to keep my lead at all costs, taking it inch by inch if necessary, she wrote later in her book, "Race Across Alaska."

Riddles' daring gamble paid off. She won the race in 18 days, 20 minutes and 17 seconds, six hours faster than her nearest competitor. As the first woman to earn the title of Iditarod champion, she became a national celebrity.

At the time, Riddles lived in Teller on the Seward Peninsula and raised dogs with her partner, Joe Garnie. Since then Riddles has lived on the Nome River, in Banner Creek and in Knik.

I was more of a cat person as a kid.

The first time I saw dogs in action was in the Fur Rendezvous in Anchorage. I was just a goner.

If you survive your first year of mushing, especially knowing as little about it as I did, it's amazing that a person would continue. People go to races and they see these nice dog teams all stretched out and doing what they're told to do, and they don't realize what it takes to get a dog team to that point.

When I started, I didn't have any intention of racing at all. I just wanted these dogs so I could haul firewood and haul drinking water so I didn't have to deal with starting a snowmachine, and basically so I didn't have to carry it myself.

I liked the dogs. I liked how much they liked to help me out and work for me and how happy they were pulling a sled. They're happiest when they have a job to do. You treat them right and give them a fair chance and they're just amazing.

I think the Iditarod fit in with what I was already doing—traveling with dogs. I love to go fast, too, but it's a different kind of racing. You can't be running a sprint race against George Attla and Roxy Wright and be looking at the sunset.

I was competitive my first year, in 1980. My objective was to get to Nome in the best fashion that I could. I wasn't going on any camping trip. I was racing. I'm glad that I started the year that I did. It was a horrible year. Half the field scratched. I was too dumb to know any better. I just thought, "It's always like this. What's the big deal?" I was able to finish eighteenth, and I was happy with that.

Winning the race changed my life. It's given me a lot of opportunities and connected me with neat people all over the country. I've met a lot of famous athletes and done lots of traveling.

I knew I had a team that could win. I knew it was a team that was as good as anybody's.

They had two freezes (stoppages) in the race. It was a heavy snow year. That definitely made an impact on the race.

I started with fifteen dogs. I didn't drop one until I got to Unalakleet on the Bering Sea coast. I had sick dogs and during the freezes I concentrated on bringing those dogs back around so I wasn't going to have to drop them. I just babied them. And I stayed among the top five.

When I took the lead it was in a moment of stubbornness. I had rested my dogs on the Yukon. Some guys had a fire going. So I stopped at their fire for about two hours and thawed out. That was around nightfall.

We went on for barely an hour, probably no more than five miles, and here's this Blackburn Lodge and all these dog teams are pulled up in there and there's a fire going, lights on. Looking through the window it looks good, and I was thinking, "Hey, we just took a big rest, we're going to keep on trooping." My dogs tried to go in and join the party. I was halfway thinking, "Hmmm, a cup of coffee might not be bad." But the fact that my dogs went in there without my permission made me feel stubborn. So I said, "C'mon, c'mon, we're going!"

I built a good lead that night because it was so cold that I didn't dare stop. I had to keep moving or freeze my feet. It was forty to fifty below.

It reached the point that if I didn't get in a cabin, or stop and start a fire, I was going to freeze my feet. I was the first one into Eagle Island at about five o'clock that morning.

I got a good twelve-hour rest there and went out the next evening, when it was even colder. It was cold enough that even with a big Eskimo-style fur pullover, the only way I was staying warm going down the trail was with my sleeping bag out, used like a cape around me.

I was sleepy in Unalakleet. I wanted to stay longer than I did. I was dragging, but I got up about five in the morning and booted up the team while it was still dark. I remembered it was so cold I could only put a few booties on and then had to thaw my hands.

It was a long forty miles to Shaktoolik.

I got there about one in the afternoon. It was blowing like hell. The weather three hours later when I left was worse.

I was nervous because I was in first place and wanted to stay there. The weather was not anything I wanted to travel in, and if I would have been at home I would never have dreamed of traveling in it, to tell you the truth. But it's different when you're in a race.

Still, having lived in that country for quite a few years, I think I had an awareness of how dangerous it could be. When it came time to get going, I didn't really think. I just did it.

Lavon Barve was rolling in as I was packing my sled and getting ready to go. He came over, shaking his head, and couldn't believe it because he'd just been battered out there. He said something like, "You're crazy if it's like what

I just came through." In a way that gave me even more incentive. I knew it was a little crazy. I knew it was more than a little crazy, actually.

And it was bad. I couldn't believe I was there. Part of what you get from dog mushing is patience. Patience, I think, was the calming factor when I was out in this storm.

It was grim. I could not see from one trail marker to the next. I let my dogs go so far that I could barely see the marker behind me, because I didn't want to lose that sucker. When that was at the edge of my visibility, I'd put my snowhook in and walk up ahead of the dogs until I could see the next marker. And we repeated that process. It was very slow. For some idiot reason the dogs trusted that I knew what I was doing.

We went fifteen miles in three hours. When it was getting dark there was absolutely no way to continue unless I wanted to do it as they did in the old days—with a compass. But when you're on sea ice and there could be open water, I didn't think it was a good idea. So I had to camp there for the night. That was an ordeal, getting settled in. It took me over two hours, I think, to get warm and halfway comfortable. My clothes had gotten damp and I had to switch into some dryer clothes inside my sled bag, which was an interesting process. It would have been hilarious to an onlooker.

It hadn't let up all night. My sled was rocking in the wind. The dogs were buried in snow the next morning. I could hardly see them. Getting started was tough, trying to get into boots and get organized without freezing my hands, doing zippers and so forth.

I was glad when I got to Koyuk. I was ready to kiss the snowbank.

It's a strange feeling coming into Nome. You've been out on the trail so long at that point that you're operating in a strange state. You're used to doing this stuff all by yourself, isolated. You think you must look like someone from Mars. I couldn't believe it was happening. It took weeks to hit me that I'd won the Iditarod.

I was unprepared for the reaction. To have so many people pulling for you. Everybody from Northwest Alaska was so proud of me. I did it the hard way and that's what people were saying. And of course I had a lot of ladies pulling for me. There were so many good feelings. I was proud of my dogs. I never doubted them.

It's hard to imagine that winning it again would be as special as winning it in 1985.

I'm not one of those lifer types who run it every year. I would love to win the race again. Of course I would. I'd love to prove that these new dogs I have are good and I miss being out there on the trail.

RICK SWENSON

RICK SWENSON, forty-one, is one of the stars of the Iditarod and one of the most recognizable faces in Alaska. He has a huge following and over the years has appeared on national TV to discuss the race.

Swenson raced in sixteen Iditarods and never has finished out of the top ten. That is the best overall record. He has won a record five times—in 1977, 1979, 1981, 1982, and again in 1991 in a storm-slowed race when he had to brave forbidding trail conditions after other competitors turned back. Swenson's famous leader in his early victories was a dog named Andy, for whom he later named his son.

Swenson lives and trains his dogs near Fairbanks. He is from Crane Lake, Minn., where he got his start in dog mushing.

I think the key element in what makes the Iditarod special is that it's in Alaska, which means it may rain, it may snow. In some sporting events, if it gets cloudy, they stop. The caution flag comes out. There have been proposals that if the weather gets too bad, the race should be stopped. That's not the Iditarod. Weather is part of the deal. If you think it's too bad for your own safety, then don't go.

When you have the attitude "I am having a good time" in storms, those situations aren't life-threatening or negative. They're positive. If you don't have that attitude, then things probably aren't going to work out for you. It doesn't matter if you're racing for first place or if you're just trying to get to the finish line. If you don't have that positive attitude, if you aren't enjoying trying to travel in those adverse conditions, then you're going to stop and crawl into a sleeping bag and wait for it to get better.

I got into dogs because I wanted to travel in the wilderness. That was when I was living up in the Boundary Waters Canoe Area, at Crane Lake, Minn., and that was the only way we could travel—either that or ski. If you wanted to go farther in a day than you could cross-country skiing, then you were going to have to step up to dogs.

Then I read about the first Iditarod and I said, "Gee, I'd sure like to do that some day." I was twenty-two. I moved to Alaska when I was twenty-three. I ran in the Iditarod in 1976. That was the dream, right? Just to run in the Iditarod. Just to get to Nome and get the belt buckle. Finish the Iditarod.

The first time it was an adventure. I had no illusions of winning that year, or ever winning. That was the only time I had any doubt as to whether I could get to Nome. Since then, I've never worried about that.

Unfortunately, because of all the sponsor pressure and media pressure, I don't have time anymore to meet those people who come for the adventure. It's not because I wouldn't like to, but running is such an intense thing now.

Any time you run in the race, whether you win or scratch, you should be able to say, "I can improve in this area and I can improve in that area." If you get to a point where you don't feel you can make any improvements, then you're going to be going downhill because there's somebody out there who's making improvements.

Just finishing gives anybody confidence. You've got twenty teams that should be in the top ten. The competition is close now. There's a personal satisfaction having won it, but back in the early days the Iditarod and sled-dog racing was different than it is now. None of us had sponsors. When I won in 1977—I've got some pictures—I don't have a single patch on. I wasn't sponsored by anybody. I won $9,600 and that was it. I had to pay my way back from Nome.

In 1979, I think I had $2,000 worth of sponsors. The personal satisfaction of winning then, I think, was a bigger deal. You were doing it for your personal satisfaction. You weren't doing it because you were getting paid money and you had all these perks and opportunity if you could win.

The sled that I won the Iditarod with the first time, I built with hand tools, and I mean non-electric hand tools. Now people talk about a handmade sled, they're using a table saw and power drills. I'm talking about hand tools.

It's a different era now. I bet half the people in the top twenty have never built a dogsled using power tools. I remember sewing harnesses. Joe Garnie is that kind of guy, every dog harness his dog wears, he still sews by hand. It's got the dog's name written on it. That guy has a tremendous wealth of knowledge of dogs.

I enjoy all the additional knowledge that I have now, but I'm nostalgic.

I could see from my first races that the event deserved attention. It deserves more attention than it's getting now. I would have never dreamed fifteen years ago that a disabled baseball player like this Bo whatever-his-name-is would be getting $100,000 a game to sit on the bench.

It's better these days for guys like me in many respects. But I still get the most satisfaction from people like Dick Wilmarth and Carl Huntington and the old champions. And when I go to a Native village, to Huslia or someplace, and talk with Bobby Vent and Warner Vent, I get more satisfaction out of that and how those guys react to what I've done. Those are the people I held up as my idols when I started racing. George Attla was at my house and had coffee. I got more satisfaction sitting there talking with him about the 1991 race than I do talking with David Letterman.

It's as if you were a boxer and you could sit down at the table with Muhammad Ali and Sugar Ray Leonard and pretend you were fighting Roberto Duran and Mike Tyson—even if it's just b.s. We can sit there and talk about the great dogs we had.

I like the sound of "Rick Swenson, five-time winner of the Iditarod." I don't consider myself to be the greatest long-distance dog-musher who ever lived. I don't think any of us should consider ourselves that. I don't think we can hold a candle to some of the old-timers, guys like Leonhard Seppala.

Seppala and those guys stayed awake days on end just to train themselves for the All-Alaska Sweepstakes (in the early years of the twentieth century). Running miles and miles and miles all the time, hard, not just out there jogging for the fun of it. Running that All-Alaska Sweepstakes was a full-time, year-round job. They weren't out making publicity appearances. They were heroes in Nome.

I'd like to win it a few more times for my own personal satisfaction. But then I think it's essential for somebody new to break into the winner's circle. That would be good for the competitors' enthusiasm.

Each year when I go into the race, I don't worry about last year's race, or having won five times versus somebody who's won four. It's this year's race. Who's going to win this year? Last year is behind us, the storms, the moose attacks. We've all been through going the wrong way and having our dogs get sick and all these things. This is a new year. And who knows what's going to happen? But it'll be interesting. It'll be the Iditarod.

SUSAN BUTCHER

IN 1985, SUSAN BUTCHER was the Iditarod favorite, but a moose attacked her team and knocked her out of the race. She came back the next year to win with a record-setting time of 11 days, 15 hours and 6 minutes flat, some seventeen hours faster than the old record. Butcher also won in 1987, 1988 and 1990, each time setting a record.

Over the years, Butcher has received many honors, including recognition from the Women's Sports Foundation as the Professional Athlete of the Year.

Probably the most famous Iditarod dog is Granite, who led Butcher's team to its first three victories, though as a pup Granite did not often show signs of becoming a great racing dog.

Butcher, thirty-seven, lives with her husband, Dave Monson, and more than one-hundred sled dogs in remote Eureka, about seventy-five air miles northeast of Fairbanks. Monson, who also has raced in the Iditarod, is a past champion of the Yukon Quest race between Fairbanks and Whitehorse, Yukon Territory, Canada.

Butcher grew up in Cambridge, Mass., and moved in the early 1970s to Colorado, where she began dog mushing. She moved to Alaska in 1975 and raced in her first Iditarod in 1978 after living alone in the wilderness in the Wrangell-St. Elias Range.

Granite is a wonderful dog. Granite has so many faults I cannot see how that dog would have made it in somebody else's kennel. But he also has some incredible natural ability, and he has such a close relationship with me.

He has no confidence. As a puppy, he didn't even look like he'd make it as a sled dog, let alone as a lead dog. He was scared of his own shadow, scared of the other dogs. He didn't understand pulling, though he was naturally intelligent. I could throw him in lead and I might get one run every two weeks out of him. But then if you put him up there again he wouldn't even leave the dog yard. He wouldn't go.

He didn't have enough confidence. But then he had this strange combination of no confidence and a stubborn streak. So sometimes he'd become confident to do the wrong thing. Most people don't tolerate that with their sled dogs, but I let him go along for a while. A long while. He wasn't a fast trotter. Now, as it turned out, he had a beautiful fast trot, but he wouldn't show it to you. He was always loping, which a long-distance racer doesn't like to see in his dogs. But I liked him and I wanted to see him do well.

I offered Granite to David (before we were married) and he didn't want him. I tried to sell him, but nobody wanted him after I listed his faults.

He's got this cool personality. He had to work so hard to become a good dog, and I had to work so hard with him, that I think he's proud of what he's done. He's not a good leader at home during training runs, never has been, never has gotten to be one. He just learned to love racing.

It started to show when I took him as a team dog to the 1984 race. I've always had a kennel of one-hundred or so dogs, but most of them were puppies and yearlings and I had few team dogs. Literally any dog that was of the right age went into the team because someone would get injured. Granite wasn't making the team on his ability, but he made it because of his age.

That year, I made it across to Koyuk with Copilot in lead, but somewhere, it must have been between Koyuk and Elim, I just didn't have any leaders. So Granite looked good.

He's just a pure mental athlete. He has good feet. But Granite doesn't eat. He'll eat one meal out of three. Makes you nervous, but he doesn't lose any weight. He eats and drinks when he needs to, and you have to have confidence that he's going to get himself fed.

In 1986, it was Granite's first year of being leader when I won. And he was a leader in 1987 when I won. The third win he was helpful. He made a big difference, but he wasn't the main leader. The next year I came in second to Joe Runyan and that year Granite wasn't much help, but I allowed him to cross the finish line in lead. He was on a sentimental journey in 1990. But he broke a toenail in Rohn, so I dropped him.

Granite was one of those neat dogs that everybody likes to have who will go up front at the beginning of the race and stay there because he loves it. He loves to be in lead in a race. What happened in 1988 is his best story.

In October of 1987 he became seriously ill. I rushed him to a vet in Fairbanks and we did the best we could for him and the vet basically said he was going to die. He had permanent heart, liver and kidney damage along with damage to his brain. I sat with him for forty-eight hours watching every breath and heartbeat. I mean, he was barely making it. He was a goner.

As best as we understand, it was a kidney infection that went undetected. He had no symptoms. And then he had heat stroke on top of it, caused by the infection, probably, because it wasn't even a hot day.

I pumped him full of fluids and we flew him down to Anchorage to Bob Sept at the Bering Sea Animal Clinic. I sat with him for two weeks and we brought him around.

Bob said that's fine, we've made him live, but he's never going to run again. I asked, "Not even with the pups?" He said no.

I knew Granite would be distraught not running. His test results were horrible. I brought him home and he was determined to get back on the team. I started taking him on puppy walks because I suppose I had this little hope. Bob wasn't even sure he was going to live long. He wasn't going to keel over tomorrow, but it didn't look good.

I took him on one-mile walks and I was testing his urine and blood twice a day. I hadn't given up. If he was to have any chance, I had to be on top of any changes in his system.

Later, Bob said go ahead and let him run the puppies. So I let him run the pups on two-mile runs. But to him it was punishment. He wanted to run with the team dogs and that's it. Every time the team dogs would go he'd be barking and jumping. Then I advanced him to the yearlings thinking he would like that better. He didn't want to go with the yearlings and he was so depressed.

Granite's tests were showing improvement, but not enough for us to feel confident. I was hooking up the dogs for a twenty-mile run when Granite had gone only ten miles that year. I put up the team dogs and he was going nuts. I thought to myself, "Well, who cares? I'll just let him run in the team because he wants to so badly. If I have to, I'll carry him home."

Well, as soon as we left the yard, and I had him in the lead, it started dumping snow. By the time we got to where we were ten miles from home, it was snowing hard and we were breaking trail through about six inches of snow.

So Granite was charging along, breaking trail, and by the time we got home, what should have been an hour-and-a-half run became a three-and-a-half-hour run.

So I ran him in the Portage 250 race in Unalakleet. I was happy with my team, with or without Granite, but I wanted him to get that third win.

In Unalakleet, I was down to two-year-olds who had never raced with Granite as their leader. My dogs were starting to tire and Rick Swenson's were feeling good, which is typical of a seasoned team. I could see him the whole time. I was timing him and he was two minutes behind me and finally caught up.

I thought, "That's it, I have tired two-year-olds." So I stopped and let Rick go by, and see, Granite is a racer, and I think he knows that we race against Rick. He knows who the competitive mushers are. He saw Rick go by and he just took off. He was literally towing those two-year-olds. Nobody was helping him pull and he was keeping up with Rick.

I stopped the team and made them sit until Granite got it out of his mind because I thought he was going to kill himself. I gave him about six minutes and off we went. Well, Rick was more tired than I knew and his dogs started faltering and Granite never stopped charging. We passed Rick and won it. So then I thought Granite was ready to run the Iditarod again.

The dogs have as much pride as any human athlete. That's why Granite's a wonderful dog. He knows when he's won. He thinks he deserves all the accolades, he expects them. He's a ham in front of the media.

When the Iditarod was organized in 1973 I knew I wanted to run it. I was a good musher and I'd been mushing for a lot of years, but I never liked racing because I'd only mushed sprint races. Although I like sprint racing now, I didn't like it then. My initial experience was in Colorado. I probably still wouldn't like sprint racing in Colorado.

I don't think my first Iditarod in 1978 was a wide-eyed experience. I'd lived in the Wrangell Mountains for so many years that I'd seen worse trail. I'd been more alone in the Bush with no one knowing where I was. The Iditarod is the biggest wilderness experience many mushers have had. It's the worst trail they've seen.

It was the funnest race. I had a great time. I met so many new friends and all the villagers. You gain confidence. I decided then that I wanted to win it.

I came to Alaska in 1975. My plan was to run the Iditarod for the experience, not for racing. I think after having trained for it, I already knew that I liked the competitive aspect. And after the first race I knew I could improve.

I always felt I was going to win the race. Your first win is in some ways your most exciting, but I feel my first race was the most exciting because everything was new. Nineteen-eighty-six was my ninth race, so there wasn't much new about the Iditarod Trail.

I felt confident in 1986. I felt confident in other years, too, and didn't win. It was a new team. My best team ever at that point was 1985. And most of the team had been obliterated by the moose. Only two were killed, but thirteen were injured. There were six veteran dogs out of sixteen in 1986. Not even all the veterans had raced with me.

I had written a plan. What I did was take my 1984 times—I ran a fabulous race in 1984, totally misjudged Dean Osmar, but ran a fabulous race—and I was planning to break the record. I thought, "Where can I take a chunk of time out?" Little bits of time, ten minutes here, twenty minutes there, and do it faster. When I added it up, it totaled eleven days, eleven hours—considerably under the record.

I thought, "I don't know if I can do it that fast." So I wrote a second, alternate plan that allowed more time, but it didn't seem to work for me. The first one worked. You were at the right places at daylight where you wanted to be at daylight, and you were at the right places at dark.

Most of the time when I win races, I'm not that excited. I'm happy but you haven't slept much and I think the joy is finishing. You almost don't realize for a day or two that you're actually done.

As soon as I'm in I don't like to talk about the race. I want to start talking about next year's race and what I plan to do. I set my goals the second I finish. That way, you don't have a letdown period. You're immediately working towards your next goal.

If I set the goal to win, then I expect to win.

☞ LEW FREEDMAN is a reporter for the *Anchorage Daily News* and the bestselling writer of many books, including *Dangerous Steps: Vernon Tejas and the Solo Ascent of Mount McKinley; Iditarod Classics: Tales of the Trail for the Men and Women Who Race Across Alaska; Spirit of the Wind: The Story of George Attla, Alaska's Legendary Sled Dog Sprint Champ;* and *Diamonds in the Rough.*

Excerpt from *Running
North: A Yukon Adventure*

ANN MARIAH COOK

Blackflies, or some large gnats of boreal origin, took advantage of the relatively mild fall days and descended on our dogs by the thousands late that September. Cold nights seemed to have no effect on lowering their population. I was beginning to think that Alaska had year-round insects. Unable to bring thirty-two dogs into the house or the shed, we watched helplessly as the dogs' ears, eye rims, and lips were bitten raw. One morning, I noticed that our big gray dog Bandit's eyelids were very swollen. His right eye was completely closed. Sticky yellow discharge flowed from the corner of his lid.

"Here, old boy," I called to him. "Let's have a look." I took Bandit's head into my arms and pried his eye open. The dog tensed but stood dutifully still. His eyeball was retracted, a sign of pain and serious injury. A veterinarian would have to be called, but what veterinarian, I wondered. "We'll find you some help," I reassured Bandit.

I returned to the house. George and Sandy were in the kitchen having their morning coffee and planning the day's training session. "We've got trouble," I told them. "Bandit's done something to his eye."

George went to get a look at the dog while Sandy and I scanned the Fairbanks yellow pages for the phone number of a veterinary clinic.

"A few years ago I read an article by an Alaskan veterinarian. It was about improving sled dogs . . . not breeding so many dogs, just better dogs," I told Sandy. "He sounded good. His name was something like Talbot. I only remember that because his brother ran the Quest a while back. You don't suppose he lives around here, do you?"

"Dr. Bill Talbot?" Sandy said, reading the name from a phone listing.

"I think that's it!" I said. "Where is he?"

"Fairbanks. Out by the airport."

"Well, let's give it a try." I dialed the number.

Bill Talbot was indeed the veterinarian whose paper I had read. He was a kind-faced young man with a dark woolly beard. He greeted George, me, and Bandit in the waiting room of the Nesbitt Veterinary Clinic and motioned us into the exam room.

George lifted Bandit onto the steel table. Bandit looked around miserably with his one open eye, while Dr. Talbot glanced at a chart.

"This is Bandit, and we haven't seen him before?" he asked.

"No, we're new here," George said. Dr. Talbot took a quick look at Bandit's eye. "That doesn't look good," he said, almost to himself. Then he turned to George. "You indicated on the chart that this is a working dog. Given his age, almost ten, I'd have to guess he's a leader."

George and I smiled. "Yes, that's right," George said.

"Mmmm," Dr. Talbot said. "Most people don't keep a ten-year-old running unless there's a good reason. He doesn't look ten though, does he?"

"He doesn't run like he's ten, either," I said.

After a brief examination of the Bandit's body, Talbot went back to the dog's eye. He poked and prodded with a light and a few instruments. Bandit stood stoically. Talbot asked us questions about the dog and the circumstances of his injury. Then he asked questions about George and me. George willingly volunteered that we were in Alaska to train for the Quest. That bit of information seemed to hold weight with Dr. Talbot.

Finally he finished the examination. "Well," he said, "Bandit has a bad ulceration of the cornea. Without help, the eye could rupture. I'd like to talk to a canine ophthalmologist in Anchorage, if you don't mind. She might be better able to advise us on our options."

Poor Bandit, I thought. Poor us! We *needed* Bandit for the Quest. He was one of our big boys, a muscle dog. What if we had to do without him? I looked into his big, broad face. He had been lucky before. Could he be lucky again?

In his youth, Bandit had belonged to Ted Thomas, a musher from Ontario. He was born and raised at Ted's farm and grew to be a big, rangy dog who could cover ground easily. Ted hitched Bandit up with Lucy, a smart female who knew her commands well. Lucy's brains and Bandit's brawn proved a winning combination, and Ted enjoyed three victorious seasons with this duo leading his team. Then Ted had a serious accident: his leg was crushed in a tractor roll. His knee was permanently damaged. Unable to balance on a sled, Ted made a pretense of facing reality and sold some of his dogs. Yet he hoped that, in time, he would overcome his handicap, so he kept just a few of his very best racers. Eventually, this group grew too old to be salable, and there they sat, in their dog yard, their glory days behind them.

Ted made a pet of Lucy. He watched the light go out of the eyes of his older team dogs, but Bandit, who was at the prime age of five when Ted had his accident, never adjusted to retirement. He would still whine and look hopefully at Ted whenever Ted passed the kennel. He never forgot what it meant to run.

When Bandit was nearly nine George and I suffered a shocking loss. Dan, our top achiever and lead dog of seven years, developed a rapidly growing brain tumor and died. We were overcome with grief. We had three young leaders coming up the ranks, all offspring of Dan's, but none were old enough to take his place. We had Minnie, Dan's co-leader and mother of the new prospects, but Minnie needed a strong partner. So Ted offered us Bandit.

I was against taking this oldster. After all, we'd lost a fast dog. George differed with me. He thought we should give the dog a try. George was so saddened over Dan that I didn't have the heart to argue with him.

Lack of exercise had greatly expanded Bandit's girth. No musher looking at him would have believed that under that blanket of fur and fat lay the heart of anything other than a house pet. Bandit would have to lose the fat and catch up with the others if he was going to make the team. We weren't at all sure he could do it, and we weren't at all sure it was in his best interest to let him try.

The first day we brought him to our training site, he could scarcely believe his good fortune. He knew from the sights and the sounds that he was going to run again. He barked, leaped, whined, and even foamed at the mouth. He was crazy to get out on the trail. At last his moment came. He was harnessed and brought up next to Minnie. Down the trail he dashed, in lead once again. He ran like a demon for about a mile, and then staggered to a halt, gasping for breath. All the while, his tail was wagging. We had to laugh.

"It's a little more work than you remember, eh Bandit!" George called out.

Despite the rough return from retirement, Bandit quickly reunited his body with his athletic soul. Each day, we increased his mileage, and he soon was back in top form. He never failed to let us know how pleased he was at his second chance. His enthusiasm took on special meaning for us. It eased our grief and longing for Dan, and allowed us to think that some good had come out of the tragedy of Dan's death.

Now, once again, the odds were against Bandit. This eye injury—this senseless injury—would now probably cost him his chance. A long recovery would put him too far behind the others to catch up. Could the eye even be saved?

Dr. Talbot called the morning after he examined Bandit. Dr. Henry, the ophthalmologist he'd consulted, had suggested three options for Bandit: remove the eye surgically, since it would rupture anyway; suture the cornea, which would deprive Bandit of a good portion of his vision but save the eye; or perform a corneal transplant, which could, if successful, restore his vision. In all three cases, an immediate decision was necessary. The most costly treatment, of course, was the transplant, and the latter two types of surgery would have to be performed at Dr. Henry's clinic in Anchorage. In his phone call, Dr. Talbot gave us full particulars on how to arrange everything with Dr. Henry, then brought the conversation to an abrupt end. I had expected him to give us some parting advice, but clearly he felt the decision was ours.

George and I tried to discuss the matter rationally while Sandy hovered. I knew that Sandy hoped we would choose the corneal transplant. Young, idealistic, and not yet independent of her parents' pocketbook, she thought an eight-hundred-dollar veterinary bill was meaningless in the face of the moral issue of whether a dog should be deprived of his vision.

"Bandit is old. Maybe he's had his chance," George said. "We could buy two new pups for what the surgery will cost."

"But we need Bandit *now*," I argued. "We need him this season. It would cost us plenty to buy an adult dog to replace him at this late date, and that is only if there is a dog available." I shook my head. "We got him for free. And we did get one good season out of him last year. Maybe it evens out."

"Yeah, nothing is ever really free," George grumbled.

Ultimately, we decided what I knew we would decide: Bandit would have a corneal transplant. None of us could bear to take anything away from this magnificent Methuselah.

Arrangements were made quickly through Dr. Henry's office. Bandit was booked on Alaska Airlines' afternoon cargo flight to Anchorage. Someone from Dr. Henry's staff would pick him up at the airport. It was all very routine. Animals from all over Alaska commonly flew in to be treated by Dr. Henry.

As we hurried to the Fairbanks airport with Bandit, I told myself that bush families often put their ailing children on medevac flights, sending them off to doctors and hospitals in the city, trusting their lives to strangers, in effect. If they could be that brave, I could certainly cope with sending a dog in, but I felt rushed, frightened.

At the air cargo building, I handed over Bandit's rabies certificate and filled out forms identifying Bandit and releasing the airlines from liability in the event of his death. These forms were also routine, but I hated signing them. They had such an air of finality about them, as if, should the worst happen, I'd have no right to mourn.

George ushered Bandit into his airline crate. Baggage handlers lifted his crate onto a trolley. George reached for my hand, and we stood together, watching until the trolley was out of sight.

There was nothing to do that night but watch the northern lights. None of us could sleep. Finally George and I put on our coats and walked out to the potato field to get a clear view of the sky. The lights were wondrous, glittering all around. Green, pink, and silver, they whirled and flashed in kaleidoscope patterns. The deity seemed quite near. Walking in such heavenly surroundings calmed us.

Dr. Henry called the next afternoon and reported that the transplant had gone very well. Bandit would stay a week in her Anchorage clinic. His environment would have to be dust free while the eye healed and adjusted to the new cornea. He would have to convalesce an additional two weeks after his release, but if there were no complications, he would again be free to run. This was indeed good news.

Bandit's homecoming was such a cause for celebration that all four of the human members of our household went to the airport. The dog greeted us with his big oafish expression and happy swings of his tail.

A few days later, Dr. Talbot called. His voice was even, guarded, as he said, "I was wondering, what did you decide to do about Bandit?"

"Oh, we did the transplant."

"You *did?*" he exclaimed. Evidently he was surprised by our choice. "How did it go?"

"Just fine. He's home and he's doing very well."

"That's . . . *great!*" Talbot seemed to gasp the second word.

It was evident to me that Dr. Talbot was not used to happy endings when it came to dogs like Bandit. Alaska has its harsh realities, and few people would burn a good eight hundred dollars on an old sled dog. In fact, I was fairly certain that Talbot himself thought we were crazy to do so. While he was genuinely interested in the medical facts of the case, a tone of incredulity crept into his voice. "Well, I guess if he's your leader, it's worth it," he said.

I sensed he was mocking me, smiling to himself about sentimental outsiders. We weren't tough Quest mushers after all, but people playing at mushing. When our conversation ended, it ended on a pleasant note, everything upbeat, but as I hung up the receiver, I swallowed hard.

"You think you know us," I told an imaginary Dr. Talbot, "but you don't. You don't know us at all."

✽ ANN MARIAH COOK is a sled dog racer, a columnist, and an American Kennel Club judge. She lives in New Hampshire with her family and thirty-five purebred Siberian Huskies.

THE GREAT EXPLORERS

IN THIS MODERN AGE of air transportation, a combination of jets and bush pilots can take a traveler from anywhere in the lower forty-eight states and set him down in the middle of the Alaskan wilderness in a matter of hours. But Alaska's early explorers suffered in their quest to discover Alaska's secrets. These selections written by some of those early explorers give a modern traveler a true perspective on the difficulties that they encountered. Included in this section are the observations of a naturalist named Georg Steller, who accompanied Captain Vitus Bering on his historic voyage of discovery in 1741, which was commissioned by Peter the Great of Russia; as well as Washington Irving's description of his travels to Alaska; the original newspaper account of an early Alaskan exploration that was used by most of the gold seekers of 1897 to make their way to Alaska's gold fields; and a stunning description by naturalist John Muir of his discovery of Glacier Bay.

GEORG STELLER

We saw land as early as July 15, but because I was the first to announce it and because forsooth it was not so distinct that a picture could be made of it, the announcement, as usual, was regarded as one of my peculiarities; yet on the following day, in very clear weather, it came into view in the same place. The land was here very much elevated; the mountains, observed extending inland, were so lofty that we could see them quite plainly at sea at a distance of sixteen Dutch miles. I cannot recall having seen higher mountains anywhere in Siberia and Kamchatka. The coast was everywhere much indented and therefore provided with numerous bays and inlets close to the mainland.

Once having determined to tell the truth and be impartial in all things, I must not fail to mention one circumstance which perhaps may not escape the notice of the high authorities but may receive an interpretation different from the actual facts. . . . It can easily be imagined how happy every one was when land was finally sighted; nobody failed to congratulate the Captain Commander, whom the glory for the discovery mostly concerned. He, however, received it all not only very indifferently and without particular pleasure, but in the presence of all he even shrugged his shoulders while looking at the land. Had the Commander survived and had he intended to take any action against his officers because of their misdoings, they would have been ready to point to his conduct then as evidence of his evil-minded disposition. But the good Captain Commander was much superior to his officers in looking into the future, and in the cabin he expressed himself to me and Mr. Plenisner as follows: "We think now we have accomplished everything, and many go about greatly inflated, but they do not consider where we have reached land, how far we are from home, and what may yet happen; who knows but that perhaps trade winds may arise, which may prevent us from returning? We do not know this country; nor are we provided with supplies for a wintering."

. . . Now that we were close to land it was great fun to listen to the conflicting expressions of great self-conceit and expectations of future reward and pathetic effusions. Some would at once make for the shore and search for a harbor. Others represented this as very dangerous. However, everybody acted for himself, and no one made any representations to the Captain Commander. Councils and commissions, that were so often called on shore in case of trivial matters, were neglected now when we had come to the most important business and the culmination of the ten years' Kamchatka Expedition, and it was quite plain that we had nothing in common and nothing to keep us united except that we were locked up together on the same ship.

Since after July 16 more noteworthy happenings occurred daily than during the six preceding weeks, I shall from now on continue my record according to what took place each day.

On the 17th, the wind being light, we gradually drew nearer the land. On Saturday, the 18th, we were so close to it towards evening, that we were enabled to view with the greatest pleasure the beautiful forests close down to the sea, as well as the great level ground in from the shore at the foot of the mountains. The beach itself was flat, level, and as far as we could observe, sandy. We kept the mainland to the right and sailed northwesterly in order to get behind a high island which consisted of a single mountain covered with spruce trees only. This had to be accomplished by continuous tacking, as the wind was contrary, the coming night being consumed with this.

On Sunday, the 19th, we were opposite the northwestern end of the island, about two miles distant. This morning there arose again a petty quarrel. We had already noticed the day before the channel between the mainland and the island, and the thought occurred at once to me that a notably large stream must be flowing from the land into the channel, the current of which could be observed two miles from shore while the difference in the water could be inferred partly from the floating matter and partly from the lesser salinity; it was consequently my opinion that an attempt could have been made to enter this channel, where it would have been just as safe to anchor as, if not safer than, in the place under the lee of the island selected on the 20th. It might even have been possible to find a harbor for our ship, with its nine feet draught, in the mouth of the river, which was large enough and therefore probably also deep enough. But the retort I got was, had I been there before and made certain of it? Yet in uncertain things it is better to act on even the slightest indication than for no reason at all and only trusting to good luck.

The day was spent in tacking in order to get close to the island, to enter the large bay seen from the distance, and at the same time to come under the lee of the land. This was also accomplished, with the greatest apprehension, when on Monday the 20th we came to anchor among numerous islands. The outermost of these had to be named Cape St. Elias, because we dropped our anchor under the lee of it on St. Elias' day. For the officers were determined to have a cape on their chart notwithstanding the fact that it was plainly represented to them that an island cannot be called a cape, but that only a noticeable projection of land into the sea in a certain direction can be so designated, the same meaning being conveyed by the Russian word *nos* (nose), while in the present case the island would represent nothing but a detached head or a detached nose.

Orderly management as well as the importance of the matter would now have demanded a harmonious consideration of what ought to be done, how to utilize the time and opportunity to the best advantage, what to explore on shore and how to go about it; furthermore, whether, considering the season and the provisions as well as the distance, the following up of the coast should be continued at this late time of the year, or whether we should winter here, or, finally, try the straight way for home. However, all this was not considered worthy the calling of a council, but everyone kept silent and did as he pleased. Only on one point were all unanimous, viz. that we should take fresh water on board, so that I could not help saying that we had come only for the purpose of bringing American water to Asia. It was agreed, besides, that the small yawl should be used for the transportation of the water, while the larger one should be given to Master Khitrov with a sufficient crew and ammunition in order that he might explore the country, a task for which he possessed the best qualifications. I asked to be sent with Khitrov, since after all he himself did not know everything, but in spite of his making the same request permission was refused. At first an attempt was made to scare me with dreadful tales of murder, to which I answered that I had never been so womanish as to fear danger and that I could not guess why I should not be allowed to go ashore, especially since that was in the line of my principal work, my calling, and my duty and that it was my determination to serve the Crown to the best of my ability in the future, as I had done in the past; moreover, that, if for reprehensible reasons I were not given the permission, I would report this action in the terms it deserved. For this I was called a wild man, who would not let himself be held back from business even when treated to chocolate, which was just then being prepared. Seeing now that it was the intention to force me against my will to inexcusable neglect of my duty, I finally put all respect aside and prayed a particular prayer, by which the Commander was at once mollified so as to let me go ashore with the water carriers, without any assistance whatever and with no other person but the cossack Thomas Lepekhin, whom I myself had brought with me. On my leaving the ship he again made a test as to how far I could distinguish between mockery and earnest, by causing the trumpets to be sounded after me, at which, without hesitation, I accepted the affair in the spirit in which it was ordered. By this time I saw only too clearly why he had wanted to persuade me to go along. I was to fulfill in my person one point of the instructions, in regard to which it would otherwise have been impossible to give an accounting, namely that which related to the investigation of the mineral resources by certain properly qualified persons. For eight years it had been forgotten to requisition them from Ekaterinburg, and the assayer Hartepol, who was staying at Okhotsk, had been sent to Yakutsk in order to accompany Spanberg, so that at the departure he could not be taken along. Under the circumstances it was intended that I, though only in name, should confer upon the whole affair a greater distinction and at the same time fill the office of ship's doctor and physician in ordinary, since with an assistant surgeon it was considered that [the expedition] was too poorly supplied.

The events of the day consequently relate to four distinct parties: Half of the command, including all of the officers except the master [Khitrov], remained on board as watch busying themselves with hauling out the empty and stowing away the filled water casks. With another party I was sent off after water, to make watery observations, while others were out on a windy expedition.

As soon as I, with only the protection and assistance of my own cossack, had landed on the island and realized how scant and precious was the time at my disposal, I seized every opportunity to accomplish as much as possible with the greatest possible dispatch. I struck out in the direction of the mainland in the hopes of finding human beings and habitations. I had not gone more than a verst along the beach before I ran across signs of people and their doings. Under a tree I found an old piece of a log hollowed out in the shape of a trough, in which, a couple of hours before, the savages, for lack of pots and vessels, had cooked their meat by means of red-hot stones, just as the Kamchadals did formerly. The bones, some of them with bits of meat and showing signs of having been roasted at the fire, were scattered about where the eaters had been sitting. I could see plainly that these bones belonged to no sea animal, but to a land animal, and I thought myself justified in regarding them as reindeer bones, though no such animal was observed on the island but was probably brought there from the mainland. There were also strewn about the remains of yukola, or pieces of dried fish, which, as in Kamchatka, has to serve the purpose of bread at all meals. There were also great numbers of very large scallops over eight inches across, also blue mussels similar to those found in Kamchatka and, no doubt, eaten raw as the custom is there. In various shells, as on dishes, I found sweet grass completely prepared in Kamchadal fashion, on which water seemed to have been poured in order to extract the sweetness. I discovered further, not far from the fireplace, beside the tree, on which there still were the live coals, a wooden apparatus for making fire, of the same nature as those used in Kamchatka. The tinder, however, which the Kamchadals make from a species of grass, was here different, namely a species of fountain moss (*Alga fontinalis*), which was bleached white by the sun and of which I have kept a sample to be forwarded. . . . From all this I think I may conclude that the inhabitants of this American coast are of the same origin as the Kamchadals, with whom they agree completely in such peculiar customs and utensils, particularly the preparation of the sweet grass, which have not been communicated even to the Siberian natives nearest to Kamchatka, for instance the Tunguses and Koryaks. But if this is so, then it may also be conjectured that America extends farther westward and, opposite Kamchatka, is much nearer in the north, since in view of such a great distance as we traveled of at least 500 miles, it is not credible that the Kamchadals would have been able to get there in their miserable craft.

The chopped-down trees, as I came across them here and there, were miscut with many dull blows in such a way that in all likelihood the cutting of trees must be done by these savages, as in Kamchatka, with stone or bone axes similar to those used by the Germans of old and known today as "thunderbolts."

After having made a brief examination of all this I pushed on farther for about three versts, where I found a path leading into the very thick and dark forest which skirted the shore closely. I held a brief consultation with my cossack, who had a loaded gun, besides a knife and ax, as to what we should do in case we met one or more persons, and I commanded him to do nothing whatever without my orders. I myself was only armed with a Yakut palma (dagger) for the purpose of digging up rocks and plants. No sooner had we taken this path than I noticed that the natives had tried to cover it up but had been prevented by our quick approach and as a results had made it only more conspicuous. We saw many trees recently bared of bark and conjectured that they must have used it for houses or *ambars* and that these must be near by, since in whatever direction we looked there was no lack of fine forests. However, as the first trail broke up into a number of paths through the forest, we explored some of them for a little distance into the wood, and after half an hour we came to a spot covered with cut grass. I pushed the grass aside at once and found underneath a cover consisting of rocks; and when this was also removed we came to some tree bark, which was laid on poles in an oblong rectangle three fathoms in length and two in width. All this covered a cellar two fathoms deep in which were the following objects: (1) lukoshkas, or utensils made of bark, one and a half ells high, filled with smoked fish of a species of Kamchatkan salmon at Okhotsk called *nerka* in the Tungus language but in Kamchatka known by the common name *krasnaya ryba*. It was so cleanly and well prepared that I have never seen it as good in Kamchatka, and it also was much superior in taste to the Kamchatkan; (2) a quantity of *sladkaya trava* [or sweet grass], from which liquor is distilled; (3) different kinds of plants, whose outer skin had been removed like hemp, which I took for nettles, which grow here in profusion and perhaps are used, as in Kamchatka, for making fish nets; (4) the dried inner bark from the larch or spruce tree done up in rolls and dried; the same is used as food in time of famine, not only in Kamchatka but all through Siberia and even in Russia as far as Khly-nov and elsewhere on the Vyatka; (5) large bales of thongs made of seaweed which, by making a test, we found to be of uncommon strength and firmness.

Under these I found also some arrows in size greatly exceeding those in Kamchatka and approaching the arrows of the Tunguses and Tatars, scraped very smooth and painted black, so that one might well conjecture that the natives possessed iron instruments and knives.

In spite of my fear of being attacked in the cellar I continued my search but, discovering nothing more, took away with me, as proof, two bundles of fish, the arrows, a wooden implement for making fire, tinder, a bundle of thongs of seaweed, bark, and grass and sent them by my cossack to the place where the water was being taken on, with instructions to bring them to the Captain Commander; at the same time I asked once more for two or three men to help me further in my investigations of nature; I also had those on shore warned not to feel too secure but to be well on their guard. I then covered over the cellar as it had been and proceeded, now all alone, with my project of investigating the noteworthy features of the three kingdoms of nature until my cossack should return. However, when I had gone about six versts, I came to a steep rock extending so far into the sea beyond the beach that it was impossible to go farther. I determined to climb the rock and after much difficulty reached the top, where I discovered that the east side was steep as a wall and that it was impossible to proceed farther. I therefore turned south in the hope of getting to the other side of the island in order to follow the beach there to the channel and thus investigate my theory regarding the existence there of a river and harbor. However, as I descended the mountain, which was covered with a thick and dark forest, without finding any trace of a path, I saw that I could not get through here. Considering at the same time that it would be impossible for my cossack to find me, also that I was too far away from the others in case something should happen, and that it might be impossible for me to return before nightfall, not to mention other dangers, which I should not have feared had I had the least assistance of companions, I climbed the mountain again and looked once more sorrowfully at the barrier to my investigations, with real regret over the action of those who had in their hands the direction of such important matters, for which nevertheless all of them had let themselves be rewarded with money and honors.

When I was once more on the top of the mountain and turned my eyes toward the mainland to take a good look at least at that country on which I was not vouchsafed to employ my endeavors more fruitfully, I noticed smoke some versts away ascending from a charming hill covered with spruce forest, so that I could now entertain the certain hope of meeting with people and learning from them the data I needed for a complete report. For that reason I returned in great haste and went back, loaded with my collections, to the place where I had landed. Through the men who were just ready to hurry back to the ship in the boat I informed the Captain Commander and asked him for the small yawl and a few men for a couple of hours. Dead tired, I made in the meantime descriptions on the beach of the rarer plants which I was afraid might wither and was delighted to be able to test out the excellent water for tea.

In an hour or so I received the patriotic and courteous reply that I should betake myself on board quickly or they would leave me ashore without waiting for me. . . . I reflected that God gives to each one the place and the opportunity to do that which he is ordered to do, so as to enable one to present one's services favorably to the highest authorities and after long waiting and untold expenses to the Empress [i.e. Government] work out one's destinies. However, as matters now stand, it is probable that at our departure we all saw Russia for the last time, since under the present circumstances it is impossible to expect the divine help on the return voyage, if wind and weather were to become as hostile [toward us] as we have been to the general object of the expedition and thereby to our own good fortune. . . . However, since there was now no time left for moralizing, only enough to scrape together as much as possible before our fleeing the country, and as evening was already nearing, I sent my cossack out to shoot some rare birds that I had noticed, while I once more started off to the westward, returning at sunset with various observations and collections. . . . Here I was given once more the strict command that, unless I came on board this time, no more notice would be taken of me. I consequently betook myself with what I had collected to the ship and there, to my great astonishment, was treated to chocolate. . . .

Although I did not need to trouble myself for the benefit of anybody except those who were capable of judging what I was doing, I nevertheless showed some of the objects and made known my ideas about various things, but only a single one of these was accepted. Namely, an iron kettle, a pound of tobacco, a Chinese pipe, and a piece of Chinese silk were sent to the cellar, but in return the latter was plundered to such an extent that, if we should come again to these parts, the natives would certainly run away even faster or they would show themselves as hostile as they themselves had been treated, especially if it should occur to them to eat or drink the tobacco, the correct use of which probably could be as little known to them as the pipe itself. . . . A couple of knives or hatchets, the use of which was quite obvious, would have aroused the interest of these savages much more. But to this it was objected that such presents might be regarded as a sign of hostility, as if the intention were to declare war. How much more likely was it, particularly if they attempted to use the tobacco in the wrong way, for them to conclude that we had intended to poison them! On the other hand, we learned later how gladly the savages had accepted a few knives from Captain Chirikov and how eager they were to have more.

I had been on the ship scarcely an hour when Khitrov with his party of about fifteen men also returned in the great boat and made the following report. He had discovered among the islands lying close to the mainland a harbor where one could anchor without any danger. Although he had seen no human beings on land, he had nevertheless come across a small dwelling built of wood, the walls of which were so smooth that it seemed as if they had been planed and in fact as if it had been done with cutting tools. Out of this building he brought with him various tangible tokens, for instance, a wooden vessel, such as is made in Russia of linden bark and used as a box; a stone which perhaps, for lack of something better, served as a whetstone, on which were seen streaks of copper, as if the savages, like the ancient Siberian tribes, possessed cutting tools of copper; further a hollow ball of hard-burned clay, about two inches in diameter, containing a pebble which I regarded as a toy for small children; and finally a paddle and the tail of a blackish gray fox.

These, then, are all our achievements and observations, and these not even from the mainland, on which none of us set foot, but only from an island which seemed to be three miles long and a half mile wide and the nearest to the mainland (which here forms a large bay studded with many islands) and separated from it by a channel less than half a mile wide. The only reason why we did not attempt to land on the mainland is a sluggish obstinacy and a dull fear of being attacked by a handful of unarmed and still more timid savages, from whom there was no reason to expect either friendship or hostility, and a cowardly homesickness which they probably thought might be excused, especially if those high in authority would pay no more attention to the testimony of the malcontents than did the commanding officers themselves. The time here spent in investigation bears an arithmetical ratio to the time used in fitting out: ten years the preparations for this great undertaking lasted, and ten hours were devoted to the work itself. Of the mainland we have a sketch on paper; of the country itself an imperfect idea, based upon what could be discovered on the island and upon conjectures.

What can be said from comparison and observations at a distance may be summed up about as follows: The American continent (on this side), as far as the climate is concerned, is notably better than that of the extreme northeastern part of Asia. For, although the land, wherever it faces the sea, whether we looked at it from near or far, consists of amazingly high mountains most of which had the peaks covered with perpetual snow, yet these mountains, in comparison with those of Asia, are of a much better nature and character. The Asiatic mountains are thoroughly broken up and long since deprived of their coherency, consequently too loose for the circulation of mineral gases and devoid of all inner heat, accordingly also without precious metals. On the other hand the American mountains are solid; not naked rocks covered with moss but everywhere with good black soil, and therefore not, as are the former, barren, with stunted dwarf trees among the rocks, but densely covered to the highest peaks with the finest trees; also they are decked with short grass and herbs, some succulent, some drier, but not with moss, marsh vegetation, and water plants. The springs, of which I discovered so many, flow out of the valleys at the base of the mountains, and not as in Siberia everywhere among the rocks, often up to the summits and in stagnant hollows. The plants are about the same size and appearance whether found on the summit of the mountains or lower down, owing to the equally distributed interior heat and moisture. In Asia, on the other hand, the plants are often so different according to their station that one is tempted to make different species of the same plant if one is not mindful of this general difference, because a plant which in the valley is two ells high often on the mountains reappears scarcely half a foot high. . . . In America on the 60th parallel one sees most beautiful forests directly on the shore, while in latitude 51° in Kamchatka willow and alder bushes only begin 20 versts from the sea, birch woods not nearer than 30 to 40 versts, not to mention that no conifers are found there but are first seen 60 versts inland from the mouth of the Kamchatka River. In latitude 62° for instance from Anadyrsk on, no tree is to be met with for 300 or 400 versts inland. I therefore hold that continuous land must extend northwards from Cape St. Elias to about 70° or farther, which by furnishing shelter against the north wind promotes the fertility of the coast, which moreover, towards the east, is protected by the mountains. On the other hand the Kamchatkan shores, particularly on the Sea of Penzhina, are directly exposed to the north winds; while the eastern side is somewhat better provided with trees, because of the protection of the Chukchi Promontory. . . . Owing to the milder temperature it also comes about that in America the fishes go up from the sea earlier than in Kamchatka. On July 20 we found there the fish supply already stored, while in Kamchatka this, the day of St. Elias, indicates the time only for the beginning of good fishing. That plants which only start to bloom in Kamchatka at this time already have mature seed here in America is only a partial argument, because in the northern regions the usually longer days and the sudden great heat and dryness contribute greatly to this result, as I had already observed in Yakutsk in 1740.

Whoever stops to consider how much one man, without assistance, can accomplish in ten hours on a small island will easily see that my failure to discover any minerals is not due to carelessness or laziness on my part. I confess freely that I observed nothing else than sand and gray rock.

Of fruit-bearing shrubs and plants I only met with a new and elsewhere unknown species of raspberry in great abundance, although not yet quite ripe. This fruit on account of its great size, shape, and delicious taste had well deserved that a few bushes of it should have been taken along in a box with soil and sent to St. Petersburg to be further propagated. It is not my fault that space for such was begrudged, since as a protester I myself took up too much space already. . . . Such well-known berries as the Chamaccerasi, red and black whortleberries, the scurvy berry, Empetrum, and such like were here as plentiful as in Kamchatka. The other plants collected by me in America I have recorded in a separate list.

The animals occurring there and supplying the natives with their meat for food and with their skins for clothing are, so far as I had opportunity to observe, hair seals, large and small sharks, whales, and plenty of sea otters, the excrements of which I found everywhere along the shore; from this circumstance it may also be concluded that the natives, because otherwise sufficiently provided with food, do not trouble themselves greatly about them, since otherwise these animals would not have come ashore, any more than they now do in Kamchatka, where there are so many people interested in their pelts. Of land animals, aside from what has been inferred above about the reindeer, I as well as others, saw at various times black and red foxes and did not find them particularly shy, perhaps because they are hunted but little. . . . Of birds I saw only two familiar species, the raven and the magpie; however, of strange and unknown ones I noted more than ten different kinds, all of which were easily distinguished from the European and Siberian [species] by their very particularly bright coloring. Good luck, thanks to my huntsman, placed in my hands a single specimen, of which I remember to have seen a likeness painted in lively colors and described in the newest account of the birds and plants of the Carolinas published in French and English, the name of the author of which, however, does not occur to me now. This bird proved to me that we were really in America. I would have enclosed the drawing herewith, were it not that I had to leave it behind, as my return voyage had to be made on foot from Avacha to the Bolshaya River, and consequently it will have to be forwarded at some future time.

☞ GERMAN-BORN GEORG STELLER was trained in botany and medicine. He joined Captain Vitus Bering's crew as naturalist in 1741. His ship, the *Saint Peter*, left Petropavlovsk on June 4, 1741. The ship wrecked on Bering Island, and the crew built a shelter and stayed there for the winter. Captain Bering died of scurvy before spring, but the crew managed to build a ship from the wreckage of their boat and return to their home port, months after they were expected and long after they'd been thought to be lost at sea. Steller's journals are the only written account of this voyage other than the ship's logs to survive, and his books on his experiences describe a number of animals that had never previously been heard of in Europe, including such marine species as seals and sea otters.

WASHINGTON IRVING

It will be recollected, that the destination of the *Beaver*, when she sailed from Astoria on the 4th of August in 1812, was to proceed northwardly along the coast to Sheetka, or New Archangel, there to dispose of that part of her cargo intended for the supply of the Russian establishment at that place, and then to return to Astoria, where it was expected she would arrive in October.

New Archangel is situated in Norfolk Sound, lat. 57° 2' N., long. 135° 50' W. It was the head-quarters of the different colonies of the Russian Fur Company, and the common rendezvous of the American trading along the coast.

The *Beaver* met with nothing worthy of particular mention in her voyage, and arrived at New Archangel on the 19th of August. The place at that time was the residence of Count Baranhoff, the governor of the different colonies; a rough, rugged, hospitable, hard-drinking, old Russian; somewhat of a soldier, somewhat of a trader; above all, a boon companion of the old roystering school, with a strong cross of the bear.

Mr. Hunt found this hyperborean veteran ensconced in a fort which crested the whole of a high rocky promontory. It mounted one hundred guns, large and small, and was impregnable to Indian attack, unaided by artillery.

Here the old governor lorded it over sixty Russians, who formed the corps of the trading establishment, besides an indefinite number of Indian hunters of the Kodiak tribe, who were continually coming and going, or lounging and loitering about the fort like so many hounds round a sportsman's hunting quarters. Though a loose liver among his guests, the governor was a strict disciplinarian among his men; keeping them in perfect subjection, and having seven on guard night and day.

Beside those immediate serfs and dependants just mentioned, the old Russian potentate exerted a considerable sway over a numerous and irregular class of maritime traders, who looked to him for aid and munitions, and through whom he may be said to have, in some degree, extended his power along the whole northwest coast. These were American captains of vessels engaged in a particular department of the trade. One of these captains would come, in a manner, empty-handed to New Archangel. Here his ship would be furnished with about fifty canoes and a hundred Kodiak hunters, and fitted out with provisions, and everything necessary for hunting the sea-otter on the coast of California, where the Russians have another establishment. The ship would ply along the California coast from place to place, dropping parties of otter hunters in their canoes, furnishing them only with water, and leaving them to depend upon their own dexterity for a maintenance. When a sufficient cargo was collected, she would gather up her canoes and hunters, and return with them to Archangel; where the captain would render in the returns of his voyage, and receive one half of the skins for his share.

Over these coasting captains, as we have hinted, the veteran governor exerted some sort of sway, but it was of a peculiar and characteristic kind; it was the tyranny of the table. They were obliged to join him in his "prosnics" or carousals, and to drink "potations pottle deep." His carousals, too, were not of the most quiet kind, nor were his potations as mild as nectar. "He is continually," said Mr. Hunt, "giving entertainments by way of parade, and if you do not drink raw rum, and boiling punch as strong as sulphur, he will insult you as soon as he gets drunk, which is very shortly after sitting down to table."

As to any "temperance captain" who stood fast to his faith, and refused to give up his sobriety, he might go elsewhere for a market, for he stood no chance with the governor. Rarely, however, did any cold-water caitiff of the kind darken the door of old Baranhoff; the coasting captains knew too well his humor and their own interests; they joined in his revels, they drank, and sang, and whooped, and hiccuped, until they all got "half seas over," and then affairs went on swimmingly.

An awful warning to all "flinchers" occurred shortly before Mr. Hunt's arrival. A young naval officer had recently been sent out by the emperor to take command of one of the company's vessels. The governor, as usual, had him at his "prosnics," and plied him with fiery potations. The young man stood on the defensive until the old count's ire was completely kindled; he carried his point, and made the greenhorn tipsy, willy nilly. In proportion as they grew fuddled they grew noisy, they quarrelled in their cups; the young-ster paid old Baranhoff in his own coin by rating him soundly; in reward for which, when sober, he was taken the rounds of four pickets, and received seventy-nine lashes, taled out with Russian punctuality of punishment.

Such was the old grizzled bear with whom Mr. Hunt had to do business. How he managed to cope with his humor; whether he pledged himself in raw rum and blazing punch, and "clinked the can" with him as they made their bargains, does not appear upon record; we must infer, however, from his gen-eral observations on the absolute sway of this hard-drinking potentate, that he had to conform to the customs of his court, and that their business trans-actions presented a maudlin mixture of punch and peltry.

The greatest annoyance to Mr. Hunt, however, was the delay to which he was subjected, in disposing of the cargo of the ship, and getting the requisite returns. With all the governor's devotions to the bottle, he never obfuscated his faculties sufficiently to lose sight of his interest, and is represented by Mr. Hunt as keen, not to say crafty, at a bargain, as the most arrant water-drinker. A long time was expended negotiating with him, and by the time the bargain was concluded, the month of October had arrived. To add to the delay he was to be paid for his cargo in seal skins. Now it so happened that there was none of this kind of peltry at the fort of old Baranhoff. It was necessary, therefore, for Mr. Hunt to proceed to a seal-catching establishment, which the Russian company had at the island of St. Paul, in the Sea of Kamtschatka. He accordingly set sail on the 4th of October, after having spent forty-five days at New Archangel boosing and bargaining with its roystering com-mander, and right glad was he to escape from the clutches of "this old man of the sea."

↝ WASHINGTON IRVING was a well-known American writer, and the author of such classics as "The Legend of Sleepy Hollow" and "Rip Van Winkle." He was the first American writer to achieve international acclaim. He spent many years in Europe, including time in England, France, and years living in a Moorish castle in Spain. He returned to the United States after a seventeen-year absence in 1832, when he began traveling throughout the American West and the Pacific Northwest. This piece was written as a result of those journeys.

YUKON AND MACKENZIE
EXPLORATION

In 1887 Mr. Wm. Ogilvie was sent in charge of a survey party to explore the Yukon district. Starting from Victoria in the spring of that year, he crossed from Chilkoot Inlet to the headwaters of the Yukon, and went down the latter to a point near the international boundary between Alaska and Canada, where he spent the greater part of the winter making astronomical observations for the purpose of ascertaining the position of the 141st degree of longitude, the international boundary at that point. His observations have not yet been completely reduced, but an approximate calculation shows that the boundary is nearly ninety miles below the point where it is marked on the United States maps. This is of great importance, as the line passes through the best gold-bearing districts yet discovered in the country.

In the first days of March, 1888, Mr. Ogilvie left his winter quarters for the mouth of the Mackenzie River, following a route never travelled before by any white man and probably by no Indian. He ascended the Ta-ton-duc, a river flowing from the north into the Yukon; and then crossing a mountain range, he discovered the true sources of the Porcupine River. From this he went to Fort McPherson, crossed the Rocky Mountains to the Mackenzie, by which he returned south, thus accomplishing a journey of 2,500 miles, through a country hitherto very little known.

The Yukon district appears to have a much greater value than was previously supposed. It would seem that for gold the best paying streams so far as discovered are in Canadian territory. About 300 miners were in the country in the summer of 1887, but it is difficult to say what quantity of gold they have taken out, as they are somewhat reticent on the subject. They all agree, however, that $8 per day is poor pay, hardly enough to cover expenses. Taking this as an average, they cannot have made less than $500 each, or $150,000 altogether. Obtained with the crudest and most primitive appliances, the result shows what may be expected so soon as communication with the interior becomes more easy, and the importation of improved mining mchinery possible. Drift coal was found at various places, indicating the existence of seams further up. Salmon abound in the rivers, but after ascending so far from the sea, it is not fit to become an article of export, although good enough as food for the Indians. The fur trade is confined to a few points; there are immense districts, teeming with game and fur-bearing animals of all kinds, where Indians never go. Part of the miners' supplies are procured in the country. The lowest estimate of this trade for 1887 is $60,000.

The whole distance travelled during Mr. Ogilvie's explorations, from Ottawa back to Ottawa was upwards of 9,000 miles. Of this, about 5,000 was by rail; about 1,000 by steamship up the Pacific, from Victoria; nearly 200 by wagon; and the balance, about 3,000 miles, in canoes or on foot. Those canoes travelled about 3,000 miles by rail; then about 1,000 by steamer; were then carried about twenty miles to the point from which they made the descent of the Lewes river to the boundary (about 700 miles); they were then drawn on toboggans made for the purpose by one of the party, about 140 miles, and again were carried over the Rocky Mountains, eight miles, after which they made the ascent of the Mackenzie river, 2,400 miles. They were sold at Fort Chipewyan and are good for some years' service yet. During the winter on the Yukon the thermometer was very seldom above zero, and often 50° below. Taking astronomic observations when it is 40° and 50° below is very trying work; more especially when it is continued for more than an hour, as all the observations taken were. In the month of February, while marking the boundary on Forty-mile river, a tramp of over 120 miles had to be made on snowshoes in deep soft snow on which one sank to the knees every step. Food and bedding for the trip were drawn on two toboggans; of course all the time this was being done the party had to live outside without even the shelter of a tent, as two men could not do more than draw the necessary instruments, food and bedding for the occasion. The work being in the valley of the river, the sun never rose above the visible horizon, and as the thermometer was most of the time 30° or 40° below zero the comforts and pleasures of the trip can be imagined better than described. In March, while crossing from the Yukon to the Mackenzie the same hardships were suffered, but over a more extended time, stretching over a period of six weeks of extremely hard labor and cold weather; as instance, the 11th March the temperature was 53° below zero, and the party had to sleep outside in that. As the whole outfit to be moved amounted to about 3,000 pounds and there were only five men to do it, the progress was necessarily very slow, and very laborious. In the soft deep snow the weight of a man would sink the snowshoe into the snow up to the knee, and the exertion of pulling the toboggan would sink it more. This was extremely fatiguing and wearying, and although the temperature was generally down about 25° and 30° below zero the perspiration would, under the exertion of drawing the heavy loads, flow as freely as in July at 90° in the shade. One would think that cooling off after a day's exertions of that kind, when the thermometer was 30° or 40° below would be sure to bring on at least a cold, more especially as there was no shelter to cool off in, but fortunately for the success of the expedition not one of the party had the slightest touch of any ailment while absent. Under the provocation of exercise of that kind, the stomach becomes very active and will dispose of about three times as much food as under ordinary circumstances. The quantity of tea one would drink, too, would surprise a prize beer drinker.

Coming up the Mackenzie river had to be done by what is locally called tracking, that is hauling the canoe by a string, the party doing so walking, or rather running along the shore; this is no easy labor, as any one who has tried to pull a loaded boat faster than a slow speed knows. This was done by each member of the party in his regular turn, and as a rule the man on shore had not a very happy time, and his misery was a source of fun for the ones in the canoe, they in their turn took the chaffing of the "passengers" good humouredly, knowing that "revenge" was coming soon.

On the way out from Lake Athabasca, in December, dogs were used to haul the necessary provisions for the party, and their own food. As a rule the team of dogs—four—will haul about 400 or 500 pounds weight, and as each dog will eat from six to eight pounds of fish each day, one can see that as a means of freighting their usefulness is limited. A rule is that four fair dogs can haul their own food and the bedding and food of two men for a seven days' trip. The distance from Lake Athabasca to Lake La Biche travelled by the party with the aid of dogs is about 425 miles. Fish for dog food was picked up along the way from Indians; were it not for this aid it would be impossible to make such long journeys with dogs. The time occupied in travelling that distance was thirteen and a half days. At the end of the journey most of the dogs were pretty well used up; in fact the team would not have gone more than a day longer. Most of the men, too, were not sorry that the "job was done."

It is needless to say that there was no riding for any of the party on the way out. The whole of the journey had to be made on snowshoes, and as the road has to be "tracked" for dogs the party had to keep ahead, each one in his turn "making track" in the trackless snow.

Dog drivers carry a whip peculiar to the "craft." The handle is about eighteen, and the lash about sixty inches long. It is heavily loaded with shot, which is plaited into it. This makes it so heavy that a good blow will almost cut through a dog's skin. One accustomed to the treatment of dogs at home will often witness treatment of them here that makes his blood boil, until he starts to drive himself; then he does not think quite so hardly of the native driver, though his animals are often punished needlessly. It may be stated generally that a kind driver makes but slow progress. A story is told about a high church dignitary, who was making a journey with dogs, and becoming quite shocked at his driver's profanity absolutely forbade him scolding the dogs any more, except in a mild way, and use his whip in the same manner. Some days after, the good man noticed that he was away behind time; at a known point he remonstrated with the driver on his slowness; that worthy demonstrated to his Reverence that it was impossible to make time with dogs, with *his* system of driving. The good man granted the driver an "indulgence" for the remainder of the drive, and finished his journey on time.

The party passed through many scenes of peril and had some strange adventures, but it is needless to refer to them here as it would take up too much time. They saw many scenes of grandeur and beauty, which will probably not be looked on again by white men for many years to come.

☞ This newspaper article from 1890 on early explorations of the Yukon and Alaska was reprinted in many places throughout the United States, and became widely used as a travel guide by the gold seekers rushing to Alaska in 1897.

JOHN MUIR

THE DISCOVERY OF
GLACIER BAY

On October 24, we set sail for Guide Charley's ice-mountains. The handle of our heaviest axe was cracked, and as Charley declared that there was no firewood to be had in the big ice-mountain bay, we would have to load the canoe with a store for cooking at an island out in the Strait a few miles from the village. We were therefore anxious to buy or trade for a good sound axe in exchange for our broken one. Good axes are rare in rocky Alaska. Soon or late an unlucky stroke on a stone concealed in moss spoils the edge. Finally one in almost perfect condition was offered by a young Hoona for our broken-handled one and a half-dollar to boot; but when the broken axe and money were given he promptly demanded an additional twenty-five cents' worth of tobacco. The tobacco was given him, then he required a half-dollar's worth more of tobacco, which was also given; but when he still demanded something more, Charley's patience gave way and we sailed in the same condition as to axes as when we arrived. This was the only contemptible commercial affair we encountered among these Alaskan Indians.

We reached the wooded island about one o'clock, made coffee, took on a store of wood, and set sail direct for the icy country, finding it very hard indeed to believe the woodless part of Charley's description of the Icy Bay, so heavily and uniformly are all the shores forested wherever we had been. In this view we were joined by John, Kadachan, and Toyatte, none of them on all their lifelong canoe travels having ever seen a woodless country.

We held a northwesterly course until long after dark, when we reached a small inlet that sets in near the mouth of Glacier Bay, on the west side. Here we made a cold camp on a desolate snow-covered beach in stormy sleet and darkness. At daybreak I looked eagerly in every direction to learn what kind of place we were in; but gloomy rain-clouds covered the mountains, and I could see nothing that would give me a clue, while Vancouver's chart, hitherto a faithful guide, here failed us altogether. Nevertheless, we made haste to be off; and fortunately, for just as we were leaving the shore, a faint smoke was seen across the inlet, toward which Charley, who now seemed lost, gladly steered. Our sudden appearance so early that gray morning had evidently alarmed our neighbors, for as soon as we were within hailing distance an Indian with his face blackened fired a shot over our heads, and in a blunt, bellowing voice roared, "Who are you?"

Our interpreter shouted, "Friends and the Fort Wrangell missionary."

Then men, women, and children swarmed out of the hut, and awaited our approach on the beach. One of the hunters having brought his gun with him, Kadachan sternly rebuked him, asking with superb indignation whether he was not ashamed to meet a missionary with a gun in his hands. Friendly relations, however, were speedily established, and as a cold rain was falling, they invited us to enter their hut. It seemed very small and was jammed full of oily boxes and bundles; nevertheless, twenty-one persons managed to find shelter in it about a smoky fire. Our hosts proved to be Hoona seal-hunters laying in their winter stores of meat and skins. The packed hut was passably well ventilated, but its heavy, meaty smells were not the same to our noses as those we were accustomed to in the sprucy nooks of the evergreen woods. The circle of black eyes peering at us through a fog of reek and smoke made a novel picture. We were glad, however, to get within reach of information, and of course asked many questions concerning the ice-mountains and the strange bay, to most of which our inquisitive Hoona friends replied with counter-questions as to our object in coming to such a place, especially so late in the year. They had heard of Mr. Young and his work at Fort Wrangell, but could not understand what a missionary could be doing in such a place as this. Was he going to preach to the seals and gulls, they asked, or to the ice-mountains? And could they take his word? Then John explained that only the friend of the missionary was seeking ice-mountains, that Mr. Young had already preached many good words in the villages we had visited, their own among the others, that our hearts were good and every Indian was our friend. Then we gave them a little rice, sugar, tea, and tobacco, after which they began to gain confidence and to speak freely. They told us that the big bay was called by them Sit-a-da-kay, or Ice Bay; that there were many large ice-mountains in it, but no gold-mines; and that the ice-mountain they knew best was at the head of the bay, where most of the seals were found.

Notwithstanding the rain, I was anxious to push on and grope our way beneath the clouds as best we could, in case worse weather should come; but Charley was ill at ease, and wanted one of the seal-hunters to go with us, for the place was much changed. I promised to pay well for a guide, and in order to lighten the canoe proposed to leave most of our heavy stores in the hut until our return. After a long consultation one of them consented to go. His wife got ready his blanket and a piece of cedar matting for his bed, and some provisions—mostly dried salmon, and seal sausage made of strips of lean meat plaited around a core of fat. She followed us to the beach, and just as we were pushing off said with a pretty smile, "It is my husband that you are taking away. See that you bring him back."

We got under way about 10 A.M. The wind was in our favor, but a cold rain pelted us, and we could see but little of the dreary, treeless wilderness which we had now fairly entered. The bitter blast, however, gave us good speed; our bedraggled canoe rose and fell on the waves as solemnly as a big ship. Our course was northwestward, up the southwest side of the bay, near the shore of what seemed to be the mainland, smooth marble islands being on our right. About noon we discovered the first of the great glaciers, the one I afterward named for James Geikie, the noted Scotch geologist. Its lofty blue cliffs, looming through the draggled skirts of the clouds, gave a tremendous impression of savage power, while the roar of the new-born icebergs thickened and emphasized the general roar of the storm. An hour and a half beyond the Geikie Glacier we ran into a slight harbor where the shore is low, dragged the canoe beyond the reach of drifting icebergs, and, much against my desire to push ahead, encamped, the guide insisting that the big ice-mountain at the head of the bay could not be reached before dark, that the landing there was dangerous even in daylight, and that this was the only safe harbor on the way to it. While camp was being made, I strolled along the shore to examine the rocks and the fossil timber that abounds here. All the rocks are freshly glaciated, even below the sea-level, nor have the waves as yet worn off the surface polish, much less the heavy scratches and grooves and lines of glacial contour.

The next day being Sunday, the minister wished to stay in camp; and so, on account of the weather, did the Indians. I therefore set out on an excursion, and spent the day alone on the mountain-slopes above the camp, and northward, to see what I might learn. Pushing on through rain and mud and sludgy snow, crossing many brown, boulder-choked torrents, wading, jumping, and wallowing in snow up to my shoulders was mountaineering of the most trying kind. After crouching cramped and benumbed in the canoe, poulticed in wet or damp clothing night and day, my limbs had been asleep. This day they were awakened and in the hour of trial proved that they had not lost the cunning learned on many a mountain peak of the High Sierra. I reached a height of fifteen hundred feet, on the ridge that bounds the second of the great glaciers. All the landscape was smothered in clouds and I began to fear that as far as wide views were concerned I had climbed in vain. But at length the clouds lifted a little, and beneath their gray fringes I saw the berg-filled expanse of the bay, and the feet of the mountains that stand about it, and the imposing fronts of five huge glaciers, the nearest being immediately beneath me. This was my first general view of Glacier Bay, a solitude of ice and snow and newborn rocks, dim, dreary, mysterious. I held the ground I had so dearly won for an hour or two, sheltering myself from the blast as best I could, while with benumbed fingers I sketched what I could see of the landscape, and wrote a few lines in my notebook. Then, breasting the snow again, crossing the shifting avalanche slopes and torrents, I reached camp about dark, wet and weary and glad.

While I was getting some coffee and hardtack, Mr. Young told me that the Indians were discouraged, and had been talking about turning back, fearing that I would be lost, the canoe broken, or in some other mysterious way the expedition would come to grief if I persisted in going farther. They had been asking him what possible motive I could have in climbing mountains when storms were blowing; and when he replied that I was only seeking knowledge, Toyatte said, "Muir must be a witch to seek knowledge in such a place as this and in such miserable weather."

After supper, crouching about a dull fire of fossil wood, they became still more doleful, and talked in tones that accorded well with the wind and waters and growling torrents about us, telling sad old stories of crushed canoes, drowned Indians, and hunters frozen in snowstorms. Even brave old Toyatte, dreading the treeless, forlorn appearance of the region, said that his heart was not strong, and that he feared his canoe, on the safety of which our lives depended, might be entering a skookum-house (jail) of ice, from which there might be no escape; while the Hoona guide said bluntly that if I was so fond of danger, and meant to go close up to the noses of the ice-mountains, he would not consent to go any farther; for we should all be lost, as many of his tribe had been, by the sudden rising of bergs from the bottom. They seemed to be losing heart with every howl of the wind, and, fearing that they might fail me now that I was in the midst of so grand a congregation of glaciers, I made haste to reassure them, telling them that for ten years I had wandered alone among mountains and storms, and good luck always followed me; that with me, therefore, they need fear nothing. The storm would soon cease and the sun would shine to show us the way we should go, for God cares for us and guides us as long as we are trustful and brave, therefore all childish fear must be put away. This little speech did good. Kadachan, with some show of enthusiasm, said he liked to travel with good-luck people; and dignified old Toyatte declared that now his heart was strong again, and he would venture on with me as far as I liked for my "wawa" was "delait" (my talk was very good). The old warrior even became a little sentimental, and said that even if the canoe was broken he would not greatly care, because on the way to the other world he would have good companions.

Next morning it was still raining and snowing, but the south wind swept us bravely forward and swept the bergs from our course. In about an hour we reached the second of the big glaciers, which I afterwards named for Hugh Miller. We rowed up its fiord and landed to make a slight examination of its grand frontal wall. The berg-producing portion we found to be about a mile and a half wide, and broken into an imposing array of jagged spires and pyramids, and flat-topped towers and battlements, of many shades of blue, from pale, shimmering, limpid tones in the crevasses and hollows, to the most startling, chilling, almost shrieking vitriol blue on the plain mural spaces from which bergs had just been discharged. Back from the front for a few miles the glacier rises in a series of wide steps, as if this portion of the glacier had sunk in successive sections as it reached deep water, and the sea had found its way beneath it. Beyond this it extends indefinitely in a gently rising prairie-like expanse, and branches along the slopes and cañons of the Fairweather Range.

From here a run of two hours brought us to the head of the bay, and to the mouth of the northwest fiord, at the head of which lie the Hoona sealing-grounds, and the great glacier now called the Pacific, and another called the Hoona. The fiord is about five miles long, and two miles wide at the mouth. Here our Hoona guide had a store of dry wood, which we took aboard. Then, setting sail, we were driven wildly up the fiord, as if the storm-wind were saying, "Go, then, if you will, into my icy chamber; but you shall stay in until I am ready to let you out." All this time sleety rain was falling on the bay, and snow on the mountains; but soon after we landed the sky began to open. The camp was made on a rocky bench near the front of the Pacific Glacier, and the canoe was carried beyond the reach of the bergs and berg-waves. The bergs were now crowded in a dense pack against the discharging front, as if the storm-wind had determined to make the glacier take back her crystal offspring and keep them at home.

While camp affairs were being attended to, I set out to climb a mountain for comprehensive views; and before I had reached a height of a thousand feet the rain ceased, and the clouds began to rise from the lower altitudes, slowly lifting their white skirts, and lingering in majestic, wing-shaped masses about the mountains that rise out of the broad, icy sea, the highest of all the white mountains, and the greatest of all the glaciers I had yet seen. Climbing higher for a still broader outlook, I made notes and sketched, improving the precious time while sunshine streamed through the luminous fringes of the clouds and fell on the green waters of the fiord, the glittering bergs, the crystal bluffs of the vast glacier, the intensely white, far-spreading fields of ice, and the ineffably chaste and spiritual heights of the Fairweather Range, which were now hidden, now partly revealed, the whole making a picture of icy wildness unspeakably pure and sublime.

Looking southward, a broad ice-sheet was seen extending in a gently undulating plain from the Pacific Fiord in the foreground to the horizon, dotted and ridged here and there with mountains which were as white as the snow-covered ice in which they were half, or more than half, submerged. Several of the great glaciers of the bay flow from this one grand fountain. It is an instructive example of a general glacier covering the hills and dales of a country that is not yet ready to be brought to the light of day—not only covering but creating a landscape with the features it is destined to have when, in the fullness of time, the fashioning ice-sheet shall be lifted by the sun, and the land become warm and fruitful. The view to the westward is bounded and almost filled by the glorious Fairweather Mountains, the highest among them springing aloft in sublime beauty to a height of nearly sixteen thousand feet, while from base to summit every peak and spire and dividing ridge of all the mighty host was spotless white, as if painted. It would seem that snow could never be made to lie on the steepest slopes and precipices unless plastered on when wet, and then frozen. But this snow could not have been wet. It must have been fixed by being driven and set in small particles like the storm-dust of drifts, which, when in this condition, is fixed not only on sheer cliffs, but in massive, overcurling cornices. Along the base of this majestic range sweeps the Pacific Glacier, fed by innumerable cascading tributaries, and discharging into the head of its fiord by two mouths only partly separated by the brow of an island rock about one thousand feet high, each nearly a mile wide.

Dancing down the mountain to camp, my mind glowing like the sun-beaten glaciers, I found the Indians seated around a good fire, entirely happy now that the farthest point of the journey was safely reached and the long, dark storm was cleared away. How hopefully, peacefully bright that night were the stars in the frosty sky, and how impressive was the thunder of the icebergs, rolling, swelling, reverberating through the solemn stillness! I was too happy to sleep.

About daylight next morning we crossed the fiord and landed on the south side of the rock that divides the wall of the great glacier. The whiskered faces of seals dotted the open spaces between the bergs, and I could not prevent John and Charley and Kadachan from shooting at them. Fortunately, few, if any, were hurt. Leaving the Indians in charge of the canoe, I managed to climb to the top of the wall by a good deal of step-cutting between the ice and dividing rock, and gained a good general view of the glacier. At one favorable place I descended about fifty feet below the side of the glacier, where its denuding, fashioning action was clearly shown. Pushing back from here, I found the surface crevassed and sunken in steps, like the Hugh Miller Glacier, as if it were being undermined by the action of tide-waters. For a distance of fifteen or twenty miles the river-like ice-flood is nearly level, and when it recedes, the ocean water will follow it, and thus form a long extension of the fiord, with features essentially the same as those now extending into the continent farther south, where many great glaciers once poured into the sea, though scarce a vestige of them now exists. Thus the domain of the sea has been, and is being, extended in these ice-sculptured lands, and the scenery of their shores enriched. The brow of the dividing rock is about a thousand feet high, and is hard beset by the glacier. A short time ago it was at least two thousand feet below the surface of the over-sweeping ice; and under present climatic conditions it will soon take its place as a glacier-polished island in the middle of the fiord, like a thousand others in the magnificent archipelago. Emerging from its icy sepulchre, it gives a most telling illustration of the birth of a marked feature of a landscape. In this instance it is not the mountain, but the glacier, that is in labor, and the mountain itself is being brought forth.

The Hoona Glacier enters the fiord on the south side, a short distance below the Pacific, displaying a broad and far-reaching expanse, over which many lofty peaks are seen; but the front wall, thrust into the fiord, is not nearly so interesting as that of the Pacific, and I did not observe any bergs discharged from it.

In the evening, after witnessing the unveiling of the majestic peaks and glaciers and their baptism in the down-pouring sunbeams, it seemed inconceivable that nature could have anything finer to show us. Nevertheless, compared with what was to come the next morning, all that was as nothing. The calm dawn gave no promise of anything uncommon. Its most impressive features were the frosty clearness of the sky and a deep, brooding stillness made all the more striking by the thunder of the newborn bergs. The sunrise we did not see at all, for we were beneath the shadows of the fiord cliffs; but in the midst of our studies, while the Indians were getting ready to sail, we were startled by the sudden appearance of a red light burning with a strange unearthly splendor on the topmost peak of the Fairweather Mountains. Instead of vanishing as suddenly as it had appeared, it spread and spread until the whole range down to the level of the glaciers was filled with the celestial fire. In color it was at first a vivid crimson, with a thick, furred appearance, as fine as the alpenglow, yet indescribably rich and deep—not in the least like a garment or mere external flush or bloom through which one might expect to see the rocks or snow, but every mountain apparently was glowing from the heart like molten metal fresh from a furnace. Beneath the frosty shadows of the fiord we stood hushed and awe-stricken, gazing at the holy vision; and had we seen the heavens opened and God made manifest, our attention could not have been more tremendously strained. When the highest peak began to burn, it did not seem to be steeped in sunshine, however glorious, but rather as if it had been thrust into the body of the sun itself. Then the supernal fire slowly descended, with a sharp line of demarkation separating it from the cold, shaded region beneath; peak after peak, with their spires and ridges and cascading glaciers, caught the heavenly glow, until all the mighty host stood transfigured, hushed, and thoughtful, as if awaiting the coming of the Lord.

The white, rayless light of morning, seen when I was alone amid the peaks of the California Sierra, had always seemed to me the most telling of all the terrestrial manifestations of God. But here the mountains themselves were made divine, and declared His glory in terms still more impressive. How long we gazed I never knew. The glorious vision passed away in a gradual, fading change through a thousand tones of color to pale yellow and white, and then the work of the ice-world went on again in everyday beauty. The green waters of the fiord were filled with sun-spangles; the fleet of icebergs set forth on their voyages with the upspringing breeze; and on the innumerable mirrors and prisms of these bergs, and on those of the shattered crystal walls of the glaciers, common white light and rainbow light began to burn, while the mountains shone in their frosty jewelry, and loomed again in the thin azure in serene terrestrial majesty. We turned and sailed away, joining the outgoing bergs, while "Gloria in excelsis" still seemed to be sounding over all the white landscape, and our burning hearts were ready for any fate, feeling that, whatever the future might have in store, the treasures we had gained this glorious morning would enrich our lives forever.

When we arrived at the mouth of the fiord, and rounded the massive granite headland that stands guard at the entrance on the north side, another large glacier, now named the Reid, was discovered at the head of one of the northern branches of the bay. Pushing ahead into this new fiord, we found that it was not only packed with bergs, but that the spaces between the bergs were crusted with new ice, compelling us to turn back while we were yet several miles from the discharging frontal wall. But though we were not then allowed to set foot on this magnificent glacier, we obtained a fine view of it, and I made the Indians cease rowing while I sketched its principal features. Thence, after steering northeastward a few miles, we discovered still another large glacier, now named the Carroll. But the fiord into which this glacier flows was, like the last, utterly inaccessible on account of ice, and we had to be content with a general view and sketch of it, gained as we rowed slowly past at a distance of three or four miles. The mountains back of it and on each side of its inlet are sculptured in a singularly rich and striking style of architecture, in which subordinate peaks and gables appear in wonderful profusion, and an imposing conical mountain with a wide, smooth base stands out in the main current of the glacier, a mile or two back from the discharging ice-wall.

We now turned southward down the eastern shore of the bay, and in an hour or two discovered a glacier of the second class, at the head of a comparatively short fiord that winter had not yet closed. Here we landed, and climbed across a mile or so of rough boulder-beds, and back upon the wildly broken, receding front of the glacier, which, though it descends to the level of the sea, no longer sends off bergs. Many large masses, detached from the wasting front by irregular melting, were partly buried beneath mud, sand, gravel, and boulders of the terminal moraine. Thus protected, these fossil icebergs remain unmelted for many years, some of them for a century or more, as shown by the age of trees growing above them, though there are no trees here as yet. At length melting, a pit with sloping sides is formed by the falling in of the overlying moraine material into the space at first occupied by the buried ice. In this way are formed the curious depressions in drift-covered regions called kettles or sinks. On these decaying glaciers we may also find many interesting lessons on the formation of boulders and boulder-beds, which in all glaciated countries exert a marked influence on scenery, health, and fruitfulness.

Three or four miles farther down the bay, we came to another fiord, up which we sailed in quest of more glaciers, discovering one in each of the two branches into which the fiord divides. Neither of these glaciers quite reaches tide-water. Notwithstanding the apparent fruitfulness of their fountains, they are in the first stage of decadence, the waste from melting and evaporation being greater now than the supply of new ice from their snowy fountains. We reached the one in the north branch, climbed over its wrinkled brow, and gained a good view of the trunk and some of the tributaries, and also of the sublime gray cliffs of its channel.

Then we sailed up the south branch of the inlet, but failed to reach the glacier there, on account of a thin sheet of new ice. With the tent-poles we broke a lane for the canoe for a little distance; but it was slow work, and we soon saw that we could not reach the glacier before dark. Nevertheless, we gained a fair view of it as it came sweeping down through its gigantic gateway of massive Yosemite rocks three or four thousand feet high. Here we lingered until sundown, gazing and sketching; then turned back, and encamped on a bed of cobblestones between the forks of the fiord.

We gathered a lot of fossil wood and after supper made a big fire, and as we sat around it the brightness of the sky brought on a long talk with the Indians about the stars; and their eager, childlike attention was refreshing to see as compared with the deathlike apathy of weary town-dwellers, in whom natural curiosity has been quenched in toil and care and poor shallow comfort.

After sleeping a few hours, I stole quietly out of the camp, and climbed the mountain that stands between the two glaciers. The ground was frozen, making the climbing difficult in the steepest places; but the views over the icy bay, sparkling beneath the stars, were enchanting. It seemed then a sad thing that any part of so precious a night had been lost in sleep. The star-light was so full that I distinctly saw not only the berg-filled bay, but most of the lower portions of the glaciers, lying pale and spirit-like amid the mountains. The nearest glacier in particular was so distinct that it seemed to be glowing with light that came from within itself. Not even in dark nights have I ever found any difficulty in seeing large glaciers; but on this mountain-top, amid so much ice, in the heart of so clear and frosty a night, everything was more or less luminous, and I seemed to be poised in a vast hollow between two skies of almost equal brightness. This exhilarating scramble made me glad and strong and I rejoiced that my studies called me before the glorious night succeeding so glorious a morning had been spent!

I got back to camp in time for an early breakfast, and by daylight we had everything packed and were again under way. The fiord was frozen nearly to its mouth, and though the ice was so thin it gave us but little trouble in breaking a way for the canoe, yet it showed us that the season for exploration in these waters was well-nigh over. We were in danger of being imprisoned in a jam of icebergs, for the water-spaces between them freeze rapidly, binding the floes into one mass. Across such floes it would be almost impossible to drag a canoe, however industriously we might ply the axe, as our Hoona guide took great pains to warn us. I would have kept straight down the bay from here, but the guide had to be taken home, and the provisions we left at the bark hut had to be got on board. We therefore crossed over to our Sunday storm-camp, cautiously boring a way through the bergs. We found the shore lavishly adorned with a fresh arrival of assorted bergs that had been left stranded at high tide. They were arranged in a curving row, looking intensely clear and pure on the gray sand, and, with the sunbeams pouring through them, suggested the jewel-paved streets of the New Jerusalem.

On our way down the coast, after examining the front of the beautiful Geikie Glacier, we obtained our first broad view of the great glacier afterwards named the Muir, the last of all the grand company to be seen, the stormy weather having hidden it when we first entered the bay. It was now perfectly clear, and the spacious, prairie-like glacier, with its many tributaries extending far back into the snowy recesses of its fountains, made a magnificent display of its wealth, and I was strongly tempted to go and explore it at all hazards. But winter had come, and the freezing of its fiords was an insurmountable obstacle. I had, therefore, to be content for the present with sketching and studying its main features at a distance.

When we arrived at the Hoona hunting-camp, men, women, and children came swarming out to welcome us. In the neighborhood of this camp I carefully noted the lines of demarkation between the forested and deforested regions. Several mountains here are only in part deforested, and the lines separating the bare and the forested portions are well defined. The soil, as well as the trees, had slid off the steep slopes, leaving the edge of the woods rawlooking and rugged.

At the mouth of the bay a series of moraine islands show that the trunk glacier that occupied the bay halted here for some time and deposited this island material as a terminal moraine; that more of the bay was not filled in shows that, after lingering here, it receded comparatively fast. All the level portions of trunks of glaciers occupying ocean fiords, instead of melting back gradually in times of general shrinking and recession, as inland glaciers with sloping channels do, melt almost uniformly over all the surface until they become thin enough to float. Then, of course, with each rise and fall of the tide, the sea water, with a temperature usually considerably above the freezing-point, rushes in and out beneath them, causing rapid waste of the nether surface, while the upper is being wasted by the weather, until at length the fiord portions of these great glaciers become comparatively thin and weak and are broken up and vanish almost simultaneously.

Glacier Bay is undoubtedly young as yet. Vancouver's chart, made only a century ago, shows no trace of it, though found admirably faithful in general. It seems probable, therefore, that even then the entire bay was occupied by a glacier of which all those described above, great though they are, were only tributaries. Nearly as great a change has taken place in Sum Dum Bay since Vancouver's visit, the main trunk glacier there having receded from eighteen to twenty-five miles from the line marked on his chart. Charley, who was here when a boy, said that the place had so changed that he hardly recognized it, so many new islands had been born in the mean time and so much ice had vanished. As we have seen, this Icy Bay is being still farther extended by the recession of the glaciers. That this whole system of fiords and channels was added to the domain of the sea by glacial action is to my mind certain.

We reached the island from which we had obtained our store of fuel about half-past six and camped here for the night, having spent only five days in Sitadaka, sailing round it, visiting and sketching all the six glaciers excepting the largest, though I landed only on three of them,—the Geikie, Hugh Miller, and Grand Pacific,—the freezing of the fiords in front of the others rendering them inaccessible at this late season.

❧ JOHN MUIR was a naturalist, inventor, and writer who penned ten books and over three hundred articles. Though he was born in Scotland, raised in Wisconsin, and made California his home base, he made many trips to Alaska in his lifetime. He founded the Sierra Club to help to preserve and protect the natural beauty he wrote so eloquently about.

GOLD RUSH

THE GOLD RUSH of 1897 and beyond made Alaska what it is today, in a very large part. What had been a sleepy territory populated by the native Alaskans and a few hardy fur traders was suddenly overrun by thousands and thousands of settlers looking to make a fortune, most of them ill-prepared for the rigors of the climate and ignorant of the mechanics of their chosen profession as miners. Many died long before they ever reached the gold fields in Alaska and the Yukon. More died after they got there, their dreams broken along with their bodies by the incredible hardships of living and working in the polar cold. The terrible conditions these settlers endured, the determination they showed in their pursuit of their dreams, and their ruthless and often destructive behavior as they sought to achieve them show man at his finest as well as at his worst. The following selections bring that amazing period of Alaska's history to life, in all its glory and desperation. This section also includes the only piece of fiction in this book, chosen mostly because it doesn't read like fiction at all, but like the honest truth of being caught in the extreme cold of the frozen North. Jack London's famous short story "To Build a Fire," joins one of his nonfiction pieces on the Gold Rush here, along with

Richard Mathews's fine history of the first rush of gold-seekers into the Yukon and Alaskan territories, a newspaper report on the first American to make it into the Yukon basin, a Yukon pioneer's actual outfit list, an 1898 newspaper article telling miners how to get to the gold fields, and a description of the abandoned sled dogs in Dawson during the summer months. Several of these selections are taken from Dawson newspapers, and Dawson is technically in Canada's Yukon Territory. But Dawson was a major staging point for Alaska's gold rush, and the words bring to life as nothing else can that time and place, and the struggles of those who ventured into Alaska to tame it and make their fortunes.

Excerpt from *The Yukon*

RICHARD MATHEWS

1898

There are two seasons on the Yukon, summer and the rest of the year. Summer begins with the river's breakup, and people in Dawson City customarily placed bets on the precise time that the ice would start to budge. After the turn of the century the ice pool became a well-organized lottery. Thousands of one-dollar tickets, each one indicating a date, hour and minute, were sold, and the resulting jackpot was worth a small fortune. To determine the exact moment when the breakup began, a stake, patriotically topped with a Union Jack, was planted on the frozen Yukon; from it a taut wire led to an electric clock in Charles Jeanerette's jewelry store and when the ice budged even a few inches the clock stopped. A gong then automatically sounded, announcing the news to Dawson, and within a few minutes every school and church bell in town was relaying the message to the surrounding countryside. In no time the entire population, leaving behind open safes, baking bread, warm beds, and incomplete sentences, would troop down to the banks of the Yukon and behold the arrival of summer.

By February or March the domain of winter on the Yukon has lasted so long and been so total that it becomes hard to imagine any other time of year; one begins to feel that not even half a dozen summers could seriously challenge its authority. Even before breakup, however, there are reassuring signs that winter, like all else, is transitory. On protected spots along the south-facing slopes tiny purple crocuses, the frailest of flowers, push forth from the dormant land, and along the watercourses yellow crowfoot blooms. The first Canadian geese and sand-hill cranes form shifting skeins across the sky, and their wonderful wild music is unmistakably the song of a new season. The snow is wet and heavy by day, and he who snowshoes or drives dogs must now travel at night. Beneath the snow, drops and trickles are forming brooks which feed into the tributary rivers of the Yukon. All winter the Yukon has been subsisting on a reduced ration of ground water, for during the six coldest months virtually all precipitation has fallen as snow and accumulated on the land. During these months the river's mean flow as recorded at the Eagle, Alaska, gauging station, has fallen to 21,300 cubic feet per second, only a third more than the annual average of the Hudson River. But now, as the days grow longer and warmer, the snow melts and the Yukon's fast ends. In May the mean flow at Eagle rises to 138,000 cubic feet per second, about five times the yearly average of the Colorado.*

At first the rising river does not carry its ice downstream, but lifts it vertically. In the fall when this ice was first formed it fit a river that was much smaller and much lower in its bed, so now as the river swells, the ice no longer reaches all the way across it. Open water appears in many places between the banks and the ice itself, which floats free in a single sheet as long as the Yukon. Along the channels of open water the Indians paddle the tiny muskratting canoes they make from flattened five-gallon cans, while on the river ice planes can safely land. As the days grow longer and warmer the ice becomes soft and honeycombed with fissures; it looks as though it had been riddled with worm borings, which is what prompted the oft-told tale of the Yukon ice worm.

So far the ice has withstood the onslaught of the sun above and the rising river beneath; it has remained intact and in place. Then suddenly it begins to

---

*The mean annual flow as measured at Kaltag, where the gauging nearest the Yukon's mouth (though still 470 miles from it) is located, is 193,800 cubic feet per second, or 140,700,000 acre-feet per year. The Yukon's discharge into the Bering Sea has not been measured, but hydrologists of the U.S. Geological Survey estimate that the annual mean is 216,000 cubic feet per second. By the criterion of flow, or volume, the Yukon system is thus the fifth largest in North America. It is exceeded by the Mississippi-Missouri system, the St. Lawrence, the Mackenzie and the Nelson-Saskatchewan system, and followed by the Columbia. All these flow calculations are based on measurements made during 1959–60.

move. It is a solid mass at first, a vast white section of the landscape slipping away downriver in an unbroken sheet. But it cannot withstand the shock of motion for more than a moment. It shatters like glass, and the sound of it breaks in upon the silence of a spring day with a groaning thunder audible for fifteen miles. The floes are five or six feet thick, weigh many tons, and move at seven to nine miles an hour. They hurtle into each other, are riven and cleaved, pound each other to bits, grind each other down. They gash the river's banks, are borne over them by the high water; they shave the spruce trees off islands and gouge out the earth. They become freighted with the debris of their work, and sometimes they carry away a doomed moose or caribou caught on the river when the ice began to move.

Then, without warning, the ice comes to a dead stop. It has dammed itself and the river behind a chaos of glistening blue-green chunks such as Coleridge might have seen in an opium dream. More water and more ice are impounded. The pressure increases, becomes unbearable. A slab that has acted as a keystone hurtles skyward with a creaking groan. The mountain of ice collapses as fast as it was formed; the lake disappears.

Many towns on the Yukon have been inundated behind these ice-dams, and such floods are particularly perilous because they occur in a matter of minutes. Usually they do not last long but the dam that formed below Galena, Alaska, in 1945 was so sturdy that it barricaded the river for more than twenty-four hours and was dislodged only after a squadron of B-17's unloaded 168,000 pounds of bombs on it. The airfield there, one of a chain of bases used in ferrying lend-lease aircraft to Russia, was largely destroyed. To the inhabitants of the river below Galena the flood had its compensations, however, for it distributed a manna of lumber, boats, drums of oil, K-rations, even tinned candies, all along the way from the base to the Bering Sea. As of September 1966, residents of Marshall, nearly four hundred miles downstream, were still digging drums of diesel oil from their sloughs.

In 1898 the Yukon ice began to move out on the seventh of May, and never before nor since did the event mean so much to so many people.

For Clarence Berry, Thomas Lippy, and a few hundred other rich claim owners it meant that frozen dumps were melting and could be sluiced. A winter's investment in the labor of burning, scraping, picking, shoveling and windlass cranking lay in these formless heaps, and now it remained only to extract the twenty-five tons of placer gold they would yield up that year. Soon Mike Bartlett, the muleskinner, would be up on these claims loading each one of his dozen pack animals with twenty-five thousand dollars' worth of gold sewn into canvas sacks a dozen layers thick. He transported the bullion to Dawson for seventy-five cents a pound.

For Tappan Adney the spring thaw meant, first of all, the inundation of his cabin. By May 3, a few days before the Yukon ice began to move, Bonanza Creek was running free, and far above its banks. The cold water, already silted from the first sluicing, unceremoniously entered Adney's cabin and covered the floor. It was only a few inches deep, but Adney was not pleased to have "to wade about the house in rubber boots, fighting mosquitoes, trying to cook a flapjack or make a cup of tea over the stove, and climbing in and out of a high bunk with boots on." He hiked off to Dawson in disgust, but soon the situation there was even worse. Shortly after the Yukon began to break up it deluged all of Lousetown and most of Dawson. Adney was forced to retreat to the flank of Midnight Dome where he pitched his tent and bivouacked for a few days. From this vantage point he had an excellent view of men sleeping on their cabin roofs, their boats tied to the eaves, and of taxi-boats working Front Street for fifty cents a fare.

The receding water left a thick coat of alluvial ooze on everything, but in exchange it took with it the last of the ice, and this was a cause for rejoicing. Soon the outside world would return to Dawson, a little out of date upon arrival, perhaps, but to be welcomed with a profound joy and sense of relief. The first boats from Bennett Lake would bring, for example, two-week-old Seattle newspapers with their reports on the Spanish-American War; the persistent rumors of New York City's destruction by an enemy naval squadron would finally be laid to rest by news of Dewey's victory in Manila Bay. And there would be mail, letters from wives and lovers and mothers and friends, who had been left after a thousand precipitous leavetakings. From the passes, and also from St. Michael, fresh food would arrive, such extraordinary marvels of creation as the potato and the turnip. Already before the breakup Mr. R. J. Gandolfo, an Italian fruit vendor, was set to leave Bennett Lake for Dawson with eight tons of oranges, bananas, lemons and cucumbers. And before long Mr. H. L. Miller would be en route with Dawson's first cow, though at $30.00 a gallon, her product would be of benefit only to the city's well-to-do. The hundreds of scow and stern-wheeler loads of food and supplies that would reach Dawson that spring would bring prices down toward a more reasonable level. A fifty pound sack of flour, for example, had fetched between $100 and $120 in October 1897, but by June the price would fall to $3.00. The arrival of abundant fresh food would also put an end to the scourge of scurvy that had taken a heavy toll during the winter. Its more fortunate victims had filled every room and hall, and even the office, at Father Judge's hospital, while the less fortunate ones were discovered as blackened and toothless cadavers in their cabins on isolated creeks.

To the ten thousand stampeders at Bennett Lake the breakup in the spring of 1898 meant that the golden grab bag was now at arm's length. As usual the ice in the lakes lingered for a time after the Yukon itself was running free and the armada didn't get under way until May 29. Colonel Sam Steele, the chief of the NWMP in the Yukon, had spent the winter at Bennett Lake, and on that day he mounted the hill in back of his headquarters to watch the exodus. It was a grand sight. He counted no less than eight hundred boats on the half of the lake visible from his vantage point. And when, a few hours later, he set out to follow them to Miles Canyon, he was never more than two hundred feet from his nearest neighbor. During May, June and July, 1898, the police post at Tagish Lake recorded the passage of 18,631 people,* more than the total population of the Yukon Territory today.

At first the boats were bunched together, as at the start of any race. And this was indeed a race, for the peculiar fever of the enterprise dictated the notion that to arrive an hour before the next fellow would assure even greater good fortune. In the case of men like Mr. Gandolfo the fruit vendor, and a number of others who were piloting scows loaded to the gunwhales with food and provisions, the haste made sense, for Dawson's absurd prices would begin to fall as soon as a few of them arrived. But most of the rest would find their haste sadly unrewarded.

Through Tagish and Marsh lakes the armada sailed, then on to Miles Canyon, which claimed one hundred and fifty boats and ten lives that season before Colonel Steele stationed a police corporal there to enforce safety measures. Across Lake Laberge they came, down the Thirty Mile River, past the Teslin, the Big Salmon, the Little Salmon, the Pelly, the White, the Stewart.

---

*According to Pierre Berton in *Klondike*, the total by the end of the navigation season rose to "more than 28,000."

The sign that says "Entering Dawson City" to the river traveler is a section of the face of Midnight Dome which has slipped down leaving a greyish scar shaped something like a stretched moosehide. It is visible for several miles upriver. By 1898 it had been drawn and photographed hundreds of times, and had appeared in the dozens of hastily written pamphlets about the Klondike. The stampeders knew what it looked like, even before they left Kalamazoo and Coeur d'Alene. For how many months had they waited for it to rise into their sight? No matter now; the Promised Land lay right around the bend.

Dawson City, just drying out from the Yukon's flood, was inundated by the hordes of stampeders early in June. Their boats, often two or three deep, formed a solid rim along the river from the north side of town to the Klondike, and across it to Lousetown—one and three-quarters miles solid with boats. Their tents turned the hillside back of Dawson white as snow, they blossomed on both banks of the Klondike and the overflow on the far side of the Yukon. Adney counted two thousand eight hundred tents from the hill behind where he was bivouacking, and estimated that each one housed three to five people.

At this time the creeks of the Klondike were producing more gold than ever before. Charlie Anderson was about to push his total to three hundred thousand dollars, and Berry to raise his to twice this. On some claims, such as Eldorado Sixteen, owned by an ex-YMCA coach named Thomas Lippy, it was becoming clear that every running foot of the five hundred was worth an average of three thousand dollars. And so it went; Eldorado was the jackpot, but Bonanza, though more spotty, yielded three million dollars, and Hunker and Bear creeks, which empty into the Klondike upstream from Bonanza, each produced over one million dollars. So too did Sulphur, Dominion, and Quartz, streams originating near the Klondike placer creeks, but flowing south to the Indian River.

It is logical to assume that the mother lode from which the placers of the Klondike and the Indian were eroded was roughly equidistant from the two rivers, in an area a few miles wide and perhaps twenty miles long. Every major creek draining this area was found to be rich, while none arising elsewhere contained any exploitable gold whatsoever. In the course of time the gold was moved down by water, and distributed along the creeks in an expanded area roughly twenty-five by thirty miles and bounded on one side by the Klondike. Outside this area there was nothing. Along the Klondike itself, for example, the north bank was devoid of gold in all places, and the south bank contained gold only along the lower fifth of its length. The placer ground of the Dawson region was by no means unlimited.

By June 1898, when the greatest of the stampeder armies marched on Dawson City, about two hundred and thirty miles of five hundred foot claims had been staked and registered in the Recorder's Office on Front Street. Near the proven placer creeks every gulch, hollow, pup and trickle showed the blazes of a claimant, and each, whether a worthless "skunk" or an Eldoradito, was baptized with a hopeful name. There was Too Much Gold Creek (a "skunk"), All Gold Creek, Gold Run, and Ready Bullion, Orogrande Gulch, Mint Gulch and Nugget Gulch, Eureka Creek, Deadwood Creek and Australia Creek. And up on the hillsides, where the old placers were deposited before the geological upthrust, smaller "bench" claims covered the ground like the patches of a quilt. These bench deposits had been first discovered in July 1897 by cheechakos, most of whom even then could find no good creek ground to stake.

Tappan Adney was back in Dawson City from a trip to the White River when the stampeder invasion reached its peak. He watched as they tied their boats to the sterns and sides of other craft on the crowded waterfront. They were exhilarated; their voices loud, their gestures expansive. They bounded from their boats and trotted with an eager stride up from the water's edge to the town. On Front Street they talked to other newcomers, to old-timers, to men in the bars where they went to celebrate their arrival, to anyone. What was the local situation? Where should one prospect? Where could one wash out the five hundred dollar pans they had heard about? By what alchemy— for the Klondike was a magic place—could a Denver millhand be transmuted into a Dawson millionaire ere the Arctic summer died?

And, slowly or quickly, depending on their conversations and their will to believe, they joined the growing throng that had already learned the answers. They trudged aimlessly now, their voices quieted. Their ardent quest for news was now only a half-hearted search for some slight shred of evidence that the expectations they had held since Topeka and Tacoma were not just a crazy dream.

Who is there [writes Adney] that can describe the crowd, curious, list-less, dazed, dragging its way with slow, lagging step along the main street? Can this be the "rush" that newspapers are accustomed to describe as the movement of gold-seekers? Have the hard, weary

months of work on the trails exhausted their vitality? or is it the heavy
shoes that make them drag their feet so wearily along the street? . . . It
is a vast herd; they crowd the boats and fill the streets, looking at Dawson. . . . The old-timer (we are all old-timers now) is lost. The mere
recognition of a face seen last winter is now excuse for a friendly nod
and a "How-de-do?"

They arrived to claim their reward and found that it was claimed already;
there was no good ground left to stake and thousands to stake it.

Probably between fifteen and twenty thousand people reached Dawson
City during the navigation season of 1898, and it is estimated that a third of
them departed within six weeks of their arrival. So many outfits were being
sold that the price of flour dropped below what its buyers had paid for it in
San Francisco. For a while everything under the sun was for sale and Front
Street looked "like a row of booths at a fair." Miners' wages, which had been
fifteen dollars a day that winter, fell to seven in August, and later there was
unemployment. Some took to sleeping in the saloons, and Colonel Steele
made provisions for the indigent to chop wood in exchange for meals.

Dawson's newborn government services sagged under the onslaught. At
the post office, generally the first place a newcomer headed, tons of unsorted
mail lay in heaps, and the chaos defied the feeble organizational genius of the
two totally inexperienced police clerks assigned there. One stampeder, who
had arrived after incredible hardships along one of the "All-Canadian routes"
(the White Pass and Chilkoot trails, of course, began in Alaska), waited at the
post office for seven hours to learn he had no mail. He then went to the
Recorder's Office where the crowds were even worse. If he had had gold dust
he might have hired a "stander," as others did, to queue up for him, but he had
none so he waited in line every day from Monday to 3 P.M. Friday. When his
turn finally came he was told by an official that "every likely spot within fifty
miles is staked out." It was the end of the week, his first in Dawson City. He
went to the North American Trading and Transportation Company's office,
bought a ticket for St. Michael, and sailed on the *John G. Healy* a few days
later.

Years later, of course, men like this could laugh at their Klondike experiences, turn them into a moving saga for their grandchildren, and reminisce
with other stampeders at the Sourdough Conventions in Seattle. But now, as

their dreams came crashing down around them, they brooded over their ill luck, their poor timing, the expectations that had defrauded them, the Klondike that had deceived them, the madness of their journey from the beginning, the houses they had mortgaged, the seniority they had lost, the savings accounts they had withdrawn, the wives they had left.

But hope dies hard, and in its terminal agonies it is not particular about its sustenance. In Dawson City in 1898, for example, a wild stampede into the circumambient bush would do. Weekly, even daily, these occurred: a man waits in line at the Recorder's Office; he is grizzled and grimy, obviously just back from a prospecting trip to some remote place. He records his claim, then gets some tools and supplies and starts back to work it. All along he has been carefully watched by dozens of the claimless throng on Front Street. So when he leaves they follow one after the other; some in fact have kept packs of grub and blankets at the ready for just such an occasion. After hours or days of slogging through the trailless wilderness, the Pied Piper leads them to a dismal creek in a boggy willow jungle where he has his discovery claim. It is a miserable place, alive with mosquitoes all summer and dead with cold all winter; and they stake it from source to mouth. Then they all scramble back to Dawson City to record. Next day they will all be seen shuffling up and down Front Street again, hoping against hope that the Pied Piper, who remained to sink a shaft, will find gold on the creek. And even before the word gets around that he discovered only mica and pyrites, they are off again on another wild goose chase. It was said at the time that shipping companies started stampedes up or down the Yukon from Dawson to augment traffic, that roadhouse keepers whispered news of bullion-paved creek beds nearby when business was slack, but it is improbable that the stampeders needed any inducement. Certainly no steamboat or roadhouse was involved when they staked the moosehide scar on Midnight Dome, just in back of Dawson, nor when they tried to claim Dawson itself, or the islands in the middle of the Yukon.

Not everybody who came to Dawson in 1898 came to grief. Most who prospered there, however, had come in search of markets instead of mines. Mr. Gandolfo sold his oranges and apples at a dollar apiece, and one of his competitors brought in a watermelon, Dawson's first, and got twenty-five dollars for it. In August a man arrived with a cargo of cats and kittens. He suffered the ridicule of his trailmates en route, but he sold the animals for ten dollars each; they were just the thing for the lonely miner in his mouse-ridden cabin. One merchant parlayed his profits on a load of ten-cent cigars he sold for a dollar fifty each into a fortune of many thousands. "These mines in Dawson can be worked winter and summer," he commented, and he never saw a placer mine the whole time, nor ever hoped to see one.

The rough census made by the police in midsummer, 1898, indicated that Dawson City had a population of seventeen thousand to eighteen thousand, with another four to five thousand on the nearby creeks. It was the biggest city in northwestern Canada. Buildings stretched solidly back from Front Street and Second Avenue all the way to Ninth Avenue. Beyond that, on the flanks of Midnight Dome, was a suburb of tents. From George Street, on the north end of town, to Craig Street, by the Klondike, it was well over a mile, and every one of the blocks William Ogilvie laid out in between was now occupied. Corner lots on Front Street went for as much as forty thousand dollars. On the banks of the Yukon it was rare not to see three or four stern-wheelers tied up at any given time between May and October, for a grand fleet of sixty now plied the river. The ACC., for years represented only by the tiny *Yukon*, dead weight tonnage about thirty, now ran a fleet of seven, three of them over a thousand tons. Dawson had by now three newspapers, two banks, a telephone service, a brewery, and two sawmills which ran night and day and were still behind on orders. The Roman Catholics were joined by the Anglicans, the Presbyterians, the Salvation Army, the Masons, and the Odd Fellows. There was an establishment offering "Russian, Turkish, Medicated and Plain Baths: Vitality Restoring" and dozens of stores, one of which advertised

DRUGS   DRUGS
Rubber boots, Shoes, Etc.
Bacon, flour, rolled oats, rice, sugar, potatoes,
onions, tea and coffee, fruits,
cornmeal, german sausage,
Dogs Dogs

Clearly, Dawson City had come of age.

JACK LONDON

Gold Hunters of the North

"Where the Northern Lights come down o'
nights to dance on the houseless snow."

Ivan, I forbid you to go farther in this undertaking. Not a word about this, or we are all undone. Let the Americans and the English know that we have gold in these mountains, then we are ruined. They will rush in on us by thousands, and crowd us to the wall—to the death."

So spoke the old Russian governor, Baranov, at Sitka, in 1804, to one of his Slavonian hunters, who had just drawn from his pocket a handful of golden nuggets. Full well Baranov, fur trader and autocrat, understood and feared the coming of the sturdy, indomitable gold hunters of Anglo-Saxon stock. And thus he suppressed the news, as did the governors that followed him, so that when the United States bought Alaska in 1867, she bought it for its furs and fisheries, without a thought of its treasures underground.

No sooner, however, had Alaska become American soil than thousands of our adventurers were afoot and afloat for the North. They were the men of "the days of gold," the men of California, Fraser, Cassiar, and Cariboo. With the mysterious, infinite faith of the prospector, they believed that the gold streak, which ran through the Americas from Cape Horn to California, did not "peter out" in British Columbia. That it extended farther north, was their creed, and "Farther North!" became their cry. No time was lost, and in the early seventies, leaving the Treadwell and the Silver Bow Basin to be discovered by those who came after, they went plunging on into the white unknown. North, farther north, till their picks rang in the frozen beaches of the Arctic Ocean, and they shivered by driftwood fires on the ruby sands of Nome.

But first, in order that this colossal adventure may be fully grasped, the recentness and the remoteness of Alaska must be emphasized. The interior of Alaska and the contiguous Canadian territory was a vast wilderness. Its hundreds of thousands of square miles were as dark and chartless as Darkest Africa. In 1847, when the first Hudson's Bay Company agents crossed over the Rockies from the Mackenzie to poach on the preserves of the Russian Bear, they thought that the Yukon flowed north and emptied into the Arctic Ocean. Hundreds of miles below, however, were the outposts of the Russian traders. They, in turn, did not know where the Yukon had its source, and it was not till later that Russ and Saxon learned that it was the same mighty stream they were occupying. In 1850, Lieutenant Barnard, of the English navy, in search of Sir John Franklin, was killed in a massacre of Russians at Nulato, on the Lower Yukon. And a little over ten years later, Frederick Whymper voyaged up the Great Bend to Fort Yukon under the Arctic Circle.

From fort to fort, from York Factory on Hudson's Bay to Fort Yukon in Alaska, the English traders transported their goods—a round trip requiring from a year to a year and a half. It was one of their deserters, in 1867, escaping down the Yukon to Bering Sea, who was the first white man to make the Northwest Passage by land from the Atlantic to the Pacific. It was at this time that the first accurate description of a fair portion of the Yukon was given by Dr. W. H. Ball, of the Smithsonian Institution. But even he had never seen its source, and it was not given him to appreciate the marvel of that great natural highway.

No more remarkable river in this one particular is there in the world—taking its rise in Crater Lake, thirty miles from the ocean, the Yukon flows for twenty-five-hundred miles, through the heart of the continent, ere it empties into the sea. A portage of thirty miles, and then a highway for traffic one tenth the girth of the earth!

As late as 1869, Frederick Whymper, fellow of the Royal Geographical Society, stated on hearsay, that the Chilcat Indians were believed occasionally to make a short portage across the Coast Range from salt water to the head-reaches of the Yukon. But it remained for a gold hunter, questing north, ever north, to be first of all white men to cross the terrible Chilcoot Pass, and tap the Yukon at its head. This happened only the other day, but the man has become a dim legendary hero. Holt was his name, and already the mists of antiquity have wrapped about the time of his passage. 1872, 1874, and 1878 are the dates variously given—a confusion which time will never clear.

Holt penetrated as far as the Hootalinqua, and on his return to the coast reported coarse gold. The next recorded adventurer is one Edward Bean, who in 1880 headed a party of twenty-five miners from Sitka into the uncharted land. And in the same year, other parties (now forgotten, for who remembers or ever hears the wanderings of the gold hunters?) crossed the Pass, built boats out of the standing timber, and drifted down the Yukon and farther north.

And then, for a quarter of a century, the unknown and unsung heroes grappled with the frost, and groped for the gold they were sure lay somewhere among the shadows of the Pole. In the struggle with the terrifying and pitiless natural forces, they returned to the primitive, garmenting themselves in the skins of wild beasts, and covering their feet with the walrus *mucluc* and the moose-hide moccasin. They forgot the world and its ways, as the world had forgotten them; killed their meat as they found it; feasted in plenty and starved in famine, and searched unceasingly for the yellow lure. They criss-crossed the land in every direction, threaded countless unmapped rivers in precarious birch-bark canoes, and with snowshoes and dogs broke trail through thousands of miles of silent white, where man had never been. They struggled on, under the aurora borealis or the midnight sun, through temperatures that ranged from one hundred degrees above zero to eighty degrees below, living in the grim humor of the land, on "rabbit tracks and salmon bellies."

Today, a man may wander away from the trail for a hundred days, and just as he is congratulating himself that at last he is treading virgin soil, he will come upon some ancient and dilapidated cabin, and forget his disappointment in wonder at the man who reared the logs. Still, if one wanders from the trail far enough and deviously enough, he may chance upon a few thousand square miles which he may have all to himself. On the other hand, no matter how far and how deviously he may wander, the possibility always remains that he may stumble, not alone upon a deserted cabin, but upon an occupied one.

As an instance of this, and of the vastness of the land, no better case need be cited than that of Harry Maxwell. An able seaman, hailing from New Bedford, Massachusetts, his ship, the brig *Fannie E. Lee*, was pinched in the Arctic ice. Passing from whaleship to whaleship, he eventually turned up at Point Barrow in the summer of 1880. He was *north* of the Northland, and from this point of vantage he determined to pull south into the interior in search of gold. Across the mountains from Fort Macpherson, and a couple of hundred miles eastward from the Mackenzie, he built a cabin and established his head-quarters. And here, for nineteen continuous years, he hunted his living and prospected. He ranged from the never-opening ice to the north as far south as the Great Slave Lake. Here he met Warburton Pike, the author and explorer— an incident he now looks back upon as chief among the few incidents of his solitary life.

When this sailor-miner had accumulated $20,000 worth of dust he con-cluded that civilization was good enough for him, and proceeded "to pull for the outside." From the Mackenzie he went up the Little Peel to its headwaters, found a pass through the mountains, nearly starved to death on his way across to the Porcupine Hills, and eventually came out on the Yukon River, where he learned for the first time of the Yukon gold hunters and their dis-coveries. Yet for twenty years they had been working there, his next-door neighbors, virtually, in a land of such great spaces. At Victoria, British Colum-bia, just previous to going east over the Canadian Pacific (the existence of which he had just learned), he pregnantly remarked that he had faith in the Mackenzie watershed, and that he was going back after he had taken in the World's Fair, and got a whiff or two of civilization.

Faith! It may or may not remove mountains, but it has certainly made the Northland. No Christian martyr ever possessed greater faith than did the pio-neers of Alaska. They never doubted the bleak and barren land. Those who came remained, and more ever came. They could not leave. They "knew" the gold was there, and they persisted. Somehow, the romance of the land and the quest entered into their blood, the spell of it gripped hold of them and would not let them go. Man after man of them, after the most terrible privation and suffering, shook the muck of the country from his moccasins and departed for good. But the following spring always found him drifting down the Yukon on the tail of the ice jams.

Jack McQuestion aptly vindicates the grip of the North. After a residence of thirty years he insists that the climate is delightful, and declares that whenever he makes a trip to the States he is afflicted with homesickness. Needless to say, the North still has him and will keep tight hold of him until he dies. In fact, for him to die elsewhere would be inartistic and insincere. Of three of the "pioneer" pioneers, Jack McQuestion alone survives. In 1871, from one to seven years before Holt went over Chilcoot, in the company of Al Mayo and Arthur Harper, McQuestion came into the Yukon from the North-west over the Hudson's Bay Company route from the Mackenzie to Fort Yukon. The names of these three men, as their lives, are bound up in the his-tory of the country, and so long as there be histories and charts, that long will the Mayo and McQuestion rivers and the Harper and Ladue town site of Dawson be remembered. As an agent of the Alaska Commercial Company, in 1873, McQuestion built Fort Reliance, six miles below the Klondike River. In 1898 the writer met Jack McQuestion at Minook, on the Lower Yukon. The old pioneer, though grizzled, was hale and hearty, and as optimistic as when he first journeyed into the land along the path of the Circle. And no man more beloved is there in all the North. There will be great sadness there when his soul goes questing over the Last Divide—"farther north," perhaps—who can tell?

Frank Dinsmore is a fair sample of the men who made the Yukon Coun-try. A Yankee, born in Auburn, Maine, the wanderlust early laid him by the heels, and at sixteen he was heading west on the trail that led "farther north." He prospected in the Black Hills, Montana, and in the Coeur d'Alene, then heard the whisper of the North, and went up to Juneau on the Alaskan Pan-handle. But the North still whispered, and more insistently, and he could not rest till he went over Chilcoot, and down into the mysterious Silent Land. This was in 1882, and he went down the chain of lakes, down the Yukon, up the Pelly, and tried his luck on the bars of McMillan River. In the fall, a per-ambulating skeleton, he came back over the Pass in a blizzard, with a rag of a shirt, tattered overalls, and a handful of raw flour.

But he was unafraid. That winter he worked for a grubstake in Juneau, and the next spring found the heels of his moccasins turned toward salt water and his face toward Chilcoot. This was repeated the next spring, and the fol-lowing spring, and the spring after that, until, in 1885, he went over the Pass for good. There was to be no return for him until he found the gold he sought.

The years came and went, but he remained true to his resolve. For eleven long years, with snowshoe and canoe, pickax and gold pan, he wrote out his life on the face of the land. Upper Yukon, Middle Yukon, Lower Yukon—he prospected faithfully and well. His bed was anywhere. The sky was his coverlet. Winter or summer he carried neither tent nor stove, and his six-pound sleeping robe of arctic hare was the warmest thing he was ever known to possess. Rabbit tracks and salmon bellies were his diet with a vengeance, for he depended largely on his rifle and fishing tackle. His endurance equaled his courage. On a wager he lifted thirteen fifty-pound sacks of flour and walked off with them. Winding up a seven-hundred-mile trip on the ice with a forty-mile run, he came into camp at six o'clock in the evening and found a "squaw dance" under way. He should have been exhausted. Anyway, his *muclucs* were frozen stiff. But he kicked them off and danced all night in stocking feet.

At the last fortune came to him. The quest was ended, and he gathered up his gold and pulled for the outside. And his own end was as fitting as that of his quest. Illness came upon him down in San Francisco, and his splendid life ebbed slowly out as he sat in his big easy chair, in the Commercial Hotel, the "Yukoner's home." The doctors came, discussed, consulted, the while he matured more plans of Northland adventure; for the North still gripped him and would not let him go. He grew weaker day by day, but each day he said, "Tomorrow I'll be all right." Other old-timers, "out on furlough," came to see him. They wiped their eyes and swore under their breaths, then entered and talked largely and jovially about going in with him over the trail when spring came. But there in the big easy chair it was that his Long Trail ended, and the life passed out of him still fixed on "farther north."

From the time of the first white man, famine loomed black and gloomy over the land. It was chronic with the Indians and Eskimos; it became chronic with the gold hunters. It was ever present, and so it came about that life was commonly expressed in terms of "grub"—was measured by cups of flour. Each winter, eight months long, the heroes of the frost faced starvation. It became the custom, as fall drew on, for partners to cut the cards or draw straws to determine which should hit the hazardous trail for salt water, and which should remain and endure the hazardous darkness of the arctic night.

There was never food enough to winter the whole population. The A. C. Company worked hard to freight up the grub, but the gold hunters came faster and dared more audaciously. When the A. C. Company added a new stern-wheeler to its fleet, men said, "Now we shall have plenty." But more gold hunters poured in over the passes to the South, more *voyageurs* and fur traders forced a way through the Rockies from the East, more seal hunters and coast adventurers poled up from Bering Sea on the West, more sailors deserted from the whaleships to the North, and they all starved together in right brotherly fashion. More steamers were added, but the tide of prospectors welled always in advance. Then the N. A. T. & T. Company came up the scene, and both companies added steadily to their fleets. But it was the same old story; famine would not depart. In fact, famine grew with the population, till, in the winter of 1897–98, the United States government was forced to equip a reindeer relief expedition. As of old, the winter partners cut the cards and drew straws, and remained or pulled for salt water as chance decided. They were wise of old time, and had learned never to figure on relief expeditions. They had heard of such things, but no mortal man of them had ever laid eyes on one.

The hard luck of other mining countries pales into insignificance before the hard luck of the North. And as for the hardship, it cannot be conveyed by printed page or word of mouth. No man may know who has not undergone. And those who have undergone, out of their knowledge claim that in the making of the world God grew tired, and when he came to the last barrowload, "just dumped it anyhow," and that was how Alaska happened to be. While no adequate conception of the life can be given to the stay-at-home, yet the men themselves sometimes give a clue to its rigors. One old Minook miner testified thus: "Haven't you noticed the expression on the faces of us fellows? You can tell a newcomer the minute you see him; he looks alive, enthusiastic, perhaps jolly. We old miners are always grave, unless we're drinking."

Another old-timer, out of the bitterness of a "home mood," imagined himself a Martian astronomer explaining to a friend, with the aid of a powerful telescope, the institutions of the earth. "There are the continents," he indicated, "and up there near the polar cap is a country, frigid and burning and lonely and apart, called Alaska. Now in other countries and states there are great insane asylums, but, though crowded, they are insufficient; so there is Alaska given over to the worst cases. Now and then some poor insane creature comes to his senses in those awful solitudes, and, in wondering joy, escapes from the land and hastens back to his home. But most cases are incurable. They just suffer along, poor devils, forgetting their former life quite, or recalling it like a dream."—Again the grip of the North, which will not let one go—for "*most cases are incurable.*"

For a quarter of a century the battle with frost and famine went on. The very severity of the struggle with Nature seemed to make the gold hunters kindly toward one another. The latchstring was always out, and the open hand was the order of the day. Distrust was unknown, and it was no hyperbole for a man to take the last shirt off his back for a comrade. Most significant of all, perhaps, in this connection, was the custom of the old days, that when August the first came around, the prospectors who had failed to locate "pay dirt" were permitted to go upon the ground of their more fortunate comrades and take out enough for the next year's grubstake.

In 1885 rich bar washing was done on the Stewart River, and in 1886 Cassiar Bar was struck just below the mouth of the Hootalinqua. It was at this time that the first moderate strike was made on Forty-Mile Creek, so called because it was judged to be that distance below Fort Reliance of Jack McQuestion fame. A prospector named Williams started for the outside with dogs and Indians to carry the news, but suffered such hardship on the summit of Chilcoot that he was carried dying into the store of Captain John Healy at Dyea. But he had brought the news through—*coarse gold!* Inside three months more than two hundred miners had passed in over Chilcoot, stampeding for Forty Mile. Find followed find—Sixty Mile, Miller, Glacier, Birch, Franklin, and the Koyokuk. But they were all moderate discoveries, and the miners still dreamed and searched for the fabled stream, "Too Much Gold," where gold was so plentiful that gravel had to be shoveled into the sluice boxes in order to wash it.

And all the time the Northland was preparing to play its own huge joke. It was a great joke, albeit an exceeding bitter one, and it has led the old-timers to believe that the land is left in darkness the better part of the year because God goes away and leaves it to itself. After all the risk and toil and faithful endeavor, it was destined that few of the heroes should be in at the finish when Too Much Gold turned its yellow belly to the stars.

First, there was Robert Henderson—and this is true history. Henderson had faith in the Indian River district. For three years, by himself, depending mainly on his rifle, living on straight meat a large portion of the time, he prospected many of the Indian River tributaries, just missed finding the rich creeks, Sulphur and Dominion, and managed to make grub (poor grub) out of Quartz Creek and Australia Creek. Then he crossed the divide between Indian River and the Klondike, and on one of the "feeders" of the latter found eight cents to the pan. This was considered excellent in those simple days. Naming the creek "Gold Bottom," he recrossed the divide and got three men, Munson, Dalton, and Swanson, to return with him. The four took out $750. And be it emphasized, and emphasized again, *that this was the first Klondike gold ever shoveled in and washed out.* And be it also emphasized, *that Robert Henderson was the discoverer of Klondike, all lies and hearsay tales to the contrary.*

Running out of grub, Henderson again recrossed the divide, and went down the Indian River and up the Yukon to Sixty Mile. Here Joe Ladue ran the trading post, and here Joe Ladue had originally grubstaked Henderson. Henderson told his tale, and a dozen men (all it contained) deserted the Post for the scene of his find. Also, Henderson persuaded a party of prospectors, bound for Stewart River, to forego their trip and go down and locate with him. He loaded his boat with supplies, drifted down the Yukon to the mouth of the Klondike, and towed and poled up the Klondike to Gold Bottom. But at the mouth of the Klondike he met George Carmack, and thereby hangs the tale.

Carmack was a squaw man. He was familiarly known as "Siwash" George—a derogatory term which had arisen out of his affinity for the Indians. At the time Henderson encountered him he was catching salmon with his Indian wife and relatives on the site of what was to become Dawson, the Golden City of the Snows. Henderson, bubbling over with good will and prone to the open hand, told Carmack of his discovery. But Carmack was satisfied where he was. He was possessed by no overweening desire for the strenuous life. Salmon were good enough for him. But Henderson urged him to come on and locate, until, when he yielded, he wanted to take the whole tribe along. Henderson refused to stand for this, said that he must give the preference over Siwashes to his old Sixty Mile friends, and it is rumored, said some things about Siwashes that were not nice.

The next morning Henderson went on alone up the Klondike to Gold Bottom. Carmack, by this time aroused, took a short cut afoot for the same place. Accompanied by his two Indian brothers-in-law, Skookum Jim and Tagish Charley, he went up Rabbit Creek (now Bonanza), crossed into Gold Bottom, and staked near Henderson's discovery. On the way up he had panned a few shovels on Rabbit Creek, and he showed Henderson "colors" he had obtained. Henderson made him promise, if he found anything on the way back, that he would send up one of the Indians with the news. Henderson also agreed to pay for this service, for he seemed to feel that they were on the verge of something big, and he wanted to make sure.

Carmack returned down Rabbit Creek. While he was taking a sleep on the bank about half a mile below the mouth of what was to be known as Eldorado, Skookum Jim tried his luck, and from surface prospects got from ten cents to a dollar to the pan. Carmack and his brothers-in-law staked and "hit the high places" for Forty Mile, where they filed on the claims before Captain Constantine, and renamed the creek Bonanza. And Henderson was forgotten. No word of it reached him. Carmack broke his promise.

Weeks afterward, when Bonanza and Eldorado were staked from end to end and there was no more room, a party of later comers pushed over the divide and down to Gold Bottom, where they found Henderson still at work. When they told him they were from Bonanza, he was nonplused. He had never heard of such a place. But when they described it, he recognized it as Rabbit Creek. Then they told him of its marvelous richness, and, as Tappan Adney relates, when Henderson realized what he had lost through Carmack's treachery, "he threw down his shovel and went and sat on the bank, so sick at heart that it was some time before he could speak."

Then there were the rest of the old-timers, the men of Forty Mile and Circle City. At the time of the discovery, nearly all of them were over to the West at work in the old diggings or prospecting for new ones. As they said of themselves, they were the kind of men who are always caught out with forks when it rains soup. In the stampede that followed the news of Carmack's strike very few old miners took part. They were not there to take part. But the men who did go on the stampede were mainly the worthless ones, the newcomers, and the camp hangers-on. And while Bob Henderson plugged away to the East, and the heroes plugged away to the West, the greenhorns and rounders went up and staked Bonanza.

But the Northland was not yet done with its joke. When fall came on and the heroes returned to Forty Mile and to Circle City, they listened calmly to the up-river tales of Siwash discoveries and loafers' prospects, and shook their heads. They judged by the caliber of the men interested, and branded it a bunco game. But glowing reports continued to trickle down the Yukon, and a few of the old-timers went up to see. They looked over the ground—the unlikeliest place for gold in all their experience—and they went down the river again, "leaving it to the Swedes."

Again the Northland turned the tables. The Alaskan gold hunter is proverbial, not so much for his unveracity, as for his inability to tell the precise truth. In a country of exaggerations, he likewise is prone to hyperbolic description of things actual. But when it came to Klondike, he could not stretch the truth as fast as the truth itself stretched. Carmack first got a dollar pan. He lied when he said it was two dollars and a half. And when those who doubted him did get two-and-a-half pans, they said they were getting an ounce, and lo! ere the lie had fairly started on its way, they were getting, not one ounce but five ounces. This they claimed was six ounces; but when they filled a pan of dirt to prove the lie, they washed out twelve ounces. And so it went. They continued valiantly to lie, but the truth continued to outrun them.

But the Northland's hyperborean laugh was not yet ended. When Bonanza was staked from mouth to source, those who had failed "to get in," disgruntled and sore, went up the "pups" and feeders. Eldorado was one of these feeders, and many men, after locating on it, turned their backs upon their claims and never gave them a second thought. One man sold a half-interest in five hundred feet of it for a sack of flour. Other owners wandered around trying to bunco men into buying them out for a song. And then Eldorado "showed up." It was far, far richer than Bonanza, with an average value of a thousand dollars a foot to every foot of it.

A Swede named Charley Anderson had been at work on Miller Creek the year of the strike, and arrived in Dawson with a few hundred dollars. Two miners who had staked No. 29 Eldorado, decided that he was the proper man upon whom to "unload." He was too canny to approach sober, so at considerable expense they got him drunk. Even then it was hard work, but they kept him befuddled for several days, and finally inveigled him into buying No. 29 for $750. When Anderson sobered up, he wept at his folly, and pleaded to have his money back. But the men who had duped him were hardhearted. They laughed at him, and kicked at themselves for not having tapped him for a couple of hundred more. Nothing remained for Anderson but to work the worthless ground. This he did, and out of it he took over three quarters of a million of dollars.

It was not till Frank Dinsmore, who already had big holdings on Birch Creek, took a hand, that the old-timers developed faith in the new diggings. Dinsmore received a letter from a man on the spot, calling it "the biggest thing in the world," and harnessed his dogs and went up to investigate. And when he sent a letter back saying that he had "never seen anything like it," Circle City for the first time believed, and at once was precipitated one of the wildest stampedes the country had ever seen or ever will see. Every dog was taken, many went without dogs, and even the women and children and weaklings hit the three hundred miles of ice through the long arctic night for the biggest thing in the world. It is related that twenty people, mostly cripples and unable to travel, were left in Circle City when the smoke of the last sled disappeared up the Yukon.

Since that time gold has been discovered in all manner of places, under the grass-roots of the hillside benches, in the bottom of Monte Cristo Island, and in the sands of the sea at Nome. And now the gold hunter who knows his business shuns the "favorable looking" spots, confident in his hard-won knowledge that he will find the most gold in the least likely place. This is sometimes adduced to support the theory that the gold hunters, rather than the explorers, are the men who will ultimately win the Pole. Who knows? It is in their blood, and they are capable of it.

George R. Adams

A RESIDENT OF DYEA
WAS THE FIRST AMERICAN IN
THE YUKON BASIN

The first American who ever set foot in the Yukon basin is in Dyea. His name is George R. Adams. He will engage in the general merchandise business in this city. He is a pioneer of pioneers. Many years have passed since first he set foot in the frozen north, yet he is still one of the handsomest and best preserved men who walk the streets of Dyea. His hair and mustache are white, but Mr. Adams is strong and active and as full of hope as ever. As he has cast his lot in Dyea, a few facts of his history will be interesting.

Nearly thirty-five years ago, Maj. Robert Kennicott, of Cleveland, Ohio, sailed from San Francisco for St. Michael, at the mouth of the mighty Yukon, in command of an expedition for exploring the coast of Alaska, for the Russian-American telegraph line. With him was a youth of twenty summers, strong, hardy and energetic—George R. Adams. The party of thirteen sailed for the north on the bark Golden Gate and late in September established winter quarters at Unalaklik, at the mouth of the river of that name. Lieut. Adams, for that was his title in the service in which he had enlisted, was placed in charge of the first expedition to penetrate the Yukon valley. He was the first American to set foot in the Yukon basin. With a half breed Russian and an Indian guide, he penetrated the interior during the winter of 1865–6 as far as Nulato, making a portage from the headwaters of the Unalaklik river to the Yukon.

Mr. Adams lived in Alaska for twelve years following this in the employ of the Alaska Commercial company. His experiences in Alaska have been extensive and his knowledge of the Yukon country is large. Back of the plain story of hardship and danger which Mr. Adams can tell when he feels like indulging in reminiscences, is a story of romance which is a part of the history of Alaska. To tell this story one would have to describe the death by his own hand of Maj. Kennicott, who was in charge of the party, and whose failure to reach Fort Yukon, where he expected to meet another party from the Frazer river, so preyed on his mind that he took a dose of strychnine. Another incident in that memorable campaign was a long, mind-killing wait at St. Michael for the steamers which were to bring supplies to the little party, and the ravings of two men who, when the steamers arrived after all hope had vanished, succumbed to the terrible mental strain and were put in irons and sent back to the states, both total wrecks.

Mr. Adams said that shortage of food is an old story in Alaska. When he organized his expedition to explore the Yukon basin from Unalaklik, food was exceedingly scarce at St. Michael. Sugar was worth $3 per pound, and they were most willing to pay that unusual price. Ice was beginning to form in the Unalaklik river when with the Russian and Indian he started in a skin canoe for its headwaters. He found an easy portage from its source to Nulato. After establishing a base of operations at this point, he returned to Unalaklik for provisions. After securing these he started again for Nulato, this time over the frozen surface of the river with dog teams, which he had obtained at Cape Romanoff. Several times the journey was made between the two points for provisions, which were very scarce and hard to get. During that winter Lieut. Adams and his two companions were forced to subsist on supplies obtained largely from the Indians. As they proceeded they found that the natives were short of food and some even on the verge of starvation. A diet of bean soup, plentifully salted, was the rule.

"Even under such circumstances," said Mr. Adams, "I grew stout and hearty. It was when we returned to Unalaklik in the summer of 1866 and waited until the surface of Norton Sound was a glittering sheet of ice, and still the supply boats did not come, that the awful terrors of a winter in that latitude without food dawned upon us. We had all arranged to scatter over the country, hoping to live with the natives during the winter. I had prepared to set out on a trip down the coast alone when a storm came up and the ice was broken. A few days later the steamer Wright, which was the flagship of the expedition, and the ship Nightingale appeared in the harbor, laden with supplies and bringing the first intelligence from civilization we had enjoyed in fourteen months. Of course we were overjoyed. The strain, however, was too much for two unfortunate fellows, Green and Cotter. Both became raving maniacs and were put in irons. Both died some years later without having fully recovered from that awful experience."

KLONDIKE OUTFIT LIST

This is the list of goods that Dan and his partner, Ned Dyers, purchased for their planned two-year stay in the Klondike gold fields, quoted from a letter sent to his sister and brother on August 1, 1897:

> Our latest improved rifles, with plenty
>   of amunition
> Two Colts Revolvers
> Six pairs snow glasses
> 2 Axes–3 shovels–3 picks
> Some pick steel & Borax for [?]
> 3 gold pans and one rocker Also Some quicksilver
> 1 Whip Saw—1 Hand Saw
> 1 Box flat files–1 claw hammer
> 1 Frying pan–1 Baking Pan
> 1–8 quart granite kettle
> 1–6 quart granite kettle
> 1 coffee pot–6 granite cups
> 2 large spoons–knives & forks & spoons
> 4 granite plates–1 Brace & set of bits

Epsom Salts–quinine–Soda

Mosquito bar (Silk)–1 tent

200 ft. ⅝" rope–Oakum

Batchelors buttons–needles & thread

Wax ends–Awls–Shor–nails

Shor tacks–Wire nails

Leather soles, already cut out

Rubber patches–rubber cement

Our large magnet, also magnifying glass

A quantity of Lime juice to keep off scurvy

Alcohol–Carbolic Acid (for gray backs)

Oiled canvas sheet to lay under blanket

Sheet iron stove–Reflector for baking

2 heavy pocket knives–Candle wicks

250 lbs. Bacon Smoked extra heavy–Matches

100 lbs. Evaporated Peaches–Baking Powder

100 lbs. Evaporated Apricots–Salt

50 lbs. Evaporated Apples–Black Pepper

100 lbs. Self rising Flour–2 cases Milk–Condensed

400 lbs. Graham Flour–250 lbs. Beans

500 lbs. Wheat Flour–Cayenne Pepper

100 lbs. Rice–20 lbs. Coffee–30 lbs.

Tea

Castile Soap–Candles–Mustard

Evaporated Potatoes & Onions

Now there are likely quite a few articles we have not thought of yet, but I put everything down as I think of it & guess we will have a good outfit. Now the next thing is clothes. We will probably get underclothes of chamois leather–2 suits outer clothes, each, made of very best woolen blankets, also 2 Suits each, either best duck or corduroy–then we will get woolen blankets–four pairs each, also two sleeping bags, these bags are made of oiled canvas and lined with wool and at night you just crawl in, close up the bag and go to sleep as warm as if you were in some other place. Then, there's Caps, Silk gloves & Heavy Mittens, Woolen Socks, German Socks & over-shoes—Leather Shoes–extra heavy–Rubber boots &c. We also have to fill up our medicine chest yet. Now after this is all packed then we have to take along enough horses, Pack Saddles etc. to carry it all over the Mountains, so you see we will have quite an outfit.

Now I have shown this list to my partners & they tell me to get it all & as much more if I want it & charge it up to them.

Article from the April 1, 1898, issue of
The Klondike News (Vol. 1, No. 1)

GETTING THERE:
HOW TO GO

In these days of rapid changes, when one reads of railroads in impossible places and steamboats that will shoot rapids, one hardly knows how to advise on this subject. What today might be an utterly impractical route, may in a few weeks be open for travel by steamboat, railroad, bicycle, or balloon. What we have to say on this subject is from our own actual experience during several years residence in the country.

The different routes by which Dawson may be reached are supposed to be as follows:

The Edmonton route
The Copper River route
The Stickine route
The Takau route
The Dalton trail
White Pass or Skaguay Trail
The Chilcoot Pass or Dyea Trail
The St. Michael's or All Water route

THE EDMONTON ROUTE

The Edmonton route is out of the question at present for anyone taking in an outfit, as it involves long portages between rivers and lakes and hundreds of miles of travel through an unknown country. It would take fully six months to reach Dawson this way.

THE COPPER RIVER ROUTE

We warn our readers against any attempt to reach the Klondike country by way of Copper River. No living man ever made the trip, and the bones of many a prospector whiten the way. In the first place it is almost impossible to ascend the Copper River. There are trackless mountains to cross, by the side of which the Chilcoot Pass trail is a boulevard, and rapids that would make the White Horse dry up and quit business. Finally the White River is not navigable for loaded boats.

Certain unscrupulous parties operating steamboats up that way are issuing gaudy pamphlets with nicely worded directions of how to travel over a country that white man never set foot in. This is worse than murder, and such crimes deserve to be punished to the full extent of the law. We would suggest that they be hung, drawn, quartered and fed to a pack of hungry Malamute dogs.

THE STICKINE ROUTE

One of the advantages this route is supposed to enjoy is its freedom from rough and dangerous water, such as the White Horse Rapids. While it is true that by going this way one would escape the danger of walking around the White Horse Rapids and the expense of sending the boat through by tramway, we would suggest that there are only a few hundred yards of rough water in the White Horse Rapids, and there are 150 miles of Stickine River, and a more swift, crooked and dangerous river does not flow.

The portage of 150 miles from Telegraph Creek to Teslin Lake is one that the traveler will never forget, even though made over a wagon road, and we would advise our friends to wait until the long-talked-of railroad is completed and go over this route by Pullman car.

THE TAKAU ROUTE

This is another back-breaking, soul-destroying way of reaching the Yukon. It has to recommend it as a possible route, grand scenery, fine fishing and a splendid opportunity for physical exercise.

In the month of August, 1897, the Editor of the 'News' was one of a party that made the pilgrimage from Juneau to Teslin Lake. Assisted by six stalwart Indians we put in ten days of terrible labour in dragging, poling and packing a canoe to the 'head of navigation.' Then we spent six delightful days in fighting our way through mud and mosquitoes to the head of the lake.

There is one mountain over which the traveler must pass that is 5,200 feet high, and where one misstep would give the climber a fast mile. This is the celebrated Sin-Wah-Clan mountain. It is twenty-two miles from the head of navigation, at the junction of the Silver Salmon and Nahkanah rivers.

To make the trip from Juneau to the head of Lake Teslin in eighteen days is considered fast traveling over that part of the country, and for the sake of comparison we will say that our trip from Dyea to Dawson in October last was accomplished in twelve days.

THE DALTON TRAIL

For those who have cattle and horses the overland route offers many inducements if the trip be made in midsummer. There is plenty of grass for stock, fine hunting and fishing, and good camping accommodations. The trail starts either at Haynes' Mission on the Lynn Canal or at Pyramid Harbor in the Chilkat Inlet. From either of these places the road follows the meanderings of the Chilkat River and over a comparatively easy summit of 2500 feet to the Altsek River, and thence along this latter water course to Dalton's Post. From the post the trail turns to the right and follows the borders of Lake Arkell to the Tahkeena River.

Ascending this river a well-defined trail leads to Hoochia. Lake Here it branches, the one to the left, although shorter, is much more difficult and rough, and will lead the traveler to the Pelly Post, otherwise known as Fort Selkirk. The regular trail keeps straight on to the Nuttsendone River, and will land one on the Yukon at a point just below Five Finger Rapids.

From here steamboats will be in operation this summer that will carry travelers to Dawson in a few days. The entire distance from the Chilkat Inlet overland to the Yukon is variously estimated from 375 to 400 miles. On this trip one needs both shotgun and rifle. There are moose, caribou, deer, mountain sheep and other animals to be encountered, as well as vast numbers of ducks, geese, grouse, and other small game.

The lakes and rivers are filled with splendid fish, including trout, bass, pickerel and white fish. In the Hoochia Lake there may be caught a yellow meated fish of exquisite flavor as yet unnamed, but one well calculated to appease 'the Yukon appetite' that is certain to be acquired.

But it must be remembered that the snow falls early and deep in this region, and in no event should the trip be attempted later than August 15th.

The writer started from Haynes Mission en route for Dawson on the 12th of September and was compelled to turn back. Other parties who started about the 1st of September were caught in the most terrible storms when half way across. Their stock perished, their provisions had to be abandoned, and it was only after fearful hardships that they succeeded in reaching the coast. The trip may be safely made, however, at any time between May 15 and August 15th.

DYEA AND SKAGUAY TRAILS

So much has been said and written of these two trails that it seems a waste of words to describe them. They start six miles apart and end at the head of the lakes, the Dyea or Chilcoot trail being 28 miles in length and the White Pass or Skaguay, 33 miles. The intending Yukoner would better make his own inquiry and investigation before choosing either. The Dyea or Chilcoot is the old reliable trail, and has been traveled for many years; but if a good wagon road is constructed over the White Pass it will be the better route, being a thousand feet lower. We would advise our readers, however, to fully satisfy themselves on this point before starting. The trip from the head of the lakes down to Dawson can be made in from eight to fifteen days. Light draught steamers will ply on Bennett, Marsh and Tagish lakes, and the dangers and difficulties encountered by the old timers will not be met with by the travelers of 1898.

THE ST. MICHAELS, OR ALL WATER ROUTE

It is well known that in the years gone by the Yukon River boats owned by the old companies had a persistent habit of sticking on the sand bars far below Circle City, and it was about an even thing whether or not they would land their passengers and freight.

There is a sneaking idea prevalent, however, that this state of affairs was not the result of carelessness, ignorance, or the natural conditions surrounding navigation, but part of a well-laid plan.

The United States government sent a representative into the Yukon country last year and his report appears in the May Bulletin of the Department of Labor, and from which we quote the words of Capt. E. D. Dixon, an old Mississippi River steamboat man, and now engaged in running a boat up the Yukon. Capt. Dixon says: "I have never seen the river with less than six feet of water at any point below Fort Yukon. The shallowest riffle is at White Eyes, and the lowest water I ever saw there was six feet, and that was the lowest water known there for years. At a medium stage of water there is sufficient depth at Fort Yukon. The steamers have been running in the wrong chanel."

"From White Eyes to Fish Camp, twelve miles above Circle City, the current averages about five and a half miles an hour. It runs swifter than that on the riffles of course. From Fish Camp to Dawson we have a narrow river, averaging about a half a mile in width, with an average current of six miles an hour. In ordinary stages of the river there is from six to seven feet of water on the highest bars. The Yukon is an ideal river for navigation. There are no rocks, no boulders, and no snags to hinder navigation. All the rocks in the river are easily located by the breaks the current throws over them, and they are all near shore. It is one of the prettiest rivers under the sun to navigate."

In the year 1897, the Yukon was opened for navigation by May 17th, and the first boat arrived at Dawson June the 2nd. The Bering Sea, however, does not open until the fore part of July, and it is useless to leave the Pacific Coast until the middle of June. The trip from St. Michaels to Dawson occupies from twelve to eighteen days, according to the swiftness of the steamer traveled upon, and the distances to the principal points are as follows: Fort Adams, 1250 miles; the Tanana, 1265 miles; Minook, 1315 miles; Fort Hamlin, 1385 miles; Fort Yukon, 1665 miles; Circle City, 1750 miles; Forty Mile, 1997 miles; Dawson, 2050 miles.

The river boats consume from one to two cords of wood per running hour, and the traveler should inquire carefully into the fuel supply of the boat he intends going on.

Many of the boats recently constructed for the navigation of the Yukon draw less than three feet of water, and will make the trip from St. Michaels to Dawson in twelve days.

Given a good modern river boat, a qualified pilot and an abundance of fuel, and it is safe to say that during the months of July and August the companies thus equipped will land their passengers safely and in due time.

The Dog Nuisance

Dogs everywhere, day and night, howling, fighting, filthy, mangy dogs—all these and more form at present one of the worst nuisances that has for a long time afflicted the citizens of Dawson.

This is the season of the year when cruel and selfish owners of dogs, with no further use for them, have turned them loose on the community to prey for an existence. . . .

There are more dogs in town today than there ever were before. It is calculated that there are at least 2,000 dogs now running loose on the streets of Dawson. Fully one-half of them are homeless by reason of their owners following the annual summer custom of driving them away to rustle for themselves with the intention of recovering them in the fall when their services shall again become valuable. Last year the government established a dog pound and passed a dog ordinance which tended to some extent in clearing the streets and sidewalks of the troublesome dogs and their filthy habits.

Unfortunately, however, the dog pound was located east of the town near the foot of the hill in the most thickly populated portion of the hillside, and the result was a howling mass of ill-assorted, half-starved canines that kept the neighborhood awake every night and drove many people to the verge of insanity.

To Build a Fire

ay had broken cold and gray, exceedingly cold and gray, when the man turned aside from the main Yukon trail and climbed the high earth-bank, where a dim and little-travelled trail led eastward through the fat spruce timberland. It was a steep bank, and he paused for breath at the top, excusing the act to himself by looking at his watch. It was nine o'clock. There was no sun nor hint of sun, though there was not a cloud in the sky. It was a clear day, and yet there seemed an intangible pall over the face of things, a subtle gloom that made the day dark, and that was due to the absence of sun. This fact did not worry the man. He was used to the lack of sun. It had been days since he had seen the sun, and he knew that a few more days must pass before that cheerful orb, due south, would just peep above the sky line and dip immediately from view.

The man flung a look back along the way he had come. The Yukon lay a mile wide and hidden under three feet of ice. On top of this ice were as many feet of snow. It was all pure white, rolling in gentle undulations where the ice jams of the freeze-up had formed. North and south, as far as his eye could see, it was unbroken white, save for a dark hairline that curved and twisted from around the spruce-covered island to the south, and that curved and twisted away into the north, where it disappeared behind another spruce-covered island. This dark hairline was the trail—the main trail—that led south five hundred miles to the Chilcoot Pass, Dyea, and salt water; and that led north seventy miles to Dawson, and still on to the north a thousand miles to Nulato, and finally to St. Michael, on Bering Sea, a thousand miles and half a thousand more.

But all this—the mysterious, far-reaching hairline trail, the absence of sun from the sky, the tremendous cold, and the strangeness and weirdness of it all—made no impression on the man. It was not because he was long used to it. He was a newcomer in the land, a *chechaquo*, and this was his first winter. The trouble with him was that he was without imagination. He was quick and alert in the things of life, but only in the things, and not in the significances. Fifty degrees below zero meant eighty-odd degrees of frost. Such fact impressed him as being cold and uncomfortable, and that was all. It did not lead him to meditate upon his frailty as a creature of temperature, and upon man's frailty in general, able only to live within certain narrow limits of heat and cold; and from there on it did not lead him to the conjectural field of immortality and man's place in the universe. Fifty degrees below zero stood for a bite of frost that hurt and that must be guarded against by the use of mittens, ear flaps, warm moccasins, and thick socks. Fifty degrees below zero was to him just precisely fifty degrees below zero. That there should be anything more to it than that was a thought that never entered his head.

As he turned to go on, he spat speculatively. There was a sharp, explosive crackle that startled him. He spat again. And again, in the air, before it could fall to the snow, the spittle crackled. He knew that at fifty below spittle crackled on the snow, but this spittle had crackled in the air. Undoubtedly it was colder than fifty below—how much colder he did not know. But the temperature did not matter. He was bound for the old claim on the left fork of Henderson Creek, where the boys were already. They had come over across the divide from the Indian Creek country, while he had come the roundabout way to take a look at the possibilities of getting out logs in the spring from the islands in the Yukon. He would be in to camp by six o'clock; a bit after dark, it was true, but the boys would be there, a fire would be going, and a hot supper would be ready. As for lunch, he pressed his hand against the protruding bundle under his jacket. It was also under his shirt, wrapped up in a handkerchief and lying against the naked skin. It was the only way to keep the biscuits from freezing. He smiled agreeably to himself as he thought of those biscuits, each cut open and sopped in bacon grease, and each enclosing a generous slice of fried bacon.

He plunged in among the big spruce trees. The trail was faint. A foot of snow had fallen since the last sled had passed over, and he was glad he was without a sled, travelling light. In fact, he carried nothing but the lunch wrapped in the handkerchief. He was surprised, however, at the cold. It certainly was cold, he concluded, as he rubbed his numb nose and cheekbones with his mittened hand. He was a warm-whiskered man, but the hair on his face did not protect the high cheekbones and the eager nose that thrust itself aggressively into the frosty air.

At the man's heels trotted a dog, a big native husky, the proper wolf dog, gray-coated and without any visible or temperamental difference from its brother, the wild wolf. The animal was depressed by the tremendous cold. It knew that it was no time for travelling. Its instinct told it a truer tale than was told to the man by the man's judgment. In reality, it was not merely colder than fifty below zero; it was colder than sixty below, than seventy below. It was seventy-five below zero. Since the freezing point is thirty-two above zero, it meant than one hundred and seven degrees of frost obtained. The dog did not know anything about thermometers. Possibly in its brain there was no sharp consciousness of a condition of very cold such as was in the man's brain. But the brute had its instinct. It experienced a vague but menacing apprehension that subdued it and made it slink along at the man's heels, and that made it question eagerly every unwonted movement of the man as if expecting him to go into camp or to seek shelter somewhere and build a fire. The dog had learned fire, and it wanted fire, or else to burrow under the snow and cuddle its warmth away from the air.

The frozen moisture of its breathing had settled on its fur in a fine powder of frost, and especially were its jowls, muzzle, and eyelashes whitened by its crystalled breath. The man's red beard and mustache were likewise frosted, but more solidly, the deposit taking the form of ice and increasing with every warm, moist breath he exhaled. Also, the man was chewing tobacco, and the muzzle of ice held his lips so rigidly that he was unable to clear his chin when he expelled the juice. The result was that a crystal beard of the color and solidity of amber was increasing its length on his chin. If he fell down it would shatter itself, like glass, into brittle fragments. But he did not mind the appendage. It was the penalty all tobacco chewers paid in that country, and he had been out before in two cold snaps. They had not been so cold as this, he knew, but by the spirit thermometer at Sixty Mile he knew they had been registered at fifty below and at fifty-five.

He held on through the level stretch of woods for several miles, crossed a wide flat of nigger heads, and dropped down a bank to the frozen bed of a small stream. This was Henderson Creek, and he knew he was ten miles from the forks. He looked at his watch. It was ten o'clock. He was making four miles an hour, and he calculated that he would arrive at the forks at half-past twelve. He decided to celebrate that event by eating his lunch there.

The dog dropped in again at his heels, with a tail drooping discouragement, as the man swung along the creek bed. The furrow of the old sled trail was plainly visible, but a dozen inches of snow covered the marks of the last runners. In a month no man had come up or down that silent creek. The man held steadily on. He was not much given to thinking, and just then particularly he had nothing to think about save that he would eat lunch at the forks and that at six o'clock he would be in camp with the boys. There was nobody to talk to; and, had there been, speech would have been impossible because of the ice muzzle on his mouth. So he continued monotonously to chew tobacco and to increase the length of his amber beard.

Once in a while the thought reiterated itself that it was very cold and that he had never experienced such cold. As he walked along he rubbed his cheekbones and nose with the back of his mittened hand. He did this automatically, now and again changing hands. But, rub as he would, the instant he stopped his cheekbones went numb, and the following instant the end of his nose went numb. He was sure to frost his cheeks; he knew that, and experienced a pang of regret that he had not devised a nose strap of the sort Bud wore in cold snaps. Such a strap passed across the cheeks, as well, and saved them. But it didn't matter much, after all. What were frosted cheeks? A bit painful, that was all; they were never serious.

Empty as the man's mind was of thoughts, he was keenly observant, and he noticed the changes in the creek, the curves and bends and timber jams, and always he sharply noted where he placed his feet. Once, coming around a bend, he shied abruptly, like a startled horse, curved away from the place where he had been walking, and retreated several paces back along the trail. The creek he knew was frozen clear to the bottom—no creek could contain water in that arctic winter—but he knew also that there were springs that bubbled out from the hillsides and ran along under the snow and on top the ice of the creek. He knew that the coldest snaps never froze these springs, and he knew likewise their danger. They were traps. They hid pools of water under the snow that might be three inches deep, or three feet. Sometimes a skin of ice half an inch thick covered them, and in turn was covered by the snow. Sometimes there were alternate layers of water and ice skin, so that when one broke through he kept on breaking through for a while, sometimes wetting himself to the waist.

That was why he had shied in such panic. He had felt the give under his feet and heard the crackle of a snow-hidden ice skin. And to get his feet wet in such a temperature meant trouble and danger. At the very least it meant delay, for he would be forced to stop and build a fire, and under its protection to bare his feet while he dried his socks and moccasins. He stood and studied the creek bed and its banks, and decided that the flow of water came from the right. He reflected awhile, rubbing his nose and cheeks, then skirted to the left, stepping gingerly and testing the footing for each step. Once clear of the danger, he took a fresh chew of tobacco and swung along at his four-mile gait.

In the course of the next two hours he came upon several similar traps. Usually the snow above the hidden pools had a sunken, candied appearance that advertised the danger. Once again, however, he had a close call; and once, suspecting danger, he compelled the dog to go on in front. The dog did not want to go. It hung back until the man shoved it forward, and then it went quickly across the white, unbroken surface. Suddenly it broke through, floundered to one side, and got away to firmer footing. It had wet its forefeet and legs, and almost immediately the water that clung to it turned to ice. It made quick efforts to lick the ice off its legs, then dropped down in the snow and began to bite out the ice that had formed between the toes. This was a matter of instinct. To permit the ice to remain would mean sore feet. It did not know this. It merely obeyed the mysterious prompting that arose from the deep crypts of its being. But the man knew, having achieved a judgment on the subject, and he removed the mitten from his right hand and helped tear out the ice particles. He did not expose his fingers more than a minute, and was astonished at the swift numbness that smote them. It certainly was cold. He pulled on the mitten hastily, and beat the hand savagely across his chest.

At twelve o'clock the day was at its brightest. Yet the sun was too far south on its winter journey to clear the horizon. The bulge of the earth intervened between it and Henderson Creek, where the man walked under a clear sky at noon and cast no shadow. At half-past twelve, to the minute, he arrived at the forks of the creek. He was pleased at the speed he had made. If he kept it up, he would certainly be with the boys by six. He unbuttoned his jacket and shirt and drew forth his lunch. The action consumed no more than a quarter of a minute, yet in that brief moment the numbness laid hold of the exposed fingers. He did not put the mitten on, but, instead, struck the fingers a dozen sharp smashes against his leg. Then he sat down on a snow-covered log to eat. The sting that followed upon the striking of his fingers against his leg ceased so quickly that he was startled. He had had no chance to take a bite of biscuit. He struck the fingers repeatedly and returned them to the mitten, baring the other hand for the purpose of eating. He tried to take a mouthful, but the ice muzzle prevented. He had forgotten to build a fire and thaw out. He chuckled at his foolishness, and as he chuckled he noted the numbness creeping into the exposed fingers. Also, he noted that the stinging which had first come to his toes when he sat down was already passing away. He wondered whether the toes were warm or numb. He moved them inside the moccasins and decided that they were numb.

He pulled the mitten on hurriedly and stood up. He was a bit frightened. He stamped up and down until the stinging returned into the feet. It certainly was cold, was his thought. That man from Sulphur Creek had spoken the truth when telling how cold it sometimes got in the country. And he had laughed at him at the time! That showed one must not be too sure of things. There was no mistake about it, it *was* cold. He strode up and down, stamping his feet and threshing his arms, until reassured by the returning warmth. Then he got out matches and proceeded to make a fire. From the undergrowth, where high water of the previous spring had lodged a supply of seasoned twigs, he got his firewood. Working carefully from a small beginning, he soon had a roaring fire, over which he thawed the ice from his face and in the protection of which he ate his biscuits. For the moment the cold of space was outwitted. The dog took satisfaction in the fire, stretching out close enough for warmth and far enough away to escape being singed.

When the man had finished, he filled his pipe and took his comfortable time over a smoke. Then he pulled on his mittens, settled the ear flaps of his cap firmly about his ears, and took the creek trail up the left fork. The dog was disappointed and yearned back toward the fire. This man did not know cold. Possibly all the generations of his ancestry had been ignorant of cold, of real cold, of cold one hundred and seven degrees below freezing point. But the dog knew; all its ancestry knew, and it had inherited the knowledge. And it knew that it was not good to walk abroad in such fearful cold. It was the time to lie snug in a hole in the snow and wait for a curtain of cloud to be drawn across the face of outer space whence this cold came. On the other hand, there was no keen intimacy between the dog and the man. The one was the toil slave of the other, and the only caresses it had ever received were the caresses of the whip lash and of harsh and menacing throat sounds that threatened the whip lash. So the dog made no effort to communicate its apprehension to the man. It was not concerned in the welfare of the man; it was for its own sake that it yearned back toward the fire. But the man whistled, and spoke to it with the sound of whip lashes, and the dog swung in at the man's heels and followed after.

The man took a chew of tobacco and proceeded to start a new amber beard. Also, his moist breath quickly powdered with white his mustache, eyebrows, and lashes. There did not seem to be so many springs on the left fork of the Henderson, and for half an hour the man saw no signs of any. And then it happened. At a place where there were no signs, where the soft, unbroken snow seemed to advertise solidity beneath, the man broke through. It was not deep. He wet himself halfway to the knees before he floundered out to the firm crust.

He was angry, and cursed his luck aloud. He had hoped to get into camp with the boys at six o'clock, and this would delay him an hour, for he would have to build a fire and dry out his footgear. This was imperative at that low temperature—he knew that much; and he turned aside to the bank, which he climbed. On top, tangled in the underbrush about the trunks of several small spruce trees, was a high-water deposit of dry firewood—sticks and twigs, principally, but also larger portions of seasoned branches and fine, dry, last year's grasses. He threw down several large pieces on top of the snow. This served for a foundation and prevented the young flame from drowning itself in the snow it otherwise would melt. The flame he got by touching a match to a small shred of birch bark that he took from his pocket. This burned even more readily than paper. Placing it on the foundation, he fed the young flame with wisps of dry grass and with the tiniest dry twigs.

He worked slowly and carefully, keenly aware of his danger. Gradually, as the flame grew stronger, he increased the size of the twigs with which he fed it. He squatted in the snow, pulling the twigs out from their entanglement in the brush and feeding directly to the flame. He knew there must be no failure. When it is seventy-five below zero, a man must not fail in his first attempt to build a fire—that is, if his feet are wet. If his feet are dry, and he fails, he can run along the trail for half a mile and restore his circulation. But the circulation of wet and freezing feet cannot be restored by running when it is seventy-five below. No matter how fast he runs, the wet feet will freeze harder.

All this the man knew. The old-timer on Sulphur Creek had told him about it the previous fall, and now he was appreciating the advice. Already all sensation had gone out of his feet. To build the fire he had been forced to remove his mittens, and the fingers had quickly gone numb. His pace of four miles an hour had kept his heart pumping blood to the surface of his body and to all the extremities. But the instant he stopped, the action of the pump eased down. The cold of space smote the unprotected tip of the planet, and he, being on that unprotected tip, received the full force of the blow. The blood of his body recoiled before it. The blood was alive, like the dog, and like the dog it wanted to hide away and cover itself up from the fearful cold. So long as he walked four miles an hour, he pumped that blood, willy-nilly, to the surface; but now it ebbed away and sank down into the recesses of his body. The extremities were the first to feel its absence. His wet feet froze the faster, and his exposed fingers numbed the faster, though they had not yet begun to freeze. Nose and cheeks were already freezing, while the skin of all his body chilled as it lost its blood.

But he was safe. Toes and nose and cheeks would be only touched by the frost, for the fire was beginning to burn with strength. He was feeding it with twigs the size of his finger. In another minute he would be able to feed it with branches the size of his wrist, and then he could remove his wet footgear, and, while it dried, he could keep his naked feet warm by the fire, rubbing them at first, of course, with snow. The fire was a success. He was safe. He remembered the advice of the old-timer on Sulphur Creek, and smiled. The old-timer had been very serious in laying down the law that no man must travel alone in the Klondike after fifty below. Well, here he was; he had had the accident; he was alone; and he had saved himself. Those old-timers were rather womanish, some of them, he thought. All a man had to do was to keep his head, and he was all right. Any man who was a man could travel alone. But it was surprising, the rapidity with which his cheeks and nose were freezing. And he had not thought his fingers could go lifeless in so short a time. Lifeless they were, for he could scarcely make them move together to grip a twig, and they seemed remote from his body and from him. When he touched a twig, he had to look and see whether or not he had hold of it. The wires were pretty well down between him and his finger ends.

All of which counted for little. There was the fire, snapping and crackling

and promising life with every dancing flame. He started to untie his moccasins. They were coated with ice; the thick German socks were like sheaths of
iron halfway to the knees; and the moccasin strings were like rods of steel all
twisted and knotted as by some conflagration. For a moment he tugged with
his numb fingers, then, realizing the folly of it, he drew his sheath knife.

But before he could cut the strings, it happened. It was his own fault or,
rather, his mistake. He should not have built the fire under the spruce tree. He
should have built it in the open. But it had been easier to pull the twigs from
the brush and drop them directly on the fire. Now the tree under which he
had done this carried a weight of snow on its boughs. No wind had blown for
weeks, and each bough was fully freighted. Each time he had pulled a twig he
had communicated a slight agitation to the tree—an imperceptible agitation,
so far as he was concerned, but an agitation sufficient to bring about the disaster. High up in the tree one bough capsized its load of snow. This fell on the
bough beneath, capsizing them. This process continued, spreading out and
involving the whole tree. It grew like an avalanche, and it descended without
warning upon the man and the fire, and the fire was blotted out! Where it had
burned was a mantle of fresh and disordered snow.

The man was shocked. It was as though he had just heard his own sentence of death. For a moment he sat and stared at the spot where the fire had
been. Then he grew very calm. Perhaps the old-timer on Sulphur Creek was
right. If he had only had a trail mate he would have been in no danger now.
The trail mate could have built the fire. Well, it was up to him to build the fire
over again, and this second time there must be no failure. Even if he succeeded, he would most likely lose some toes. His feet must be badly frozen by
now, and there would be some time before the second fire was ready.

Such were his thoughts, but he did not sit and think them. He was busy all
the time they were passing through his mind. He made a new foundation for
a fire, this time in the open, where no treacherous tree could blot it out. Next
he gathered dry grasses and tiny twigs from the high-water flotsam. He could
not bring his fingers together to pull them out, but he was able to gather them
by the handful. In this way he got many rotten twigs and bits of green moss
that were undesirable, but it was the best he could do. He worked methodically, even collecting an armful of the larger branches to be used later when
the fire gathered strength. And all the while the dog sat and watched him, a
certain yearning wistfulness in its eyes, for it looked upon him as the fire
provider, and the fire was slow in coming.

When all was ready, the man reached in his pocket for a second piece of birch bark. He knew the bark was there, and, though he could not feel it with his fingers, he could hear its crisp rustling as he fumbled for it. Try as he would, he could not clutch hold of it. And all the time, in his consciousness, was the knowledge that each instant his feet were freezing. This thought tended to put him in a panic, but he fought against it and kept calm. He pulled on his mittens with his teeth, and threshed his arms back and forth, beating his hands with all his might against his sides. He did this sitting down, and he stood up to do it; and all the while the dog sat in the snow, its wolf brush of a tail curled around warmly over its forefeet, its sharp wolf ears pricked forward intently as it watched the man. And the man, as he beat and threshed with his arms and hands, felt a great surge of envy as he regarded the creature that was warm and secure in its natural covering.

After a time he was aware of the first faraway signals of sensation in his beaten fingers. The faint tingling grew stronger till it evolved into a stinging ache that was excruciating, but which the man hailed with satisfaction. He stripped the mitten from his right hand and fetched forth the birch bark. The exposed fingers were quickly going numb again. Next he brought out his bunch of sulphur matches. But the tremendous cold had already driven the life out of his fingers. In his effort to separate one match from the others, the whole bunch fell in the snow. He tried to pick it out of the snow, but failed. The dead fingers could neither touch nor clutch. He was very careful. He drove the thought of his freezing feet, and nose, and cheeks, out of his mind, devoting his whole soul to the matches. He watched, using the sense of vision in place of that of touch, and when he saw his fingers on each side the bunch, he closed them—that is, he willed to close them, for the wires were down, and the fingers did not obey. He pulled the mitten on the right hand, and beat it fiercely against his knee. Then, with both mittened hands, he scooped the bunch of matches, along with much snow, into his lap. Yet he was no better off.

After some manipulation he managed to get the bunch between the heels of his mittened hands. In this fashion he carried it to his mouth. The ice crackled and snapped when by a violent effort he opened his mouth. He drew the lower jaw in, curled the upper lip out of the way, and scraped the bunch with his upper teeth in order to separate a match. He succeeded in getting one, which he dropped on his lap. He was no better off. He could not pick it up. Then he devised a way. He picked it up in his teeth and scratched it on his leg. Twenty times he scratched before he succeeded in lighting it. As it flamed he held it with his teeth to the birch bark. But the burning brimstone went up his nostrils and into his lungs, causing him to cough spasmodically. The match fell into the snow and went out.

The old-timer on Sulphur Creek was right, he thought in the moment of controlled despair that ensued: after fifty below, a man should travel with a partner. He beat his hands, but failed in exciting any sensation. Suddenly he bared both hands, removing the mittens with his teeth. He caught the whole bunch between the heels of his hands. His arm muscles not being frozen enabled him to press the hand heels tightly against the matches. Then he scratched the bunch along his leg. It flared into flame, seventy sulphur matches at once! There was no wind to blow them out. He kept his head to one side to escape the strangling fumes, and held the blazing bunch to the birch bark. As he so held it, he became aware of sensation in his hand. His flesh was burning. He could smell it. Deep down below the surface he could feel it. The sensation developed into pain that grew acute. And still he endured it, holding the flame of the matches clumsily to the bark that would not light readily because his own burning hands were in the way, absorbing most of the flame.

At last, when he could endure no more, he jerked his hands apart. The blazing matches fell sizzling into the snow, but the birch bark was alight. He began laying dry grasses and the tiniest twigs on the flame. He could not pick and choose, for he had to lift the fuel between the heels of his hands. Small pieces of rotten wood and green moss clung to the twigs, and he bit them off as well as he could with his teeth. He cherished the flame carefully and awkwardly. It meant life, and it must not perish. The withdrawal of blood from the surface his body now made him begin to shiver, and he grew more awkward. A large piece of green moss fell squarely on the little fire. He tried to poke it out with his fingers, but his shivering frame made him poke too far, and he disrupted the nucleus of the little fire, the burning grasses and tiny twigs separating and scattering. He tried to poke them together again, but in spite of the tenseness of the effort, his shivering got away with him, and the twigs were hopelessly scattered. Each twig gushed a puff of smoke and went out. The fire provider had failed. As he looked apathetically about him, his eyes chanced on the dog, sitting across the ruins of the fire from him, in the snow, making restless, hunching movements, slightly lifting one forefoot and then the other, shifting its weight back and forth on them with wistful eagerness.

The sight of the dog put a wild idea into his head. He remembered the tale of the man, caught in a blizzard, who killed a steer and crawled inside the carcass, and so was saved. He would kill the dog and bury his hands in the warm body until the numbness went out of them. Then he could build another fire. He spoke to the dog, calling it to him; but in his voice was a strange note of fear that frightened the animal, who had never known the man to speak in such way before. Something was the matter, and its suspicious nature sensed danger—it knew not what danger, but somewhere, somehow, in its brain arose an apprehension of the man. It flattened its ears down at the sound of the man's voice, and its restless, hunching movements and the liftings and shiftings of its forefeet became more pronounced; but it would not come to the man. He got on his hands and knees and crawled toward the dog. This unusual posture again excited suspicion, and the animal sidled mincingly away.

The man sat up in the snow for a moment and struggled for calmness. Then he pulled on his mittens, by means of his teeth, and got upon his feet. He glanced down at first in order to assure himself that he was really standing up, for the absence of sensation in his feet left him unrelated to the earth. His erect position in itself started to drive the webs of suspicion from the dog's mind; and when he spoke peremptorily, with the sound of whip lashes in his voice, the dog rendered its customary allegiance and came to him. As it came within reaching distance, the man lost his control. His arms flashed out to the dog, and he experienced genuine surprise when he discovered that his hands could not clutch, that there was neither bend nor feeling in the fingers. He had forgotten for the moment that they were frozen and that they were freezing more and more. All this happened quickly, and before the animal could get away, he encircled its body with his arms. He sat down in the snow, and in this fashion held the dog, while it snarled and whined and struggled.

But it was all he could do, hold its body encircled in his arms and sit there. He realized that he could not kill the dog. There was no way to do it. With his helpless hands he could neither draw nor hold his sheath knife nor throttle the animal. He released it, and it plunged wildly away, with tail between its legs, and still snarling. It halted forty feet away and surveyed him curiously, with ears sharply pricked forward.

The man looked down at his hands in order to locate them, and found them hanging on the ends of his arms. It struck him as curious that one should have to use his eyes in order to find out where his hands were. He began threshing his arms back and forth, beating the mittened hands against his sides. He did this for five minutes, violently, and his heart pumped enough blood up to the surface to put a stop to his shivering. But no sensation was aroused in the hands. He had an impression that they hung like weights on the ends of his arms, but when he tried to run the impression down, he could not find it.

A certain fear of death, dull and oppressive, came to him. This fear quickly became poignant as he realized that it was no longer a mere matter of freezing his fingers and toes, or of losing his hands and feet, but that it was a matter of life and death with the chances against him. This threw him into a panic, and he turned and ran up the creek bed along the old, dim trail. The dog joined in behind and kept up with him. He ran blindly, without intention, in fear such as he had never known in his life. Slowly, as he plowed and floundered through the snow, he began to see things again—the banks of the creek, the old timber jams, the leafless aspens, and the sky. The running made him feel better. He did not shiver. Maybe, if he ran on, his feet would thaw out; and, anyway, if he ran far enough, he would reach camp and the boys. Without doubt he would lose some fingers and toes and some of his face; but the boys would take care of him, and save the rest of him when he got there. And at the same time there was another thought in his mind that said he would never get to the camp and the boys; that it was too many miles away, that the freezing had too great a start on him, and that he would soon be stiff and dead. This thought he kept in the background and refused to consider. Sometimes it pushed itself forward and demanded to be heard, but he thrust it back and strove to think of other things.

It struck him as curious that he could run at all on feet so frozen that he could not feel them when they struck the earth and took the weight of his body. He seemed to himself to skim along above the surface, and to have no connection with the earth. Somewhere he had once seen a winged Mercury, and he wondered if Mercury felt as he felt when skimming over the earth.

His theory of running until he reached camp and the boys had one flaw in it: he lacked the endurance. Several times he stumbled, and finally he tottered, crumpled up, and fell. When he tried to rise, he failed. He must sit and rest, he decided, and next time he would merely walk and keep on going. As he sat and regained his breath, he noted that he was feeling quite warm and comfortable. He was not shivering, and it even seemed that a warm glow had come to his chest and trunk. And yet, when he touched his nose or cheeks, there was no sensation. Running would not thaw them out. Nor would it thaw out his hands and feet. Then the thought came to him that the frozen portions of his body must be extending. He tried to keep this thought down, to forget it, to think of something else; he was aware of the panicky feeling that it caused, and he was afraid of the panic. But the thought asserted itself, and persisted, until it produced a vision of his body totally frozen. This was too much, and he made another wild run along the trail. Once he slowed down to a walk, but the thought of the freezing extending itself made him run again.

And all the time the dog ran with him, at his heels. When he fell down a second time, it curled its tail over its forefeet and sat in front of him, facing him, curiously eager and intent. The warmth and security of the animal angered him, and he cursed it till it flattened down its ears appeasingly. This time the shivering came more quickly upon the man. He was losing in his battle with the frost. It was creeping into his body from all sides. The thought of it drove him on, but he ran no more than a hundred feet, when he staggered and pitched headlong. It was his last panic. When he had recovered his breath and control, he sat up and entertained in his mind the conception of meeting death with dignity. However, the conception did not come to him in such terms. His idea of it was that he had been making a fool of himself, running around like a chicken with its head cut off—such was the simile that occurred to him. Well, he was bound to freeze anyway, and he might as well take it decently. With this new-found peace of mind came the first glimmerings of drowsiness. A good idea, he thought, to sleep off to death. It was like taking an anesthetic. Freezing was not so bad as people thought. There were lots worse ways to die.

He pictured the boys finding his body next day. Suddenly he found himself with them, coming along the trail and looking for himself. And, still with them, he came around a turn in the trail and found himself lying in the snow. He did not belong with himself any more, for even then he was out of himself, standing with the boys and looking at himself in the snow. It certainly was cold, was his thought. When he got back to the States he could tell the folks what real cold was. He drifted on from this to a vision of the old-timer on Sulphur Creek. He could see him quite clearly, warm and comfortable, and smoking a pipe.

"You were right, old hoss; you were right," the man mumbled to the old-timer of Sulphur Creek.

Then the man drowsed off into what seemed to him the most comfortable and satisfying sleep he had ever known. The dog sat facing him and waiting. The brief day drew to a close in a long, slow twilight. There were no signs of a fire to be made, and, besides, never in the dog's experience had it known a man to sit like that in the snow and make no fire. As the twilight drew on, its eager yearning for the fire mastered it, and with a great lifting and shifting of forefeet, it whined softly, then flattened its ears down in anticipation of being chidden by the man. But the man remained silent. Later the dog whined loudly. And still later it crept close to the man and caught the scent of death. This made the animal bristle and back away. A little longer it delayed, howling under the stars that leaped and danced and shone brightly in the cold sky. Then it turned and trotted up the trail in the direction of the camp it knew, where were the other food providers and fire providers.

NATURAL WONDERS

ALASKA IS HUGE, untamed, and so beautiful that it resonates in the soul. No matter what measure is used—the most public land set aside as nature reserves, the tallest mountain, the longest coastline, the biggest population of wildlife, the most species of birds—the statistics only serve to emphasize what a visitor senses from the moment he sets foot in the state. The place is stunning. Within Alaska's borders are the largest populations in the world of bald eagles, vast bear and wolf and moose populations and millions of seabirds of every description. What follows is a small peek into the world of Alaska's natural wonders, written by two of the world's most famous naturalists.

Excerpt from *Monarch of Deadman Bay:*
The Life and Death of a Kodiak Bear

ROGER A. CARAS

Selecting the highest ground she could find, the sow forced her way through some bushy debris that blocked the entrance to a rock tunnel running a dozen feet into the hill. The natural cave had the preferred southern exposure and she set about lining the floor at the far end. She managed to accumulate a fair pile of alder branches and mosses and, sweeping with her amazingly dexterous paws, spread them about until the floor was covered to a depth of a foot. This was a refinement some bears do not bother with. As if to sample her work she entered the den several times during the first few days and slept for two or three hours at a stretch. After these short naps she would emerge and feed on whatever was at hand.

The cave site was on a prominence 2,851 feet above sea level behind Alpine Cove at the northeast end of Deadman Bay, which is itself an extension of Alitak Bay. There was little to be had on the higher portions of the slope and the sow worked her way down to feed. She stopped from time to time to nose along grass tunnels in open areas and gulp down the diminutive tundra voles she found.

In a general mopping-up operation she ate whatever she could find— dead grass, high-bush cranberries, a few old salmon carcasses found beside a stream, a few blueberries that had survived the late summer. She found the lost or abandoned jacket of a hunter and worried it for several minutes. She finished by eating bits and pieces of it. The fact that it reeked of man-smell yet was inanimate seemed to please her. Her almost puppy-like postures as she tossed it about and pounced on it were ludicrous because of her great size. It is such unexpected behavior as this that has earned bears an altogether unsuitable reputation as natural clowns.

Twenty-six years earlier, in 1924, a small herd of Sitka black-tailed deer had been transported to the Island by men seeking to establish new sport, and although most of the descendants of these imports now lived to the northeast, a few had wandered toward the west. One of these, a prime buck, had been shot at earlier in the year by an amateur hunter and had stumbled off into a thicket to die in agony. The sow came upon the rotting carcass and found it just to her liking. Had she made the kill herself she would have eaten very little before burying it and waiting for it to putrefy. Her crushing-type premolars and molars were better able to handle flesh that had been dead for some time, and the higher the flesh the better she liked it.

The good fortune the sow had realized in finding first a bull fur seal, then a gray whale, and lastly the buck, in addition to her normal quota of salmon and small game, had given her more animal food in one year than she had consumed in the previous three combined.

The last food she consumed before finally retiring consisted of a few frozen berries and then, one very rainy, cold afternoon, she disappeared into her den for nearly half a year of sleep.

It took her some time to settle down and she lay awake for many hours, listening. She was unlikely to be disturbed but still she listened, her nerves strangely taut. Quite aside from the fact that she had laid claim to the cave, this was a nursery. Without any real understanding of the situation, she sensed that she must defend this place. The chemical changes within her body were releasing behavioral patterns, and she would be held prisoner by them for months to come. She could not reason them out, but she could and did respond to them.

In terms of human knowledge and understanding, the whole matter of territorialism among bears is a perfect muddle. Bears, whose behavior is contradictory at best, have kept this secret well. They *appear* to be more concerned with the specifics of life than with abstracts like territory. If there are cubs, a sow is likely to defend them; if a male has a mate, he is likely to drive off other males. Similarly, if there is a food cache or a preferred fishing spot along a stream, the largest and strongest animal is likely to prevail in any dispute. But whether or not a bear actually establishes a territory is open to question and, on some evidence at least, even doubtful. The so-called "bear tree," a well-clawed tree often described as a territory boundary marker, may have other meanings entirely. We do not know.

This cave behind Deadman Bay, however, was a specific, and the sow would not allow another bear to share it with her. Her temper, short at all times, would be even worse when her winter sleep was upon her. Perhaps unwittingly, she had left enough of her signs around to warn off any intruder. Only a fool would ignore them.

As the sow slipped slowly off to sleep, forces in nature were transforming the Island. The steadily declining temperature was causing minute changes that would continue to accumulate until the land, its lakes, and its streams were no longer recognizable. These changes, although microscopic at first, carried the insistence of universal laws. Their chemistry and their physics were basic to the nature of matter itself and as open to influence as the orbits of planets and the forward surge of time. The fresh water that had flowed so freely throughout the spring, summer and early fall was changing form. As a liquid it consisted mostly of dihydrol molecules. As it slipped downward, away from the boiling point it had never approached even on the hottest day, the percentage of *tri*hydrol molecules increased. On the third day of the sow's sleep the temperature reached 32 degrees Fahrenheit and heat flow out of the water was sufficient to allow a trihydrol saturation to occur. Ice appeared, first as a colloid, without crystalline form. Small disklike particles formed and then began to congeal. Soon it was visible to the naked eye. In the quieter waters on the Island it was feathery and light. In the more agitated streams, broken spicules marked the transformation. On the fourth day, only the fastest flowing streams remained uncoated and even in these the ground gru or bottom-forming ice appeared. The new ice on the quieter ponds, the lolly ice, was without the buoyancy it would have later. It was still highly plastic but hardened hour by hour. The fog rolling in from the relatively milder sea began to freeze and soon every blade of dead grass, every branch on every tree was covered with rime. Rain fell and turned to sleet. And still the temperature fell. The sky was ashen and the sun was a pale yellow disk in the sky.

The weasels and the foxes, the wintering birds, and all of the other life on the Island that had been ordered by nature to face the winter awake and exposed to its dangers, huddled in whatever cover was available. Their winter coats had grown over the preceding weeks but it would take days for them to acclimate to the sudden change. In time, atmospheric water vapor precipitated out and fell as billions of hexagonal crystals. Although each was a masterpiece of sculpture, a thing of unparalleled beauty, no one appreciated the fact. All eyes, human and animal alike, were focused on grosser facts. The land was white again and winter had retaken Kodiak Island.

Cold air flowed steadily across the warmer waters in the harbors and bays that indented the coast. Weird frost smoke drifted across peninsulas and changed the once green and vital shores to mysterious etchings. Rocks and trees drifted in and out of the freezing fog like ghost ships. The difference between night and day seemed less well defined. Winds blew down from the north and compacted the snow. By the end of the first week the smaller animals could walk across the wind-crust without breaking through. As the bretts formed under the incessant hammering, ever larger animals would be able to do the same. This packed snow meant, though, that foraging became more difficult. In these first weeks of winter a selection would be made. Many wintering animals that were old, past their prime, would die. The young born that spring and summer that were not fit to live and breed the following year would also be lost. The toll mounted and the carrion eaters rejoiced in the new bounty. But their good fortune was of brief duration, and many of them were soon in trouble as well. Having created blindly, having created too much, nature had come full circle to the time of culling.

Inside of her cave the sow was oblivious to the transformations taking place in the land, killing animals by the hundreds. Her great body, luxurious in its winter coat and insulated with fat, moved rhythmically in her sleep. She was not hibernating, for she did not have that strange power. The ground squirrels *were* hibernating, their respiration, temperature, and heart rate reduced almost to the point of death. But the sow slept, her vital processes nearly normal. If disturbed, she could awake and, although it would take her some minutes to collect herself, she would be quick enough to meet any threat, real or imagined. The rodents, sleeping in deeper places, could not do this. The two phenomena—hibernation and winter sleep—are quite different.

On two occasions during the long winter months the sow would wake and shuffle out of her den in an almost drunken stupor. Finding nothing to eat and not quite understanding what she was doing out in the cold in the first place, she would return to her den. Her tracks, for no snow crust could bear her weight; would soon be filled in by fresh snowfalls and wind-driven diamond dust, incredibly fine flakes no more than five one-thousandths of an inch wide. Inside her den her huge body, acting like a radiator, would soon raise the temperature again to a comfortable level and her snoring would attest to her comfort and security. There are decided advantages to being the largest animal in the land.

Outside, the wind and the cold continued and the transformation of the world progressed. Snow that had fallen as cottony flakes, huge aggregates of tiny crystals, began to firnicate and lose its form. Snow, like everything else, must age and firn snow, or névé, replaced the fresher falls. The winter fix was complete. Only the hardiest, and those able to sleep, could survive. The cold itself was more than a measurement on a thermometer. It was a vital force that maimed and killed.

Once she had fallen asleep the sow's body accelerated the business of creation. Embryonic growth was rapid, for a new timetable had to be met. Within her, two cubs grew. Protected from the harsh reality of the winter world, and even from the relative warmth and calm of the cave, their tiny bodies were nourished by the store the sow had instinctively provided. By early December their bodies were each about one fifteen-thousandth the weight of their mother. If they were to survive their birth they would have to increase that weight tenfold in eight or nine weeks. This, their first challenge, was an unconscious one. Deeply implanted in the magic chemicals, they grew, were nurtured, guarded, truly created in a repetition of the most ancient and marvelous miracle of all.

On the last day of January, the sow gave birth. Her two cubs each weighed eleven ounces. Blind, toothless, hairless, the cubs could not survive without the protection of their mother's body. She curled around them, approximating a pouch with the rolls of fat that girded her, and slept again as they began to suckle. For at least nine months and perhaps much longer, she would feed them from her own body. The fact that the cubs had been born was a significant change in status, to be sure. It required of her different chemical processes. In the longer view, however, the change was almost academic. She was no more or less the provider now than before. Her life was their life and her death would be followed in hours by theirs.

At the end of forty days the cubs' eyes were open and they had cut their first teeth. Although more active each day, and more demanding, they seldom moved more than inches away from the great fount of warmth and nourishment. Their bodies were furred now and there was a measure of coordination in their movements. But had the mother moved away from them for even a few minutes they would have panicked and whined piteously.

No one can know how many hours the sow slept and how many she lay awake, caressing, cleaning and generally attending to her cubs. She was almost unbelievably gentle with them and tolerant of their increasingly bad manners. Her own vent was stopped with a resinous plug and the den remained surprisingly clean. The bear stench was unmistakable, though, and her own particular smell was so firmly implanted in the senses of the cubs that they would not forget it until chased away by her more than a year later. For the two cubs, the male and the female, the world was dark, soft and rich in smell. The only thing that changed was themselves. Everything else was a reassuring constant.

Winter passed, finally, and a satisfying richness returned to the land. The animals that had survived began to move with a new freedom and there were fresh crops to harvest everywhere. The table was reset and the feast began again.

April came, unlocking a land long gripped in severe winter conditions. Yet the sow did not emerge. Her cubs were by now truly playful and she slowly began to exert the first slight pressure of her authority. By the time she brought her cubs out into the open, in mid-May, they would weigh fifteen pounds and be far too active for her to allow them a free hand. Immediate response to her demands was a prerequisite to their survival. The dangers for the young, even the young of giants, are very real. The grumpy males would be about and the flesh of a newly emerged cub is sweet. If the cub is poorly trained, it can be easy prey. This the sow knew instinctively, as she knew everything, and against this she protected her young with the evenly applied rudiments of education. By mid-May they would know the meaning of a grunt or woof and would know well the sting of a ponderous paw on the rump.

And so nature's will was done. A new generation had been born, soon to emerge into a world freshly culled and newly seeded. The sow had made a down payment on her debt, a debt that could be discharged only when her own body was no longer productive. For the moment, however, she had a task to perform. The lives she had created within her body and had nurtured in the den needed to be readied until they could be set free to incur, in their turn, the same indebtedness. Nature works only in cycles. There are no straight lines. The forward movement is provided by time. Everything within it must revolve.

The world of change into which the cubs emerged was already far advanced. Cubs of previous seasons, the yearlings, sows that had not bred the summer before, and the unpredictable males were about. The influx of bird life and the offshore flow of marine mammals heading for the newly liberated Arctic Ocean pastures were in progress. Rain was a daily and sometimes hourly occurrence and the ground underfoot was mushy. Spring was unmistakable on all sides and summer was on the way. Her advance scouts were everywhere.

Shortly after leaving the cave, ahead of her cubs and extremely alert to the possible appearance of a mature bear, the sow began to eat cathartic grasses and herbs and quickly voided the black, resinous plug that had blocked her intestinal passage. Her feet were tender from the long period of inactivity and she limped slightly. During the first days she stayed close to her den, eating what she could find on the higher slope. Not at all unlike a cow, she would take a mouthful of grass and crop it by a slightly abrupt lift of her head. She was still fat but would lose weight rapidly during the first two weeks. Following that she would again begin to lay on fat against the needs of her coming sleep.

This concentration on food is typical of bears. The demands increase as spring progresses into summer and the sow, never a fastidious eater, took whatever she could find. While she might consume surprisingly little for so large an animal at any one feeding, her meals were so frequent as to be almost continuous. The total volume of food consumed was larger than might be suspected by the casual observer.

Seeking the tender pooshka, or wild parsnip, the sow would grasp a mouthful of vegetation and plant her front paws firmly on the ground. With a convulsive movement she would thrust backward with her body until a clump of sod tore loose. Turning it over with her paw she freed the roots, up to a half inch or more in diameter, and slowly ate them. In her quest for these tender morsels, and for grubs and beetles as well, she turned over whole areas of the hillside until it looked as if it had been plowed by a drunken farmer. Food-getting for a bear is more a matter of drudgery than of reliance on keen senses. Having given the bear a varied appetite, having delivered it from the agony other predators know when game is short, nature has either taken back or denied altogether the razor-edge alertness that wolves, weasels, and cats must have to survive.

At regular intervals the sow returned to her cubs, for their feeding demands were no less insistent than hers. Unlike their mother, however, they could accomplish nothing on their own.

Often, as she worked the fields close to the mouth of the cave, she would leave her cubs at its entrance, but she was never out of range and she constantly tested the wind for signs of danger. When she came to them they whined eagerly and climbed over each other to get at her. She would sometimes lie on her side and watch them feed, making the softest of satisfied sounds. At other times she would lie on her back and move her hind legs rhythmically as they tugged and gorged. And at yet other times she would sit square on her bottom with her back against a tree or mound and place a paw on the back of each cub. With her hind legs thrust out in front like a comical old woman she would point her nose straight up and slowly rotate her head as if to exercise a stiff neck. The cubs thrust hard with their hind feet and shuddered with satisfaction at what she gave them. Always she was tender, always alert. Her life was divided between feeding herself, and through herself her cubs, and worrying about their safety. There seemed to be no other forces, no other concerns.

The cubs grew daily. Their emergence weight of fifteen pounds would have to increase to a hundred pounds or more by mid-autumn. By the late fall of their second year they would weigh as much as four hundred pounds. A difference in weight between them would not occur until about their fourth year. For the moment, there was little to distinguish between the two. They were liver-gray in color but it was impossible to predict the tones they would finally achieve. The genes they inherited from their parents had been too confused over the preceding generations by the influx of brown bear color variation to take a predictable form. Since no survival factor had existed in any one tone before man arrived there was no particular trend. Before nature can make that miraculous adjustment man will almost certainly see to it that the bear is extinct.

As the cubs' size and strength grew and as their coordination improved the sow increased the length and duration of her excursions. Calling to them and constantly bolstering their confidence with the sounds she made, she took them further and further away from the cave. At last she began keeping them away for days and nights at a time, always bedding down before dark in the deepest cover she could find. Their demands on her never faltered and their treks were often interrupted for a feeding session. The further they moved away from their den site the more alert she became. She seldom relaxed for more than a few minutes at a time.

One afternoon as the family was edging down through a clearing between two rings of stunted alders that girded a hill, the sow stopped short and rose to her hind legs. The movement was smooth and effortless. Straining against the inadequacy of her vision she moved her head from side to side. The cubs came tumbling up against her legs and began to frolic. She issued three rapid, harsh commands and in a comic imitation of their mother they attempted to rise up to see what had caught her attention. The longer she held the position the more nervous the cubs became. They sank to all fours and moved in close against her legs. The female cub began to whine and again the sow grunted peremptorily. She was listening to the winds, and sampling their chemistry. She sensed another bear in the vicinity—and it was close by.

On the lower portion of the slope, another sow stood among the alders and stared myopically up to where the bronze female towered. Victim of a natural freak, this bear had *four* cubs huddled by her legs. This extremely rare occurrence does happen from time to time and the sows involved are generally all but overwhelmed by the ordeal. With so much more to do, with so much more to worry about, their whole attitude is one of profound bewilderment.

A small current of moving air that had begun at sea and picked its way across seaweed-covered rocks, through patches of brush and trees, was working up the slope. The energy behind it was reinforced by other currents from over the surface of the water and it flowed and rippled across the clearing. It passed the sow in the alders, snatched away her secret and eddied past the female on the slope peering down, alert but uninformed. Instantly, the bronze sow located the intruder in the valley. Her sudden head movement and grunt caused the stranger to move, and to shift her position ever so slightly. The bronze sow was able to detect the movement and determine her shadowy outline. She gave a sharp bark and lumbered two steps forward on her hind legs before dropping to all fours, facing downhill. Her cubs were already on their way up to the ridge. They bawled in terror as they ran.

With front legs stiff, each step jarring her great frame, the sow hurried down the slope.

In the alder growth the other female, too, had gone to all fours and, determining that her cubs were well concealed, started out into the open.

The two sows faced each other over a distance of a couple of dozen yards and circled slowly until they were on the same level. In a kind of displacement activity, as if to relieve the unbearable tension that had been mounting, the intruder stopped and pulled free a mouthful of grass. Jerking her head up she quartered away and stood with her head turned to the side, looking in the direction of her opponent with the grass drooping comically from the corner of her mouth. In an imitative movement the bronze sow did the same.

Then, without warning, after having given it all the thought of which she was capable, the bronze sow charged. She hurtled across the intervening yards and caught the intruder in the shoulder as she turned and half rose to bring her great forepaws into play. They slapped ineffectually as she was rolled over twice by the weight of the impact. Her reflexes had been a beat too slow and the blood flowed from an open wound where the sow had sunk her teeth.

The momentum of her charge carried the bronze sow well beyond her target and when she pulled up and whirled about to charge again she was struck by the intruder barreling down on top of her. She felt a terrible, stunning shock as a paw as large as a platter with powerful claws spread wide and angry descended with the full force of half a ton behind it. One of the bronze sow's cheeks was opened and her teeth showed through the wound. Again she charged, snapping furiously, but the intruder had already begun to retreat. She caught up with the darker female and managed to sink her teeth into her rump before she vanished into the brush. The crashing of her great body sounded as if a truck were hurtling through the growth.

The sow patrolled the edge of trees, coughing and grunting. She didn't dare enter the thicket with an opponent so aroused and with the benefit of cover. The air currents between the trees could not be trusted and her eyesight would be all but useless.

The bronze sow's two cubs and the intruder's four had witnessed the battle huddled in two groups a hundred yards apart. They would have played together had they been allowed, for they were still endowed with a social sense that enabled them to tolerate their litter mates. They would lose it in time, though, and were learning the lesson of distrust that would stay with them as long as they lived.

Both females bedded down almost immediately after returning to their cubs. They were no more than a hundred and fifty yards apart in the two groups of alders that bounded the small clearing. Throughout the night they both remained awake, sniffing, listening for the sound of any movement. On several occasions each moved to the edge of the trees and stood facing each other, although neither could know for sure the other was there.

On the following morning the sows again spotted each other. They did not clash, although some short charges were made by each as gestures of threat. They drifted apart after a few minutes and did not see each other again for several hours, when once again they came within sensing distance of each other. Several defiant movements were made, but again there was no direct conflict.

On the morning of the third day, shortly after feeding her cubs their first meal of the morning, the bronze sow moved down to the edge of the trees. There, not more than a dozen feet away, the intruder grazed with her four cubs strung out behind her. The wind was blowing again from the sea and the scent and sound of the intruder carried clearly and unmistakably. The sow sank back on her haunches and sorted out the messages. With a wild roar, almost a scream, she burst from her cover. The four cubs scattered but one was too slow. Snatching it up in her great jaws she ended its life with a single snapping action, dropped its small body and spun again to re-enter the woods where her own cubs were wailing.

Whether or not it was immediately clear to the intruder that she had lost her smallest cub we cannot know. Her remaining three were running and tumbling down the slope in abject terror. The charge of the great bronze sow out of the brush so close at hand came with stunning impact. Only their training enabled them to break away from the paralyzing effect of the attack and get away at all.

The intruder spun around, perhaps seeing the body of her cub lying limp and oozing blood, and crashed into the brush after her opponent. Roaring, wailing, grunting, and chopping her jaws, she smashed down brush and with a gesture of wild defiance clubbed a sapling an inch and a half thick to the ground with one sweep of her forepaw. Rising to her full height, her jaws still chopping in anger, the great sow circled slowly, worrying everything in her way. In her passage she destroyed the nests of three ground-nesting birds. The yellow yokes from a dozen shattered shells seeped out and the parent birds circled overhead, bemoaning their loss. Diminutive mammals of several species fled before the onslaught and a mouse nest toppled, spilling its pink inhabitants to the ground. When the sow had passed a weasel emerged and took the little bodies before the female mouse could find them.

The furious charge of the intruder into the brush was to no avail. While she beat her way through the bushes and between the trees the bronze sow and her cubs had vanished over the ridge above and were close to a mile away when the intruder emerged grunting and coughing on the downslope side to sit wailing beside her dead cub. She left the valley that day and never returned.

As if her cruelly violent deed had reminded her of the danger that surrounded her own two cubs, the sow was unusually alert in the days that followed. She was even short-tempered with her charges and their obedience had to be ever more unquestioning to satisfy her. She cuffed them often and bit one on the flank hard enough to make it whimper for several minutes. Thoroughly cowed, it returned to her to be fed and found her forgiving.

The intruder that had come to the valley to lose her cub remained confused and miserable for days. She never quite realized that he was gone and grunted angrily several times when her commands brought only three cubs to her side. She would look for him and stand bawling when he did not appear.

The savage cruelty of this encounter cannot be overstated. There was food enough in the area for both families and the females need not have fought. The killing of the cub was senseless and indeed an unthinking man would despise a species whose behavior is seemingly so cruel. Such a man must only reflect on his own behavior, though, and think of cities bombed and the young of his own kind dead in their smashed beds and broken gardens to understand and forgive that which is savage in nature. Although it is bewildering in any species, man and animal alike, at least among bears it can be accounted for. Bears are not equipped to feel pity and cannot reflect on agony they cause another. Bears know only how to survive. They instinctively destroy what seems threatening to them and are extremely intolerant of any annoyance, however slight. They have no capacity for guilt. Man, who has that capacity, seems unable to act upon it. The most imaginative of living creatures, he is also the most cruel, and he is in no position to judge another species harshly.

✍ NATURALIST ROGER CARAS was the author of more than sixty books on animals, as well the president of the American ASPCA and a special correspondent for ABC on issues involving animals.

Excerpts from *Travels in Alaska*

JOHN MUIR

ALEXANDER ARCHIPELAGO AND THE HOME I FOUND IN ALASKA

To the lover of pure wildness Alaska is one of the most wonderful countries in the world. No excursion that I know of may be made into any other American wilderness where so marvelous an abundance of noble, newborn scenery is so charmingly brought to view as on the trip through the Alexander Archipelago to Fort Wrangell and Sitka. Gazing from the deck of the steamer, one is borne smoothly over calm blue waters, through the midst of countless forest-clad islands. The ordinary discomforts of a sea voyage are not felt, for nearly all the whole long way is on inland waters that are about as waveless as rivers and lakes. So numerous are the islands that they seem to have been sown broadcast; long tapering vistas between the largest of them open in every direction.

Day after day in the fine weather we enjoyed, we seemed to float in true fairyland, each succeeding view seeming more and more beautiful, the one we chanced to have before us the most surprisingly beautiful of all. Never before this had I been embosomed in scenery so hopelessly beyond description. To sketch picturesque bits, definitely bounded, is comparatively easy—a lake in the woods, a glacier meadow, or a cascade in its dell; or even a grand master view of mountains beheld from some commanding outlook after climbing from height to height above the forests. These may be attempted, and more or less telling pictures made of them; but in these coast landscapes there is such indefinite, on-leading expansiveness, such a multitude of features without apparent redundance, their lines graduating delicately into one another in endless succession, while the whole is so fine, so tender, so ethereal, that all penwork seems hopelessly unavailing. Tracing shining ways through fiord and sound, past forests and waterfalls, islands and mountains and far azure headlands, it seems as if surely we must at length reach the very paradise of the poets, the abode of the blessed.

Some idea of the wealth of this scenery may be gained from the fact that the coast-line of Alaska is about twenty-six thousand miles long, more than twice as long as all the rest of the United States. The islands of the Alexander Archipelago, with the straits, channels, canals, sounds, passages, and fiords, form an intricate web of land and water embroidery sixty or seventy miles wide, fringing the lofty icy chain of coast mountains from Puget Sound to Cook Inlet; and, with infinite variety, the general pattern is harmonious throughout its whole extent of nearly a thousand miles. Here you glide into a narrow channel hemmed in by mountain walls, forested down to the water's edge, where there is no distant view, and your attention is concentrated on the objects close about you—the crowded spires of the spruces and hemlocks rising higher and higher on the steep green slopes; stripes of paler green where winter avalanches have cleared away the trees, allowing grasses and willows to spring up; zigzags of cascades appearing and disappearing among the bushes and trees; short, steep glens with brawling streams hidden beneath alder and dogwood, seen only where they emerge on the brown algæ of the shore; and retreating hollows, with lingering snow-banks marking the fountains of ancient glaciers. The steamer is often so near the shore that you may distinctly see the cones clustered on the tops of the trees, and the ferns and bushes at their feet.

But new scenes are brought to view with magical rapidity. Rounding some bossy cape, the eye is called away into far-reaching vistas, bounded on either hand by headlands in charming array, one dipping gracefully beyond another and growing fainter and more ethereal in the distance. The tranquil channel stretching river-like between, may be stirred here and there by the silvery plashing of upspringing salmon, or by flocks of white gulls floating like waterlilies among the sun spangles; while mellow, tempered sunshine is streaming over all, blending sky, land, and water in pale, misty blue. Then,

while you are dreamily gazing into the depths of this leafy ocean lane, the little steamer, seeming hardly larger than a duck, turning into some passage not
visible until the moment of entering it, glides into a wide expanse—a sound
filled with islands, sprinkled and clustered in forms and compositions such as
nature alone can invent; some of them so small the trees growing on them
seem like single handfuls culled from the neighboring woods and set in the
water to keep them fresh, while here and there at wide intervals you may
notice bare rocks just above the water, mere dots punctuating grand,
outswelling sentences of islands.

The variety we find, both as to the contours and the collocation of the
islands, is due chiefly to differences in the structure and composition of their
rocks, and the unequal glacial denudation different portions of the coast were
subjected to. This influence must have been especially heavy toward the end
of the glacial period, when the main ice-sheet began to break up into separate
glaciers. Moreover, the mountains of the larger islands nourished local glaciers, some of them of considerable size, which sculptured their summits and
sides, forming in some cases wide cirques with cañons or valleys leading
down from them into the channels and sounds. These causes have produced
much of the bewildering variety of which nature is so fond, but none the less
will the studious observer see the underlying harmony—the general trend of
the islands in the direction of the flow of the main ice-mantle from the
mountains of the Coast Range, more or less varied by subordinate foothill
ridges and mountains. Furthermore, all the islands, great and small, as well as
the headlands and promontories of the mainland, are seen to have a rounded,
over-rubbed appearance produced by the over-sweeping ice-flood during the
period of greatest glacial abundance.

The canals, channels, straits, passages, sounds, etc., are subordinate to the
same glacial conditions in their forms, trends, and extent as those which
determined the forms, trends, and distribution of the land-masses, their
basins being the parts of the pre-glacial margin of the continent, eroded to
varying depths below sea-level, and into which, of course, the ocean waters
flowed as the ice was melted out of them. Had the general glacial denudation
been much less, these ocean ways over which we are sailing would have been
valleys and cañons and lakes; and the islands rounded hills and ridges, landscapes with undulating features like those found above sea-level wherever the
rocks and glacial conditions are similar. In general, the island-bound channels are like rivers, not only in separate reaches as seen from the deck of a ves-

sel, but continuously so for hundreds of miles in the case of the longest of them. The tide-currents, the fresh driftwood, the inflowing streams, and the luxuriant foliage of the out-leaning trees on the shores make this resemblance all the more complete. The largest islands look like part of the mainland in any view to be had of them from the ship, but far the greater number are small, and appreciable as islands, scores of them being less than a mile long. These the eye easily takes in and revels in their beauty with ever fresh delight. In their relations to each other the individual members of a group have evidently been derived from the same general rock-mass, yet they never seem broken or abridged in any way as to their contour lines, however abruptly they may dip their sides. Viewed one by one, they seem detached beauties, like extracts from a poem, while, from the completeness of their lines and the way that their trees are arranged, each seems a finished stanza in itself. Contemplating the arrangement of the trees on these small islands, a distinct impression is produced of their having been sorted and harmonized as to size like a well-balanced bouquet. On some of the smaller tufted islets a group of tapering spruces is planted in the middle, and two smaller groups that evidently correspond with each other are planted on the ends at about equal distances from the central group; or the whole appears as one group with marked fringing trees that match each other spreading around the sides, like flowers leaning outward against the rim of a vase. These harmonious tree relations are so constant that they evidently are the result of design, as much so as the arrangement of the feathers of birds or the scales of fishes.

Thus perfectly beautiful are these blessed evergreen islands, and their beauty is the beauty of youth, for though the freshness of their verdure must be ascribed to the bland moisture with which they are bathed from warm ocean-currents, the very existence of the islands, their features, finish, and peculiar distribution, are all immediately referable to ice-action during the great glacial winter just now drawing to a close.

We arrived at Wrangell July 14, and after a short stop of a few hours went on to Sitka and returned on the 20th to Wrangell, the most inhospitable place at first sight I had ever seen. The little steamer that had been my home in the wonderful trip through the archipelago, after taking the mail, departed on her return to Portland, and as I watched her gliding out of sight in the dismal blurring rain, I felt strangely lonesome. The friend that had accompanied me thus far now left for his home in San Francisco, with two other interesting travelers who had made the trip for health and scenery, while my fellow passengers, the missionaries, went direct to the Presbyterian home in the old fort. There was nothing like a tavern or lodging-house in the village, nor could I find any place in the stumpy, rocky, boggy ground about it that looked dry enough to camp on until I could find a way into the wilderness to begin my studies. Every place within a mile or two of the town seemed strangely shelterless and inhospitable, for all the trees had long ago been felled for building-timber and firewood. At the worst, I thought, I could build a bark hut on a hill back of the village, where something like a forest loomed dimly through the draggled clouds.

I had already seen some of the high glacier-bearing mountains in distant views from the steamer, and was anxious to reach them. A few whites of the village, with whom I entered into conversation, warned me that the Indians were a bad lot, not to be trusted, that the woods were well-nigh impenetrable, and that I could go nowhere without a canoe. On the other hand, these natural difficulties made the grand wild country all the more attractive, and I determined to get into the heart of it somehow or other with a bag of hard-tack, trusting to my usual good luck. My present difficulty was in finding a first base camp. My only hope was on the hill. When I was strolling past the old fort I happened to meet one of the missionaries, who kindly asked me where I was going to take up my quarters.

"I don't know," I replied. "I have not been able to find quarters of any sort. The top of that little hill over there seems the only possible place."

He then explained that every room in the mission house was full, but he thought I might obtain leave to spread my blanket in a carpenter-shop belonging to the mission. Thanking him, I ran down to the sloppy wharf for my little bundle of baggage, laid it on the shop floor, and felt glad and snug among the dry, sweet-smelling shavings.

The carpenter was at work on a new Presbyterian mission building, and when he came in I explained that Dr. Jackson* had suggested that I might be allowed to sleep on the floor, and after I assured him that I would not touch his tools or be in his way, he goodnaturedly gave me the freedom of the shop and also of his small private side room where I would find a wash-basin.

---

*Dr Sheldon Jackson, 1834–1909, became Superintendent of Presbyterian Missions in Alaska in 1877, and United States General Agent of Education in 1885. [W.F.B.]

I was here only one night, however, for Mr. Vanderbilt, a merchant, who with his family occupied the best house in the fort, hearing that one of the late arrivals, whose business none seemed to know, was compelled to sleep in the carpenter-shop, paid me a good-Samaritan visit and after a few explanatory words on my glacier and forest studies, with fine hospitality offered me a room and a place at his table. Here I found a real home, with freedom to go on all sorts of excursions as opportunity offered. Annie Vanderbilt, a little doctor of divinity two years old, ruled the household with love sermons and kept it warm.

Mr. Vanderbilt introduced me to prospectors and traders and some of the most influential of the Indians. I visited the mission school and the home for Indian girls kept by Mrs. MacFarland, and made short excursions to the nearby forests and streams, and studied the rate of growth of the different species of trees and their age, counting the annual rings on stumps in the large clearings made by the military when the fort was occupied, causing wondering speculation among the Wrangell folk, as was reported by Mr. Vanderbilt.

"What can the fellow be up to?" they inquired. "He seems to spend most of his time among stumps and weeds. I saw him the other day on his knees, looking at a stump as if he expected to find gold in it. He seems to have no serious object whatever."

One night when a heavy rainstorm was blowing I unwittingly caused a lot of wondering excitement among the whites as well as the superstitious Indians. Being anxious to see how the Alaska trees behave in storms and hear the songs they sing, I stole quietly away through the gray drenching blast to the hill back of the town, without being observed. Night was falling when I set out and it was pitch dark when I reached the top. The glad, rejoicing storm in glorious voice was singing through the woods, noble compensation for mere body discomfort. But I wanted a fire, a big one, to see as well as hear how the storm and trees were behaving. After long, patient groping I found a little dry punk in a hollow trunk and carefully stored it beside my matchbox and an inch or two of candle in an inside pocket that the rain had not yet reached; then, wiping some dead twigs and whittling them into thin shavings, stored them with the punk. I then made a little conical bark hut about a foot high, and, carefully leaning over it and sheltering it as much as possible from the driving rain, I wiped and stored a lot of dead twigs, lighted the candle, and set it in the hut, carefully added pinches of punk and shavings, and at length got a little blaze, by the light of which I gradually added larger shavings, then twigs all set on end astride the inner flame, making the little hut higher and wider. Soon I had light enough to enable me to select the best dead branches and large sections of bark, which were set on end, gradually increasing the height and corresponding light of the hut fire. A considerable area was thus well lighted, from which I gathered abundance of wood, and kept adding to the fire until it had a strong, hot heart and sent up a pillar of flame thirty or forty feet high, illuminating a wide circle in spite of the rain, and casting a red glare into the flying clouds. Of all the thousands of camp-fires I have elsewhere built none was just like this one, rejoicing in triumphant strength and beauty in the heart of the rain-laden gale. It was wonderful,—the illumined rain and clouds mingled together and the trees glowing against the jet background, the colors of the mossy, lichened trunks with sparkling streams pouring down the furrows of the bark, and the gray-bearded old patriarchs bowing low and chanting in passionate worship!

My fire was in all its glory about midnight, and, having made a bark shed to shelter me from the rain and partially dry my clothing, I had nothing to do but look and listen and join the trees in their hymns and prayers.

Neither the great white heart of the fire nor the quivering enthusiastic flames shooting aloft like auroral lances could be seen from the village on account of the trees in front of it and its being back a little way over the brow of the hill; but the light in the clouds made a great show, a portentous sign in the stormy heavens unlike anything ever before seen or heard of in Wrangell. Some wakeful Indians, happening to see it about midnight, in great alarm aroused the Collector of Customs and begged him to go to the missionaries and get them to pray away the frightful omen, and inquired anxiously whether white men had ever seen anything like that sky-fire, which instead of being quenched by the rain was burning brighter and brighter. The Collector said he had heard of such strange fires, and this one he thought might perhaps be what the white man called a "volcano, or an *ignis fatuus*." When Mr. Young was called from his bed to pray, he, too, confoundedly astonished and at a loss for any sort of explanation, confessed that he had never seen anything like it in the sky or anywhere else in such cold wet weather, but that it was probably some sort of spontaneous combustion "that the white man called St. Elmo's fire, or Will-of-the-wisp." These explanations, though not convincingly clear, perhaps served to veil their own astonishment and in some measure to diminish the superstitious fears of the natives; but from what I heard, the few whites who happened to see the strange light wondered about as wildly as the Indians.

I have enjoyed thousands of camp-fires in all sorts of weather and places, warm-hearted, short-flamed, friendly little beauties glowing in the dark on open spots in high Sierra gardens, daisies and lilies circled about them, gazing like enchanted children; and large fires in silver fir forests, with spires of flame towering like the trees about them, and sending up multitudes of starry sparks to enrich the sky; and still greater fires on the mountains in winter, changing camp climate to summer, and making the frosty snow look like beds of white flowers; and oftentimes mingling their swarms of swift-flying sparks with falling snow-crystals when the clouds were in bloom. But this Wrangell camp-fire, my first in Alaska, I shall always remember for its triumphant storm-defying grandeur, and the wondrous beauty of the psalm-singing, lichen-painted trees which it brought to light.

AURORAS

I set out with Professor Reid's party to visit some of the other large glaciers that flow into the bay, to observe what changes have taken place in them since October, 1879, when I first visited and sketched them. We found the upper half of the bay closely choked with bergs, through which it was exceedingly difficult to force a way. After slowly struggling a few miles up the east side, we dragged the whale-boat and canoe over rough rocks into a fine garden and comfortably camped for the night.

The next day was spent in cautiously picking a way across to the west side of the bay; and as the strangely scanty stock of provisions was already about done, and the ice-jam to the northward seemed impenetrable, the party decided to return to the main camp by a comparatively open, roundabout way to the southward, while with the canoe and a handful of foodscraps I pushed on northward. After a hard, anxious struggle, I reached the mouth of the Hugh Miller fiord about sundown, and tried to find a camp-spot on its steep, boulder-bound shore. But no landing-place where it seemed possible to drag the canoe above high-tide mark was discovered after examining a mile or more of this dreary, forbidding barrier, and as night was closing down, I decided to try to grope my way across the mouth of the fiord in the starlight to an open sandy spot on which I had camped in October, 1879, a distance of about three or four miles.

With the utmost caution I picked my way through the sparkling bergs, and after an hour or two of this nerve-trying work, when I was perhaps less than half-way across and dreading the loss of the frail canoe which would include the loss of myself, I came to a pack of very large bergs which loomed threateningly, offering no visible thoroughfare. Paddling and pushing to right and left, I at last discovered a sheer-walled opening about four feet wide and perhaps two hundred feet long, formed apparently by the splitting of a huge iceberg. I hesitated to enter this passage, fearing that the slightest change in the tide-current might close it, but ventured nevertheless, judging that the dangers ahead might not be greater than those I had already passed. When I had got about a third of the way in, I suddenly discovered that the smooth-walled ice-lane was growing narrower, and with desperate haste backed out. Just as the bow of the canoe cleared the sheer walls they came together with a growling crunch. Terror-stricken, I turned back, and in an anxious hour or two gladly reached the rock-bound shore that had at first repelled me, determined to stay on guard all night in the canoe or find some place where with the strength that comes in a fight for life I could drag it up the boulder wall beyond ice danger. This at last was happily done about midnight, and with no thought of sleep I went to bed rejoicing.

My bed was two boulders, and as I lay wedged and bent on their up-bulging sides, beguiling the hard, cold time in gazing into the starry sky and across the sparkling bay, magnificent upright bars of light in bright prismatic colors suddenly appeared, marching swiftly in close succession along the northern horizon from west to east as if in diligent haste, an auroral display very different from any I had ever before beheld. Once long ago in Wisconsin I saw the heavens draped in rich purple auroral clouds fringed and folded in most magnificent forms; but in this glory of light, so pure, so bright, so enthusiastic in motion, there was nothing in the least cloud-like. The short colorbars, apparently about two degrees in height, though blending, seemed to be as well defined as those of the solar spectrum.

How long these glad, eager soldiers of light held on their way I cannot tell;

for sense of time was charmed out of mind and the blessed night circled away in measureless rejoicing enthusiasm.

In the early morning after so inspiring a night I launched my canoe feeling able for anything, crossed the mouth of the Hugh Miller fiord, and forced a way three or four miles along the shore of the bay, hoping to reach the Grand Pacific Glacier in front of Mt. Fairweather. But the farther I went, the ice-pack, instead of showing inviting little open streaks here and there, became so much harder jammed that on some parts of the shore the bergs, drifting south with the tide, were shoving one another out of the water beyond high-tide line. Farther progress to northward was thus rigidly stopped, and now I had to fight for a way back to my cabin, hoping that by good tide luck I might reach it before dark. But at sundown I was less than half-way home, and though very hungry was glad to land on a little rock island with a smooth beach for the canoe and a thicket of alder bushes for fire and bed and a little sleep. But shortly after sundown, while these arrangements were being made, lo and behold another aurora enriching the heavens! and though it proved to be one of the ordinary almost colorless kind, thrusting long, quivering lances toward the zenith from a dark cloudlike base, after last night's wonderful display one's expectations might well be extravagant and I lay wide awake watching.

On the third night I reached my cabin and food. Professor Reid and his party came in to talk over the results of our excursions, and just as the last one of the visitors opened the door after bidding good-night, he shouted, "Muir, come look here. Here's something fine."

I ran out in auroral excitement, and sure enough here was another aurora, as novel and wonderful as the marching rainbow-colored columns— a glowing silver bow spanning the Muir Inlet in a magnificent arch right under the zenith, or a little to the south of it, the ends resting on the top of the mountain-walls. And though colorless and steadfast, its intense, solid, white splendor, noble proportions, and fineness of finish excited boundless admiration. In form and proportion it was like a rainbow, a bridge of one span five miles wide; and so brilliant, so fine and solid and homogeneous in every part, I fancy that if all the stars were raked together into one windrow, fused and welded and run through some celestial rolling-mill, all would be required to make this one glowing white colossal bridge.

After my last visitor went to bed, I lay down on the moraine in front of the cabin and gazed and watched. Hour after hour the wonderful arch stood perfectly motionless, sharply defined and substantial-looking as if it were a permanent addition to the furniture of the sky. At length while it yet spanned the inlet in serene unchanging splendor, a band of fluffy, pale gray, quivering ringlets came suddenly all in a row over the eastern mountain-top, glided in nervous haste up and down the under side of the bow and over the western mountain-wall. They were about one and a half times the apparent diameter of the bow in length, maintained a vertical posture all the way across, and slipped swiftly along as if they were suspended like a curtain on rings. Had these lively auroral fairies marched across the fiord on the top of the bow instead of shuffling along the under side of it, one might have fancied they were a happy band of spirit people on a journey making use of the splendid bow for a bridge. There must have been hundreds of miles of them; for the time required for each to cross from one end of the bridge to the other seemed only a minute or less, while nearly an hour elapsed from their first appearance until the last of the rushing throng vanished behind the western mountain, leaving the bridge as bright and solid and steadfast as before they arrived. But later, half an hour or so, it began to fade. Fissures or cracks crossed it diagonally through which a few stars were seen, and gradually it became thin and nebulous until it looked like the Milky Way, and at last vanished, leaving no visible monument of any sort to mark its place.

I now returned to my cabin, replenished the fire, warmed myself, and prepared to go to bed, though too aurorally rich and happy to go to sleep. But just as I was about to retire, I thought I had better take another look at the sky, to make sure that the glorious show was over; and, contrary to all reasonable expectations, I found that the pale foundation for another bow was being laid right overhead like the first. Then losing all thought of sleep, I ran back to my cabin, carried out blankets and lay down on the moraine to keep watch until daybreak, that none of the sky wonders of the glorious night within reach of my eyes might be lost.

I had seen the first bow when it stood complete in full splendor, and its gradual fading decay. Now I was to see the building of a new one from the beginning. Perhaps in less than half an hour the silvery material was gathered, condensed, and welded into a glowing, evenly proportioned arc like the first and in the same part of the sky. Then in due time over the eastern mountain-wall came another throng of restless electric auroral fairies, the infinitely fine pale-gray garments of each lightly touching those of their neighbors as they swept swiftly along the under side of the bridge and down over the western mountain like the merry band that had gone the same way before them, all keeping quivery step and time to music too fine for mortal ears.

While the gay throng was gliding swiftly along, I watched the bridge for any change they might make upon it, but not the slightest could I detect. They left no visible track, and after all had passed the glowing arc stood firm and apparently immutable, but at last faded slowly away like its glorious predecessor.

Excepting only the vast purple aurora mentioned above, said to have been visible over nearly all the continent, these two silver bows in supreme, serene, supernal beauty surpassed everything auroral I ever beheld.

BLACK GOLD

THE PETROLEUM INDUSTRY has been one of Alaska's largest employers and biggest sources of income since the discovery of oil there in 1957. Prudhoe Bay started pumping crude in 1968, and made the state's dependence on oil even more overwhelming. There are ongoing battles in Washington today about expanding oil exploration and production into land currently reserved for nature preserves. The industry is both a boon for Alaska's economy and a threat to it—Alaska's other major industry is tourism, and incidents like the wreck of the Exxon Valdez and the resulting oil spill can have a terrible effect on the flow of tourist dollars, as well as on everything living in the path of destruction. There's no denying that the United States needs Alaska's oil, and that Alaska needs the dollars the oil brings into the economy. Balancing those needs with the goal of preserving and protecting Alaska's natural treasures is a constant battle for petroleum engineers and environmentalists alike. Here's a look into that struggle. . . .

Excerpt from *Who Killed Alaska*

DAVE BROWN AND
PAULA CRANE

D ave Brown never lived in Alaska "before oil." But he did live in Alaska before the oil boom which resulted from construction of the pipeline from the North Slope to Valdez. By that time, the Kenai Peninsula had already been given a good dose of then-legal drilling muds into the earth. Anchorage experienced the full pipeline boom in the mid-1970's. After Dave moved there, the Kenai Peninsula had its own growth spurt.

But the peninsula did not experience the full force of oil development, with the natural accompaniment of a mushrooming state bureaucracy and its resulting jobs and sprawling development, until about 1983. So Dave was able to live in both Anchorage, and then the Kenai Peninsula, before they exploded with people and problems.

Until this era, Alaska was getting along fine with minimal oil development. Its economy was based on the United States military, commercial fishing, logging, mining, construction, guiding, trapping, and a growing tourism business.

Many of the people who came from other states and settled in Alaska were pioneer types—individualistic and adventurous. Anyone who wanted to work could usually find work. These early settlers, unlike the drifters who came to Alaska strictly for employment, came to Alaska to live because they wanted to become Alaskans, not because they wanted to get rich. They liked the outdoor lifestyle and the opportunity that the land offered them. It was a serene atmosphere, made to order for folks who didn't care for life in the fast lane. A man wasn't judged, or given a job, on the basis of his family tree, nor by his position in the social register, nor by where he'd been or what he'd done. All that mattered was a person's character. If your word was good, you were good. You were accepted. A lot of people like Dave Brown, who had problems or didn't fit in in the Lower Forty-eight, came up to Alaska. The state and its people gave them fresh starts and the opportunity to succeed when they had failed elsewhere.

Oil changed everything.

Oil was first discovered in the state at Katalla, not far from Cordova and the Gulf of Alaska, in the 1920's. A refinery was built at Katalla, but it burned down in 1933, and was never rebuilt.

In 1923, a well was drilled at Cold Bay on the Alaska Peninsula. It was a dry hole. Other locations were tested, and, finally, in July 1957, oil was discovered on the Kenai Peninsula at Swanson River by the Richfield Oil Company. Richfield's well was a gusher, and from that moment on, Alaska would never be the same.

After Swanson River's beginning, construction of offshore drilling platforms in the Cook Inlet began at a feverish pace. Then, by the late 1960's, two major industrial companies began to take shape on the Kenai Peninsula. The Collier Carbon and Chemical Company started building a chemical plant near Kenai to produce ammonia and urea for fertilizer, using the excess reserves of natural gas that existed on the Kenai Peninsula. The plant went through several name changes, and today it is known as Unocal Chemicals Division. Shortly after Colliers, Phillips built its liquefied natural gas plant. The gas is compressed at extremely low temperatures, transforming it into a liquid state. It is then shipped across the ocean to Japan in refrigerated tanker ships. Two other refineries were then built—the Tesoro Refinery, which refines crude oil into gasoline and jet fuel, and the Chevron Refinery, which mostly makes asphalt, along with other oil products.

Today there are fifteen offshore drilling platforms anchored to the bottom of Cook Inlet by steel legs, serving four hundred and sixty-five wells that have been drilled in the bottom of the inlet. Oil and natural gas flow from these platforms through pipelines to refineries and other onshore installations. Some goes to Kenai, some goes to Anchorage, and some of it is loaded onto tanker ships for shipment to the Lower Forty-eight and to Japan and Korea. There are also currently three major on-shore oil and gas fields—Marathon's Beaver Creek field which is about five miles from Kenai's city limits; Chevron and ARCO's Swanson River oil field which began the first oil rush; and Unocal's Kenai Gas Fields just outside the city limits of Kenai and the Cannery Loop unit, in the city limits. Across Cook Inlet there are several other oil support facilities—Drift River, West Forelands, McArthur River, Nicolai Creek, Granite Point, Beluga River and Ivan River. The Drift River terminal, with its storage tanks, was built at the base of an active volcano, Mt. Redoubt, and recently had to undergo major flood prevention work in order for the state to allow it to continue to operate. A 1990 eruption caused some flooding of the storage tanks, and it was feared a major eruption could cause a major oil spill into Cook Inlet.

During the late 1960's, while Dave was selling heavy equipment to the construction and oil industries, he got a taste of what it takes to do business with the oil industry. The company for which Dave worked was the Alaskan distributor for a particular brand of welding machines. The company sold a lot of those machines to a major international oil field contractor. Although there were only two salesmen working for the company, and Brown was one of the two, Todd, the lanky, dark-haired general manager of the company, said in a secretive one, "Dave, don't go near the head man of that oil field contractor. The account with that contractor is one which I handle personally."

Dave and Todd became pretty good friends, fishing together, and tilting quite a few bottles of Oly together. One night, after more than a few Olys, Todd became more talkative, "Dave, you probably have guessed there are some kickbacks involved in doing business with that particular company." Todd hiccuped as he went on, "Those welding machines sell for a certain price to anyone who wants them—the manufacturer's suggested retail price plus the freight to Anchorage. But, for you-know-who, we sell the welding machines for the listed price plus a little extra." Dave was a little shocked, but he leaned forward to listen more closely. "Is there more I should know?" Dave asked.

"Probably not," Todd said, "but tonight I'm gonna" he slurred the next word, "tell you."

"The bills go directly to the contractor's home office. When they're paid, I pay the head man with the contractor his take." Dave's company benefited only in that it was able to sell the welding machines to the contractor. The contracting company itself paid a slightly higher price than it should. The head man with the contractor was the one who pocketed the extra cash.

"Why would you go along with that kind of nonsense?" Dave asked, puzzled. "You don't make enough to take the risk." Todd confided to Dave that although he really didn't like doing it, if he didn't, the contractor would just buy another brand of welders from another source instead.

Not too long after this discreet conversation, Dave and Betty were shopping in J. C. Penney's, and saw Bart Jamison, the top man with the oil field contractor buying new furniture and appliances for his new home.

As Betty and Dave watched speechless, Jamison rolled back a wad of one hundred dollar bills and paid for the furniture and appliances in cash. Dave made a mental note of the transaction, and couldn't help but wonder how many of those bills were kickback bills.

Dave continued to learn bits and pieces that made up the interesting, bureaucratic and corrupt nature of the oil business. He noticed that when he sold a major piece of equipment to a non-oil contractor, the question always before the contractor was how was he going to pay for it. However, whenever Dave sold a major piece of equipment to an oil field contractor or an oil company itself, paying for it was never even a consideration. Their question was, "How soon can we get it?"

Another major international oil field contractor had an office in Anchorage. They had a young purchasing agent named Ted Tanner, whose wife was still in the Lower Forty-eight. He didn't know anyone in Alaska, and he was lonely. Dave's wife was an excellent cook, so Dave invited Ted over for dinner. At the same time, Dave had a neighbor who was out of town working at a remote location. Janet, his young wife, was lonely and frequently came over to visit Betty. On the afternoon of the day Ted came to dinner, Janet was there, and she eventually invited herself to stay for dinner. Dinner turned into a long evening after which Ted took Janet home. The Browns later learned he spent the night. After that night Dave could do no wrong with Ted's company, but Dave didn't like it. Ted was never asked for dinner again, and Janet was never allowed to hang around Betty. Dave wanted no part of an irate husband who might just come home and choose to do away with the perpetrator or accomplices in his wife's adultery.

With oil came men, without wives, and women lonely for their husbands,

so one-night stands became commonplace in Alaska, and slowly morality
crept down the gutter. Topless and bottomless bars appeared overnight, along
with plentiful massage parlors.

While the Swanson River and Cook Inlet platforms brought the first oil
boom, the real big one—Prudhoe Bay—was still to come. One Alaskan, Tennessee Miller, hitched himself to the oil boom and, as owner of Frontier Rock
and Sand, pioneered for the oil companies all over the North Slope with cat
trains, pulling men, equipment and supplies wherever the oil companies
wanted them to go. The pioneering paid off for Tennessee and it paid off for
the oil industry. On April 22, 1967, Atlantic Richfield had spudded in a well
named Prudhoe Bay State #1. Fourteen months later and 12,016 feet deeper,
on July 24, 1968, ARCO and Humble Oil and Refining Company publicly
announced that a major oil discovery had been made at Prudhoe Bay on
Alaska's frozen North Slope. Both companies had brought in two spectacular
wells near Prudhoe Bay, just seven miles apart from each other. Humble Oil
and Refining Company later became known as the Exxon Company.

D ave worked on the Trans-Alaska Pipeline for almost three years as a
heavy equipment operator. He terms it "the most interesting fiasco I
have ever been allowed to participate in."

The waste in time, money, material and labor was so ridiculous that a normal person couldn't even begin to fathom it. The problem was, according to
Dave, "the way it was bid." If it had been a "hard money" project, each phase of
the job would be put up for bid with engineer estimates and the jobs would go
to the lowest bidders provided they were qualified—that they had the man-
power, the equipment, the capability and the bonding to get the job done. In
those kinds of jobs, the contractor who is awarded the job hurries to get it
done as efficiently as possible, so he can get paid and go on to another job.

But the pipeline was built as a "cost plus" job, where the philosophy is to
put twice or three times as many men, or twice or three times as much equipment, on the job as are needed, and then go as slow as possible, because the
longer the contractor takes, the more money he makes.

The contractors were all paid "cost plus" by the Alyeska consortium of
oil companies which built the pipeline, and Alyeska—and therefore the
oil companies—were paid "cost plus" at the gas pumps by the American
people. Dave reported that most of his fellow workers had the feeling

they weren't working the pipeline to get it done, but just to take up time and money. Dave saw criminal waste of equipment—materials, supplies and labor at all the camps he worked—Valdez, Livengood, Five Mile Camp and Coldfoot.

At Valdez, he walked out on the job one crisp morning with a fellow worker, Don Peters.

"Look over there," Don said, pointing.

Dave looked in the direction. Two crane operators were fighting a duel along the dock with their cranes, tipping one of them over and bending it out of shape.

"What the hell do you think they are doing?" Dave protested.

"It's all in the name of fun," Don retorted sarcastically.

Dave's face wore a grim look, "Well, I guess we and the rest of the American people will pay for that stupidity at the gas pumps."

At Valdez, there were two 977 caterpillar loaders owned by the contractor. Dave operated one, and a man called Goose Loring operated the other. Goose would sit all day in his loader with one pane of glass broken out of the front of his cab. Occasionally, he would lean out through the missing window and drop an empty soft drink can down his exhaust stack. Then he would climb back in the operator's seat, pull back on his throttle, and see how high up in the sky he could blow the empty can.

Later, Goose was put on a bobcat loader. His favorite trick was to drive the loader inside an empty container van, closing the doors behind him. There he would hide all afternoon. Several times during the winter, his foreman followed his loader tracks through the snow to the doors of the van, and kicked him out. But nobody ever fired him.

There was really no point to firing him. All he was supposed to do was to stay awake, anyway. There was no real work for him to do.

Dave did his best to stay busy. If he couldn't find any dirt to move, he would carry tools for the laborers, steel for the iron workers or oxygen and acetylene for the welders. Dave felt he earned his pay, but it was hard. He had to look for work.

One day, on his way to the main gate, he passed a small pond with a 225 cat backhoe next to it. The operator and oiler, at two hundred dollars an hour, were playing with the machine, killing time. With the backhoe, they had put a big rock in the little pond. On top of the big rock they had placed a medium-sized rock, and on top of that they were trying to balance a small rock, sort of like building a snowman with rocks. It was a silly game, but, considering the concept of cost plus, it wasn't senseless. The contractor was getting paid only for the hours that machine was running. It didn't matter what the machine was actually doing.

Dave was older than a lot of the men on the job, and brought to the pipeline some of his 1950's views, including anti-drug opinions. Although he drank his share of beer, his hard drug views got him a quick "red neck" label. But whereas Dave's pay day night beer never got in the way of his performance, the men who smoked pot and snorted cocaine on the job could, with their drug-induced incompetence, endanger everyones' lives, including Dave's. Once, he watched a pot-stoned surveyor in Valdez step back too far while using his transit, and fall into a twenty-foot deep hole. He survived, unhurt, but a lot of the men on the pipeline weren't so lucky. Carelessness and overconfidence, much of it under a drug cloud or while hung over, caused many deaths.

One of Dave's friends, Jess Straight, was killed at Valdez. In his case, it was his own overconfidence, not drugs nor booze. A heavy equipment and diesel mechanic—and a good one—he jacked up a truck and crawled under it without setting any blocks. The jack slipped and Jess died.

A laborer lost his arm at Valdez his first night on the job because the crane he was working with was operated by the oiler and not by the operator. Alyeska normally held safety meetings once a week. The workers could always tell when someone was killed, because there would be an extra safety meeting. Dave and his buddies would first hear the ambulance screaming through camp, and then there would be a safety meeting—like a death knell everyone tried to, but couldn't avoid.

At Livengood Camp, Dave worked as a relief operator, covering other operators while they were on R & R (rest and relaxation) or while they were sick. As a relief operator, he operated 'dozers, scrapers, loaders and, for a while, a six-inch Gorman Rupp pump. Operating this pump opened Dave's eyes to the absurdity of a "cost plus" job. The six-inch pump was used to fill a shiny yellow Kenworth water truck, and it was situated on the bank of Hess Creek. For two weeks, while the pump operator was on R & R, Dave ran his pump.

A six-inch Gorman Rupp pump has an electric starter. This pump also had a suction hose down in the creek, and a discharge hose mounted high in the air on a pipe frame. The water truck backed down under the discharge hose. All Dave had to do was turn the key on the pump, then push the starter button and wait five or ten minutes while the tank filled with water. When it was finished, he would turn off the switch. He did this three or four times every day. But when he wasn't turning the key or pushing the button, he was sitting down in the dry shack reading magazines. He worked a total of not more than half an hour three or four times a day, yet got paid for twelve hours a day, seven days a week, and cleared slightly more than $1,000 a week, after taxes.

It wasn't just Dave. It took four men every day to get that water truck filled. A teamster drove the truck because that was a teamster's job. The teamster couldn't run the pump because that was an operator's job. Dave was the operator. The Kenworth water truck had two bucket seats; a laborer rode on the other seat. The laborer had to climb on the side of the truck's water tank and open the lid. Later, he had to climb back up and close the lid. That's three men. In addition, the operator, Dave, had to get to and from the dry shack from Hess Creek. The foreman—the one who hated Alaska—would drive Dave three or four times a day to the creek, just so he could turn his key and push his button.

Union labor required the division of labor, and that added to the cost; that was the way Alyeska wanted it. Using union labor, the company could generate more cash flow and justify raising the price of gas at the pumps. When the job was completed, and the "cost plus" was gone, Alyeska got rid of the union labor and replaced them with less expensive, non-union workers, mostly from the Lower Forty-eight. That policy has continued until today, with the marriage between the unions and the oil industry nearly completely broken.

Life on the pipeline wasn't all irony and absurdity. There were just plain jovial incidents, and some simple hilarity. Dave always got a kick out of relating this story:

"At Valdez, a laboring crew was drilling rock one day, all of them covered with dirt and wearing coveralls, goggles, and hard hats. One of the men had to urinate and apparently didn't have time or didn't feel like walking to one of those little green plastic outhouses that Alyeska had scattered all over the site, so he unzipped his coveralls and started to go. One of his fellow laborers tapped him on the arm and said, 'Hey, do you see that guy over there in the coveralls? Well, under those coveralls, hard hat and goggles is a girl, not a guy!' The urinating laborer wet his pants trying to turn it off in mid-stream and put it away."

Women were hired on the pipeline, working as laborers, teamsters, operators, oilers, welders and helpers. Some were ornamental, some were foreman's and superintendent's helpers. Most were there to make money, and they worked hard.

At Valdez, the women were separated from the men. One two-story barracks was filled with women only. Another two-story barracks had women on the floor and men on the other. All the other barracks were filled with men.

The other pipeline camps in which Dave worked were smaller, so the arrangements were more haphazard. Dave's first night at one of the smaller camps gave him quite a surprise. At ten p.m. he made a trip to the men's room. There were four or five urinals in a row followed by a row of sinks along the same wall. No one was in the room that he could see, so he stepped up to the urinal next to the sinks. Just as he started to urinate, a female voice said, "Hi there. How are you?" A girl in her twenties stood at the sink, just three or four feet away, getting ready to brush her teeth. Dave zipped his wet fly and tried to look casual as he sauntered out of the room.

While women in camp sometimes created an invasion of privacy, there was a much more threatening invasion. Bears, both black and brown, were everywhere—in dry shacks, in dumpsters, in pick-up trucks and busses. They would even occasionally get into the mess halls and barracks. Dave watched once as a man dropped some trash into a steel dumpster in Valdez, not knowing there was a bear inside until the bear stood up. The man shouted and scrammed. A couple of black bears walked into a dry shack at Valdez while the men inside were eating lunch. That created quite a scramble.

Dave had his own bear problems at Livengood Camp. He was operating a D-7 winch cat near a steep hill. A mechanic had driven him to the foot of the hill where his 'dozer was supposed to be, but the night shift had instead left it on top of the hill. In the morning rain, the mechanic drove the truck as far as he could, but the hill was much too steep for a flat-bed truck to climb. They both noticed a black bear ambling about two hundred feet away.

"Are you afraid of bears?" the mechanic asked Dave.

"Heck, no!" Dave huffed proudly. "Bears and I get along just fine."

"Well, good. I'll just drop you off here and get back to work. I can't climb that hill, and the foreman will be here shortly to drive you up in his four-wheel-drive pickup."

As the mechanic drove off, Dave instantly regretted his macho reply about bears. Here he was with no trees to climb, and no weapon except a stainless steel vacuum thermos. Sure enough, the bear decided to check him out, or at least try to see what was in Dave's lunch. But Dave didn't feel like sharing his lunch. Another quick glance at the local scenery revealed only a JLG manlift. Dave wasn't very familiar with a manlift, but he knew it required two people—one person on the platform, and another actually on the machine doing the lifting. The box platform had pipes on all four corners and safety chains all around and was about four feet off the ground—slightly safer than standing in the middle of an open field.

Dave climbed the platform, with the bear close behind, placing front paws on the edge of the platform and looking at Dave through his little beady eyes.

Dave shrugged nervously, "Coffee, tea or me, huh?" The bear was four feet away.

A quick glance around the platform revealed a case of insect spray in one corner.

"Hey, big fella," Dave said calmly. "There isn't room for both of us up here."

The bear waved his head back and forth. Brown bears may have poor eyesight, but Dave knew this one could smell lunch and, at four feet, he could see pretty well, too.

Slowly, Dave reached for a can of insect spray, then quickly hurled it just above the bear's head. The bear whirled around, chasing the can and biting into it. Bug spray is pretty nasty stuff; it sure made the bear mad. But it kept him away from Dave. So Dave threw another one, and another one. The bear chased after them like a dog. Finally, Dave reached out and realized he had hold of the last can. He was running out of luck. Then he noticed something else on the platform—a sledge hammer. He would make his last stand. Either he would kill that bear with a blow from the sledge hammer or die trying.

Just as Dave was reaching for the last can with one hand and for the sledge hammer with the other, his foreman drove up. He slowly rolled down the window, looked at all the bitten up cans and laughed till tears came to his eyes.

But Dave's sense of humor had been seriously imperiled by the ordeal, and he snapped, "Just shut up, run that bear out of here, and come pick me up!"

The foreman did run the bear off, at least a little ways. Far enough to be able to pick Dave up and take him to the top of the hill where two 'dozers were parked—Dave's and another operator's, Ron Caine. Two other pick-ups were parked with men waiting for the busses and drill rigs to come so they could go to work. Ron was in one of the pick-ups, but he had left his lunch in his 'dozer.

Pretty soon, that disagreeable and hungry bear, full of the taste of bug dope in his mouth, came ambling up the hill. He climbed up onto the D6 'dozer, sat down in the seat, and promptly started to eat Ron's lunch. Run jumped out of his truck and ran to his 'dozer, thinking he could scare the bear off. But bears around there—accustomed to people—didn't scare very easily. This one just got out of the seat and climbed down the track, ready to defend his lunch from this harassing man. The bear won. After he had successfully chased Ron back to his pick-up, he put his front paws on the hood and glared. He must have recognized Dave as the perpetrator of the bug-dope melee, because the bear came over to Dave's side, jumped up, and pressed his nose against the glass of the window, this time just six inches from Dave. Dave grinned back, thinking he had won.

But the ordeal wasn't over. The Fourth of July was coming up and the company had planned a big celebration with fireworks. The fireworks were in the other pick-up. The men started lighting them and throwing them at the bear. The first three or four firecrackers didn't impress the bear much, so the men threw a cherry bomb directly in front of him. That got his attention, and he slowly walked away, then stopped, stood up and pawed the air, as if to say, "Okay, I'm going, but don't push your luck or I'll come right back."

The pipeline brought all sorts of people to Alaska; so it wasn't really unusual that Dave would meet an old friend and former co-worker from a Seattle job he had before moving to Alaska. Sten Berg was working as a mechanic on the same job Dave was. One day, at lunch time, the lunch bus parked in the gravel pit and all the men piled into it to eat lunch. Sten was in his mechanics truck, so Dave joined him there.

Soon, as if hearing a dinner bell, a huge black bear ambled out of the woods. Although it was against the rules to feed black bears, it was done regularly, and, as a result, the bears became dangerously accustomed to men, associating men with food—and not just a few measly scraps. Bears ate side orders of prime rib, steak, king crab, and, of course, sandwiches, so they soon forgot all about their supposed main course of berries, bugs and mice.

As this particular black bear sauntered up, he got what he wanted. The men in the bus dropped food from the side windows. But lunch does end, and the bear had not gotten its fill. It simply waited by the door. Soon the day began to get hot, so he crawled under the bus to get into the shade. Nobody dared to leave. A water truck arrived and sprayed water all around and underneath the bus. The bear appeared to enjoy the mid-day bath and he kept the men trapped in the bus for about an hour.

Dave and Sten were watching the shenanigans from the truck, also leery about stepping out. Finally, Dave turned to Sten and said, "Drive me over to my loader and I'll get rid of the bear before the whole crew gets fired."

Dave drove the loader to the side of the bus and shoved his four-yard loader bucket under the edge of the bus. He rocked the loader bucket up and down and shook the entire bus, almost like an earthquake. The bear wasted no time in getting out. Dave chased the bear a half mile across the gravel pit, but the bear didn't give up easily. He thought he might try sparring with that yellow monster. Three times, he whirled around on his hind legs, ready to charge the yellow machine.

"Damn fool!" Dave yelled, hitting the brakes to keep from running the bear over.

☞ DAVE BROWN has been a resident of Alaska since the 1960s and, after working in the petroleum industry, served as head of Alaska Environmental Industries, Inc. PAULA CRANE is a freelance writer and the former associate editor for one of Alaska's largest newspapers.

FAR TREK

ate on a February afternoon, the Kuparuk field's Central Processing Facility One looms out of the dark like something from the dreams of J.R.R Tolkien or George Lucas. Totally alight in a world where darkness rests heavy on deep snow for miles in every direction, from a distance its brightness calls to mind a fairy castle. Closer, and you notice a flare shaking a 5-foot finger of flaming gas against the bitter cold sky, and the efficient space-colony modularity of the structures becomes apparent. From here, Kuparuk could be an isolated outpost station on a distant frozen planet, or perhaps the setting for a "Road Warrior on Ice."

And all of these images are fitting, because popular fantasy and science fiction abound with imaginary worlds that are far more welcoming to human life than the North Slope in winter. Frodo and Bilbo, Skywalker and Obi-wan, the characters of our media's speculative mythologies have acted out most of their adventures in environments that are more, well, more *Earth-like* than this. The air itself near the Central Processing Facility bites at the back of the throat and coats the taste buds, a cocktail of hanging diesel fumes and hard cold that almost makes one wish for a space helmet.

In this alien place, almost 300 miles north of the Arctic Circle, Atlantic Richfield Co. (ARCO), British Petroleum (BP) and other firms have established corporate colonies, outposts that, through a combination of high-tech componentry, human ingenuity (and occasionally sheer toughness), and an almost paranoid concern for safety are harvesting oil from the depths of the frozen soil.

The petroleum prospectors, engineers and construction crews responsible for founding these virtual cities were not, of course, the first people here on the shores of the Beaufort Sea. The earliest European explorers to reach these waters, back in the days of sail, found Eskimos thriving in this unlikely place. These Native people, passing a chain of wisdom down from generation to generation, with their Elders serving as living repositories of the knowledge and skills needed to sustain life in the Arctic, developed a culture that grew into its setting. They are a part of the land they inhabit, as much so as the white bear, the raven, the cold.

But in order to draw the oil from beneath the sand and gravel of this Arctic seashore and pipe it down to Valdez, today's petroleum companies have had to take a different route. They've designed and imported modular villages, places in which oil workers from Alaska, yes, but also from Oklahoma, California and Texas, many of them men and women with no traditional knowledge of, or even experience in, the ways of the Arctic, could live and work. The "space stations" of the North Slope are the result.

And, also as a result, these corporate "cities" are studies in contradiction, where off-duty workers can see a movie or visit a library; play racquetball or shuffleboard, ride a stationary bike or work with free weights while the wind-chill beyond the skin of their shelters drops beyond 100 below. And where—in a land in which a few lone caribou survive the winter by simply *starving* their way through it, where each hunting white fox is constantly monitored by at least one desperately hungry raven—there is food in startling abundance. The dining halls here offer as many as a dozen courses per meal, and all you can eat, while snack rooms stocked with everything from cookies to sandwich makings to design-it-yourself ice cream sundaes are open 24 hours a day.

It's a world where the delicate tundra, which in the summer presents a soft and spongy 12 inches of living "skin" atop the permafrost, can, when temperatures drop to 10 below or lower, be sprayed with layer upon layer of water to create ice roads of up to 30-miles long. These "instant highways" are capable of supporting 5-million-pound drilling rigs that move, at a speed of one mile per day, on the kind of mobile platforms used to ease space shuttles into launch position.

It is a world where man-eating polar bears poke their heads through rec hall windows, and where some doorways to the outside open into stout cages to protect workers from ambush attack, a place where, on varying schedules from one-week-on-one-off to four-weeks-on-three-off, people from vastly different climates come together to form temporary communities.

And despite the deadly winter cold and the caribou-killing insects of summer, it is a world that has called to someone every Alaskan knows. Our husbands and wives, our friends and neighbors, boldly take that far trek north, drawn into the orbit of oil.

≈ Long-time Alaska resident BRUCE WOODS is a writer and the editor of *Alaska Magazine*.

T. A. BADGER

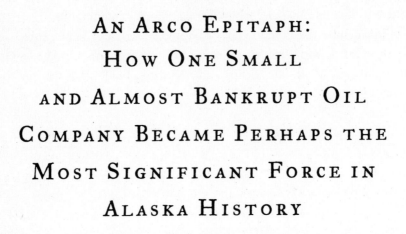

An Arco Epitaph: How One Small and Almost Bankrupt Oil Company Became Perhaps the Most Significant Force in Alaska History

In the spring of 1957 a geologist with a struggling exploration company strides into the scrappy spruce woods of the Kenai Peninsula, confidently grinds the heel of his boot into the snow and tells his crew, "Drill here." The roughnecks start driving the steel bit into the earth. About two miles down and still no pay dirt, they're thinking about abandoning the hole. Just a little farther, the geologist urges. Soon the bit catches the edge of a large pool of crude they will name after the nearby Swanson River. The down-at-heel territory of Alaska is suddenly a player in the oil game.

Leap ahead a decade to the North Slope. Belief in the region's oil potential is flagging as wildcatters poke dry hole after expensive dry hole, but a struggling exploration company isn't ready to pack it in. Just one more well, it says. That last try is successful beyond anyone's dreams, tapping into Prudhoe Bay, one of the biggest oil troves ever found.

Swanson and Prudhoe. Both names are woven into the fabric of Alaska's frontier legend, in large part because their significance carried far beyond the oil fields. The first discovery persuaded Congress that Alaska could support itself as a state, the second made the state a multi-billionaire and ignited a northward stampede of fortune seekers that dwarfed those of the turn-of-the-century gold rushes.

And in both places, the struggling exploration company was the same: Atlantic Richfield.

"They were the history makers in Alaska's oil development—they were the beginning," said Jack Roderick, a 1950s oil-lease buyer who later wrote a book about Alaska's early days of oil exploration. "It was not inevitable that oil would be found on the Kenai . . . They took immense risks, and Alaska has been very good to them."

Like many an Alaska pioneer, Arco showed up without much money—for an oil company, that is—and by dint of smarts, hard work and a little luck, ended up very rich. Prudhoe was quickly followed by other North Slope discoveries that kept the oil flowing and the cash rolling in.

"For the last 25 to 30 years there is no doubt that Alaska has been the cornerstone of Arco's success," said Kevin Meyers, who used to head Arco's Alaska operation. "When you talk Arco, you talk Alaska. They go hand in hand."

But when you talk Arco nowadays, you talk memories . . . because that's all that's left. The company itself is gone, its considerable assets divvied up and sporting new corporate logos. BP Amoco got most of Arco, but not the Alaska assets it badly wanted to add to its already large stake on the North Slope. After a long antitrust fight, federal regulators made the British oil giant spin off Arco's valuable Alaska properties. Those massive deposits of oil and gas, along with tens of thousands of acres to explore, now belong to Phillips Petroleum.

While Arco went through its year-long death throes, Alaskans too were convulsing. The impending loss cracked the foundation of their world, and many feared what lay ahead for Alaska. Plenty of oil companies had come and gone over the years, but this was Arco, the Old Reliable. And the idea of BP controlling nearly three-quarters of the North Slope's oil didn't sit well with most Alaskans. That discomfort birthed an unusual coalition—conservative ex-governors joined with the most fervent environmentalists to fight for a better deal for the state.

"We were protecting our sovereignty," said Christy McGraw, a leader in that effort. "Alaskans are the owners of their resources. We saw this combination as concentrating control not in the hands of the people, but in the hands of a company."

Alaska's relationship with Arco was familylike—complex and multilayered, with expectations from both sides. Arco expected oil-dependent

Alaskans to support the company's quest to find more sources of crude and not to tax away too much of its profit. Alaska expected Arco to keep the maximum number of Alaskans working at high salaries and to kick back part of the company's profit into local public works, charities and the arts.

Sure, there were small betrayals. The state occasionally tinkered with the rules to extract more revenue out of the oil industry, prompting Arco and the others to threaten to pull out of Alaska. Arco also didn't hesitate to lay off workers when low oil prices squeezed its cash flow. It also spilled some crude and several times had to be hauled into court for shortchanging the state treasury. It was, after all, an oil company, and acted every bit the corporate giant when money was on the line.

But rocky times aside, Alaskans expected Arco, here at the dawn of oil time, to be here for them forever.

Arco's demise began in late 1998, when crude prices were in the tank and the industry was rapidly consolidating into fewer, bigger players. The company had tried to vault into the top tier by pouring billions of exploration dollars into the Gulf of Mexico and overseas prospects, but it couldn't duplicate its golden touch in Alaska on a global scale. It was teetering under a heavy debt load when North Slope oil bottomed out at less than $9 a barrel.

"One of Arco's greatest strengths was Alaska, and in a way, it was also its weakness," said Meyers, who has signed on to run Phillips' Alaska operation. "If we ran into difficulties here, we did not have a broad-based, diversified portfolio to turn to elsewhere in the world. So we had to be successful in Alaska for the corporation to succeed."

But being successful in Alaska, the source of half of Arco's crude production, wasn't enough at 1998 prices. Arco's top executives in Los Angeles, less than hopeful that the company could make its way against beefed-up competitors, decided their best option was to lay the company at the feet of BP Amoco.

Arco chairman and chief executive Mike Bowlin essentially told shareholders last August that the only way to save Arco was to kill it. "BP Amoco's scale and financial strength will significantly enhance the value of Arco's assets and allow greater value to be realized than if Arco remains an independent oil and gas company," said Bowlin, whose parting gift was millions of dollars in severance pay and other benefits.

Others say Bowlin and the rest of Arco's top brass panicked during what proved to be a temporary downturn. By last November, a year after prices hit their nadir, North Slope oil had rocketed up to $26 a barrel on its way to $32, the highest in a decade.

"From what I see, they gave the shop away," said Gil Mull of Fairbanks, a former Arco geologist who had a hand in the Prudhoe Bay discovery. "Management had a golden parachute, and they didn't worry about the rest of it."

Meyers, however, suggests that Alaskans, accustomed to seeing only Arco successes, might not have the proper vantage point to second-guess the deal's merits. "It's safe to say that if all of Arco as a corporate entity had the vision, teamwork and performance that (Arco) Alaska did, perhaps we wouldn't have reached this conclusion."

Alaska had no oil industry back in the mid-1950s, when the first geologists from the tiny Richfield Oil Co. joined a few other companies poking around in the Cook Inlet region. The territory's oil potential remained alluring despite its abysmally consistent failure rate—more than 150 consecutive dry holes.

Richfield had survived bankruptcy and was still on wobbly legs, but that didn't stop Alaska's development boosters from avidly courting the company, along with anyone else with access to a drilling rig. Initially Richfield begged off, even when offered free oil leases in exchange for a commitment to drill. The firm later decided to venture north after one of its California geologists saw a promising rock formation while studying a map of the Kenai Peninsula.

Bill Bishop, a young Texan, was dispatched to Alaska. After doing some seismic testing and walking the wilderness, Bishop was confident he had found an area near the Swanson River where there might be oil. He went to Anchorage and bought up 60,000 acres in oil leases from a group of local businessmen—among them, former *Anchorage Times* publisher Robert Atwood and his brother-in-law Elmer Rasmuson, owner of National Bank of Alaska—for 25 cents an acre.

"Richfield was used to dealing with small landowners from their leasing in California. That's what they did when they came up here, and they were very good at it," said Roderick, who in those days published a newsletter that tracked goings-on in the fledgling oil patch.

It was Bishop who ground his boot heel into the snow in April 1957 to mark where he wanted to drill. Three months later, a powerful stream of oil gushed out of the ground.

"When we tested the well at an estimated 900 barrels a day, it was a big day for me, for Richfield and Alaska," the late Bishop said in a 1985 speech at Alaska Pacific University.

"Richfield Hits Oil," boomed the front-page headline in Atwood's daily. The discovery at Swanson River made him and many other Alaskans wealthy and quickly set off a rush by major oil companies to get a piece of the action. More oil and natural gas fields were found on the Kenai and under Cook Inlet. Soon Alaska's stalled crusade to become a state was roaring forward.

"The Swanson River discovery provided the economic justification for statehood for Alaska," said the late William A. Egan, the state's first governor.

Not only was Bill Bishop's timing good, so was his aim. If he had sunk his heel into the snow just a few hundred feet away, the rig would have missed the Swanson River reservoir entirely, and who knows whether the oil hunters would have stuck around for another try. Perhaps that's why Bishop's cowboy-style boots were bronzed and now stand on display in Anchorage's history museum.

The strike at Swanson River also refueled the zeal to explore for oil in arctic Alaska, and Richfield was a front-runner in the first wave. The North Slope presented a whole new set of challenges to overcome, including transporting tons of equipment across nearly 500 miles of roadless tundra, and enduring 50-below-zero cold in winter and man-devouring mosquito swarms in summer.

A pair of young geologists, Gil Mull and Gar Pessel, were sent north in 1963 to scout out the North Slope and map its rocks.

"I was constantly amazed at the level of confidence our boss gave us, because Pessel and I hadn't been out of school very long," said Mull, who now works as a state geologist. "We were given a level of responsibility we certainly never would have had with a large oil company. Richfield being the way it was, it wasn't burdened under layers of management. They were able to be more aggressive, and that was an advantage."

Mull and Pessel found lots of oil potential, but Richfield was short on drilling cash, a crucial disadvantage in a high-cost environment like the North Slope. It shopped around for a partner with deep pockets, and persuaded Humble Oil, later called Exxon, to pony up half the drilling costs in trade for half of whatever was found. It was one of the greatest oil deals ever made—for Exxon. By fronting a mere $20 million, it got half of Arco's stake at Prudhoe Bay, an investment that so far has yielded more than two billion barrels of oil for Exxon.

By the time drilling started at Prudhoe in April 1967, Richfield had merged with Atlantic Refining Co. to become Atlantic Richfield. At its helm was the brilliant and flamboyant Robert O. Anderson, described in the epic oil history *The Prize* as "a man who was one of the last of the great wildcatters and oil tycoons of the 20th century."

But even Anderson, comfortable with high-stakes gambles, was losing faith in the North Slope after a series of dry holes. Everyone else had walked away, but Arco decided to go ahead with one more well at a flat, lonely spot on the tundra near the Arctic Ocean coast.

"It was a rank wildcat hanging way out, 60-something miles from the nearest well," recalled Mull, who worked on the rig. "None of us in our wildest imaginations could have envisioned what it turned out to be."

The well, named Prudhoe Bay State No. 1, revealed that the oil prize was there all along. That revelation came just before Christmas 1967, with the Slope shrouded in darkness and temperatures at about 35 below zero.

"When we opened the (drilling) tool at Prudhoe Bay, immediately there was gas to the surface in a huge flare with tremendous pressure that sounded like a jet plane overhead, and that continued for the better part of a day," Mull said. "That was the first 'Wow!', and it just went from there."

And Arco's fortunes just went from there, too. With Prudhoe's 13 billion barrels at the hub, the company's exploration radiated out in all directions and more huge reserves were found, beginning in 1969 with Kuparuk River, the continent's second-largest field.

Overall production from the North Slope peaked in the mid-1980s and then started a steady decline that continues to this day. Many in the industry came to see Alaska as yesterday's news and lit out for more promising frontiers.

Arco went hunting with the others, but it also kept prowling the North Slope. In the early 1990s, the company once again demonstrated its Alaska prowess by making the nation's largest find of the decade—the 400-million-barrel Alpine field, which will start flowing this fall. And even last summer, with the clock ticking down toward the BP takeover, Arco had a crew of geologists sniffing around on the Slope for more prospects.

In transient Alaska, people come up for a while and then go away, and so do companies. Arco had a nice run here for more than 40 years, and now Alaska and Alaskans are left with what they remember.

"A corporation develops a body and soul and tradition, and it's too bad to see that disappear," said Mull. "It's why people carve their names in birch trees. After a while, fewer and fewer people will be aware there was an entity called Atlantic Richfield."

The process of forgetting Arco will likely be a long one for Alaska. The name has been changed on the golden-hued tower in downtown Anchorage, but locals still call it the Arco building. And many of those who used to work for the company are still here. Maybe they draw a paycheck from BP or Phillips now, but that doesn't stop them from gathering to laugh and cuss and relive those bygone days when their Arco was strong and bold and proud.

Meyers, the last head of Arco's Alaska operation, summed up the company's legacy in a few words that stitch together its time in the Last Frontier— from modest beginnings to glorious heyday to abrupt departure. "We'll be remembered as the company that believed in Alaska when a lot of people didn't."

T. A. BADGER is an Anchorage-based reporter with The Associated Press. He has covered the state's oil industry since 1991.

MODERN ADVENTURERS

JUST BECAUSE WE'VE entered a new millennium of cell phones, jet flights, the Internet, and global communications, it doesn't mean that the wild frontier is gone. Here are tales of modern adventurers in Alaska, seeking out the wildest places and making their homes the old-fashioned way, crafting them from the wilderness in rugged and individual styles.

DANA STABENOW

Males for Sale: Cheap, Hairy

Talkeetna, population 330, zip code 99676, is about 120 miles from Anchorage. It began life as a Tanaina village, in 1916 became a work camp for construction of the Alaska Railroad, and now serves as the staging area for climbing Denali (known to people from Ohio as Mount McKinley). Talkeetna is Tanaina for "river of plenty;" Denali is either "home of the sun" or "the high one," or both.

Talkeetna also is the town that celebrates Winterfest.

What is Winterfest? Ah, thereby hangs my tale.

Make that tail. A foxtail, in fact.

Hanging from a fox-fur G-string.

But I'm getting ahead of myself. Winterfest is a December-long party featuring the Wilderness Women's Contest, the Talkeetna Bachelor Auction, a parade and a tree-lighting ceremony, bazaars and craft shows, appearances by Santa with real reindeer, cookie decorating, ice skating, snowshoe softball, broomball (whatever that is), the Taste of Talkeetna, a food drive, steak night at the Veterans of Foreign Wars post, and anything and everything else Talkeetnans can think up to get them through the solstice and into a new year.

Did I mention the Wilderness Women's Contest? And the Bachelor Auction? I did? I thought so.

The Wilderness Women's Contest commences at noon on the first Saturday of Winterfest. It was 22 degrees out with a light breeze, and the bonfire on Main Street was entirely too small. Hillary Schaefer of Ester, returning two-time champion, was heard to say that if she won a third time she was thinking of retiring.

The first round was hauling water in plastic buckets, with encouragement from bachelors (identified by badges) along the likes of "Hurry it up, woman, I want my tea!"

The next round consisted of making a sandwich, opening a beer and delivering both to a bachelor seated on a lawn chair in front of a television perched on a snowbank. The bachelors wore garbage bag slipcovers as a defensive measure against the, er, exuberance of the delivery. Each contestant then piled onto a snowmobile, drove to a woodpile, loaded wood into a sled, drove a circular course, unloaded the wood and raced back over the starting line.

The third round began with snagging a plastic foam salmon, followed by shooting three balloon "ptarmigan," crawling through a culvert, being surprised by a "moose," back through the culvert, up a tree to ring a bell, back through the culvert, grab a rifle, shoot the moose and run home. There were snowshoes in there somewhere, too, but by then, in spite of my father's parka and three pairs of socks, I was too cold to take notes.

Contest over, winner to be announced before the auction that evening. I went back to the Talkeetna Alaskan Lodge (about which more later) and thawed out in front of the lobby fireplace.

Let it be understood, here and now, that the Talkeetna Bachelor Auction is a charitable event. It is held to raise money for the Valley Women's Resource Center in Palmer. In this good cause, Talkeetna bachelors suffer themselves to be led up on a stage at the VFW and put themselves up for bid by any single woman with enough cash in her wallet. The winning bid buys a drink and a dance with the bachelor.

The annual event has been raising money since 1981, when a bunch of Talkeetna bachelors was sitting around the Fairview Inn and lamenting the lack of bachelorettes. "Let's throw a party and invite some," one guy said. "Let's call it a ball," another guy said. *Yeah!* everybody else said.

See? Altruists, every one of them.

Here I feel it appropriate to interject some Talkeetna mating calls. "*Want some!*" and "*I have a job!*" seemed popular, although "Puh-*leeze!*" was simple, direct and appeared remarkably effective. (I suppose this could have gone below, under "Do It Yourself," but oh well.)

There would be no shortage of bidders, as the packed room was proof positive that there is no fire marshal in Talkeetna. There was a steady stream of traffic between the bidding room and the bar next door, which goes a long way toward explaining the rest of the evening. Hillary Schaefer won her third Wilderness Woman title and was awarded a fur hat and a gold nugget. I asked her if she was going to retire; she looked thoughtful and said, "Well, this friend said she was going to kick my butt next year . . ."

Before I describe the auction, a word about the bachelors: Some of them clean up pretty well. Hell, some of them could answer the phone for 1-800-HUNK. Plus, they live in Talkeetna, which means they've got to have a sense of humor. What more do you want in a guy?

It was announced that the opening bid had been raised to $20 from the previous year's $5, cause for some grumbling. "Used to be you could get a perfectly good bachelor for 10 bucks," remarked one habitual bidder. Another said anxiously, "They don't take Visa? You can't charge a guy?"

One bachelor got things rolling, literally, by hootchy-kootchying up the aisle wearing a fox-fur G-string and a few strategically placed tatoos. Local songwriter Steve Durr sang "Wilderness Woman" ("She leaves man-sized tracks/she has a double-bladed ax/she's got a house of logs/she's got 36 dogs").

The first bachelor, tall, dark and wearing a tux, no less, brought $35, the second only $30. After that the crowd warmed up, $65, $75, $100. "Can I give mine away as a present?" one bidder wanted to know. "Can I bid on another?" a second inquired.

One bidder doubled her bid if her bachelor would take it off, take it *all* off. The crowd hummed "The Stripper," and he did, but he hid behind the podium so I didn't see anything. Honest. It happened twice and I didn't see anything twice. Would I lie?

Visiting author Peter Jenkins (*A Walk Across America*), under the influence of who knows what, bid $50 dollars on perennial bachelor Gak (no, that can't be right, that's Klingon worm food). Grok (no, that's Heinlein zenspeak) was beside himself, especially after Peter asked, "He's gotta dance with me, right?"

Regrettably, it was at this point that I lost any pretense of journalistic objectivity and gave Peter $5 to help with his bid. After that I completely lost my head and gave $10 to Penny, the woman bidding against him. Gorp (no, that's trail mix) begged over clasped hands, on his knees, plastered up against the wall, please, please, *please*, somebody, anybody outbid this guy! The bidding picked up: $50, $60, $75, $100, $150. A steady stream of people funneled cash to the two bidders, who waved fistfuls of bills and shouted out new bids, greeted with boisterous cheers and offers of more money.

The final bid? $250. The winning bidder? Penny. Grog (that's it!) made a beeline for Penny and very nearly prostrated himself before her in gratitude.

Let it be known, Grog has been bought before, and a past date ended the evening wading out of the Talkeetna River. You have been warned.

Alaska resident DANA STABENOW is the author of the bestselling Kate Shugak mysteries, including *Breakup*, *A Cold Day for Murder*, and *A Fatal Thaw*. She also writes a regular column for *Alaska Magazine*.

Excerpt from *Arctic Son*

JEAN ASPEN

The fifth of August and already the air smelled of fall. We had arrived near the solstice, six weeks before, and it was now too dark to read at night. It's hard to grasp how brief the Arctic summer really is. Ice is king of these northern latitudes, winter the true temperament of the land.

Hunting season opened in less than three weeks, and we would need to shift our attention from building to getting in our winter meat. Once rut starts, bull moose run off most of their summer fat in the ancient rituals of procreation. Domestic animals are never devoid of fat, but wild ones can be. Because truly lean meat has very few calories, it was critical that we hunt as soon as the weather was cool enough for meat to keep.

There were signs that it was going to be an early autumn. It remained cool, though mostly sunny. Blueberries were ripe (what we could find of them), their turning leaves like sprays of tiny rose petals to our knees. More gold showed in the willows across the river. The high peaks were russet ("sun-burned" as Luke put it) and birds were flocking up. We often heard their groups rushing like wind through the trees, talking excitedly of the coming migration. The moose too were restless with the advancing season and we would see them from time to time striding on long legs across the river bars. The trees seemed alive with busy squirrels, claiming territory and storing cones.

A sense of change vibrated the air, building like inaudible music. The land itself was aware, with a consciousness older than thought, dancing in interlocking patterns of perfect symmetry as it celebrated and released the harvest of summer. With the wisdom of millennia, each species embraced autumn and prepared in its own way for the coming cold and dark.

Perhaps we, like the symphony of life around us, sensed in some dim way that it was time to release our summer roles, for we seemed less jocular and became more tender with one another. Whatever became of our little band would be entirely up to us. If we were to survive the coming winter, we would need to set aside modern thinking and listen to the deeper wisdom of our beings, learning to harmonize with the cycles of the planet. We could not confront this land with the arrogance of our species, for it was vast and powerful beyond our imagination and cared nothing for our opinions.

The morning after John left, Tom fell ill with a severe migraine. I tucked him into the tent with a cold wash-cloth over his eyes, and he stayed there most of the day. It was sobering to work with Laurie on the unfinished cabin, worrying if Tom was okay.

"When I'm sick, I like to be fussed over," I told her as we sat twisting the augers, "but Tom hates it. So I've learned to leave him alone. Still, I'd rather keep an eye on him." Below us, Luke and the invisible Zaza were engrossed in a debate as they swung on the hammock. Shylo was sacked out in the sunlight, snoring loudly.

"You think it's more than a headache?" she asked, raising her gray eyes to mine.

"Mmmm . . . probably not. I keep thinking that his father died of a stroke at fifty and he's only four years short of that. But his blood pressure and cholesterol are fine. I'm sure it's nothing."

"Would you use the Emergency Transmitter?"

I sighed. "He wouldn't want me to. I don't know. I try to respect his wishes about his body. We've given one another permission to die, and neither of us is afraid of it. More afraid of medical bills than death."

Laurie listened and said nothing. She was willing to express her thoughts but never added anything to mine. It was a freedom that took some getting used to.

"There wouldn't be any point in using it if he died," I went on. We had all agreed on this in principle, but I found it disquieting to consider.

"I guess it depends on how we feel about going on alone," she said thoughtfully. "I think we'd be fine."

"We might have to settle on a smaller cabin. I don't know if the two of us could get those huge ridgepoles up. You and Tom maybe, but not me." It was hard to admit my limitations, but it was true.

"So forget the loft," she shrugged. "We could do it. The main thing I'm concerned about is the chain saw. Can you run it?"

"Yes . . . but it's been a long time, and I don't know the maintenance. Truthfully, I'm afraid of the damn thing. How about you?"

"I think I could learn," she answered.

It's good to specialize, I thought, but everyone should be competent. My aunt and uncle had told me how they started exchanging skills as they got older, preparing one another for life alone. He showed her how to manage investments and she taught him to cook. It made sense.

I glanced fondly at Laurie. She was thriving, her face open and happy, body tough and limber. A strong walker, she was daily more at home in the woods. I wondered if she was becoming me and I was becoming my mother. Perhaps that was as it should be: that we give away what we have learned and relinquish our roles. Certainly I was no longer the wild Arctic girl I fancied myself. It was painful to watch part of me die, but necessary to the birth of something new. It's unnatural (and in the end fruitless) to deny the next step.

There's always a gift in releasing the past, but it's sometimes hard to recognize. When I became a mother I thought I would expand, super-woman-like, to this new challenge. But pregnancy was hard on me; my body let me down. I discovered my weakness and my great strength. For the first time in my life I had to ask for help. I had to be vulnerable. Nor the lesson I wanted, but the one I needed to become a deeper, more compassionate, person.

My thoughts were interrupted by Luke. He was standing below us, blackened coffee pot gripped in both dirty hands.

"May I have grown-up coffee?" he asked.

"No, it wouldn't be good for you. And there's none made."

"I already made it," he told me, holding out the pot of cold water to which he had added grounds.

"That's just a waste of coffee," I blurted before I thought.

His face fell. "I made it for everyone," he said.

How quickly we forget our moments of inspiration when confronted with wasted coffee, I thought, shaking my head. "Come on," I said to Laurie. "Maybe it's time we did take a little break. Let's heat up Luke's coffee and have a snack."

To our great relief, Tom was his old self the next day.

Three days later we set off for more logs. We had cut and yarded the day before and hoped to finish up and raft them home. There was a strong south wind and the temperature hovered in the forties as we climbed the river bluff east of Lake Eugene across from John's Stone. It was a ways from camp, but we had cleaned the snags from the shoreline closer to home. The area looked promising from below but had proved a disappointment, for many of the larger trees were punky or riddled with ant colonies and the smaller ones were very twisted.

An expanse of brilliant autumn colors stretched below us as we topped the bluff and looked back: scarlet alpine berry, blueberry bushes ranging from pink-gold to purple festooned with smoky-blue droplets, scrubby arctic birch of salmon and flame orange, bright yellow poplar, and willows with leaves of pale gold edged in red. The river ran turquoise, muskegs were tawny expanses delineated with the somber olive of spruce forests, and the peaks shown forth in burgundy. Close at hand, lime green moss and pale lichens were laced with bright red and green cranberry plants, their berries shiny as enamelled jewelry. The sky was clear, but a high gray smudge stretched along the southern horizon, creeping towards us even as we watched.

"I should be able to drop these downhill," Tom said. "It won't be much fun working on this slope, but they ought to pull easy, if they don't run over us." His eyes were squinted into the wind and his hair and beard whipped about his shoulders.

"I don't like cutting in this wind," I stated.

"Well, I think it'll be okay. It's the river I'm not looking forward to. Where's Luke?"

"Sliding down the cutbank. Laurie is down there."

We stepped near the edge and could see eighty feet down to the water. Luke had climbed the steep hill and onto the loose cut. "Luke, that's danger-ous!" I bawled into the wind. And hard on your pants, I thought. "Don't climb so high!"

"It is not!" he yelled and launched himself on his bottom in a cascade of dirt and stones.

Tom shook his head and turned away, angry at Luke's defiance. I felt a wave of sadness. I could love my family, but I couldn't direct their lives. Not even Luke.

"There are ducks on Horseshoe Lake," Tom said, pointing east across the river. "Want me to try to get a couple for dinner?" He was observant and was often the first to spot wildlife. He seemed at home in this country, looking wild and somewhat aloof, as if he had traveled a step beyond the need for companionship.

I shook my head. "It's a shame to kill them for such a small amount of food."

"You're probably right, but I'm sure tired of beans."

"It won't be long, we'll have moose." Somehow it was easier to justify killing something big, for it would feed us a long time. I grinned at him sheepishly. "I'm an old softy, aren't I?"

That set me to wondering about how we value life. Why would a moose be more important than a duck? They both have the same components, only one is obviously larger.

I turned from the view and set off to scout for dead trees. Soon the whine of Tom's saw marked his progress along the bluff. I followed, balancing on the steep slope as I limbed the dead trees. The butts of several were riddled with ant collonies. Tom had cut the nest sections free and carefully replaced them on top of their stumps, capping each with a little hat of sod.

Earlier in the summer I had pulled one of these honey-combed logs over to the cabin site. When Tom sawed it into sitting stumps, three-quarter-inch carpenter ants boiled out. Thinking they would infest our home, we set the stumps over the fire. Several quarts of pearly eggs fell while the frantic members of the colony tried to rescue their brood, and the smell of burning flesh soiled the air. Since then we had been careful to respect ant trees.

The fate of an ant isn't the issue, I decided, but what it does to us when we approach the miracle of life without respect. If we carelessly wipe out another being, dismissing it as unimportant, we are spiritually impoverishing ourselves.

By the time we took our lunch break the sky was gray overhead and our patch of blue was being pushed north up the valley. A cold wind kicked spray off the river, blasting our cheerless fire and blowing sand into our eyes. After a hasty lunch we decided to take what we had and go home.

I gathered up tools and loaded the canoe while Tom and Laurie hefted logs over the slippery rocks and into the icy river, allowing me to keep my feet dry. I wasn't looking forward to paddling the light canoe into the wind and I knew they would be miserable on the raft.

"I'll try to get down through the rapids first in case you need help getting to shore," I said as they shoved it into the gray current and stepped aboard, poles in hand.

"Don't worry about us," Tom answered. "You'll have all you can manage with the canoe."

"Come on Luke," I called. "I'm gonna need your help paddling. Shylo! It's a long swim home girl. Better join us." I tied Shylo behind the first thwart and put Luke in the bow with his short paddle.

"How come I never get to steer?" he asked.

It was a rough trip home. Like a giant leaf the canoe spun in the wind, carried this way and that by the blasting air. It took all my strength to control it. Fortunately the wind didn't affect the heavy raft, and Tom and Laurie arrived home safely long before me. We were all cold by the time we had the logs pulled up on the bank beside our camp. It was to be our last trip.

The next day Tom and I were straddling a stockpile of logs near the cabin. "Okay, so what about these two?" I said, pointing out a modest pair as roof supports for the utility room. The ones I indicated were smaller than I wanted for purlins, but an acceptable compromise. "They need to be strong enough to hold up the snow."

"They will be. Look, it's only a ten-foot-span."

"Okay," I nodded. "I'll skin them."

It had been the same over the loft, me insisting that the supports be large and higher than our heads, Tom wanting to just get them up. I had a tendency to overbuild, but I was sure the effort would pay off.

It was late afternoon and had been overcast much of the day, but now the sun slanted toward the mountains and streaked brightly beneath the layer of dove gray, illuminating the autumn colors in an almost unnatural radiance. Across the river, Mt. Laurie stood forth in black silhouette, but the foreground was a blaze of yellow, green and red.

The other two were in the forest near camp gathering the deep sphagnum moss for chinking, and I could hear their voices through the woods. Large cracks showed between the logs of our new home, and one might justifiably call it a "moss cabin," the logs forming only a framework. But moss was plentiful and with careful gathering would not be harmed by our harvest.

"Okay," I heard Laurie say reasonably as they climbed the bench toward me, "do you want me to help you carry it?" Up the trail they trudged, each with a large duffel bag of moss. Laurie had hers on one shoulder. Luke seemed upset and was yanking his along the ground. Perhaps the strain of our long efforts and lack of a home was telling on him, but he had been volatile of late, angry and demanding even with Laurie.

"No! I want to do it myself!" he snapped. As she turned again he kicked the bag and yelled, "You're just stupid!"

Generally I allowed them their own relationship, but Laurie was so gentle there were times I felt obliged to step in. "That's enough, Luke," I informed him, reaching for the bag. He began to hop with rage, yanking the strap from my hand. "Stop!" I commanded. "You are very close to a smack!"

Furiously he kicked the bag. In one gesture I pulled him forward and delivered several sharp whacks to the dusty seat of his pants.

"You have no right to hit me!" he glared. "It's my body and no one has a right to touch it without my permission!"

"That's true, but sometimes I don't know what else to do. I can't allow one little kid to terrorize three adults. Are you going to settle down?"

"No!"

I forcefully gathered up my furious, kicking son and sat on a log while he struggled in my arms. His eyes filled with hurt and he whispered violently, "Don't make me cry in front of her! She's not part of the family!"

"Yes, she is," I informed him. "For the next year this is the only family we've got. You better start taking better care of your Laurie. You need her; we all do."

I held him until his enraged struggles ceased. Laurie had seated herself cross-legged on the ground and was chinking between the bottom logs, tongue sticking out the corner of her mouth in concentration as she packed the damp moss with a wedge-shaped tool Tom had fashioned from wood.

"You have a right to your feelings," I told Luke. "And you have a right to express them. But you don't get to abuse anyone. You don't get to scream at people or hit them. Can I release you now?"

"Uh-huh."

He walked away with as much dignity as he could muster and took refuge in the hammock with his imaginary friends. Then he moved to where Shylo was napping on the sawdust pile and began covering her with wood shavings until she got up and left. After a while I saw him laughing with Laurie, teasing her to blow on his tummy as he rolled in the moss beside her.

My eyes swept the clearing and the burgundy hills. Everywhere the alpine bearberry plants were arrayed in scarlet and the blueberry bushes were layered in shades of pink and purple. This was the day Phil and I had stopped walking upriver and started work on a cabin twenty years before. How glad I was that ours was now nearing completion! By next August, I thought, I will have spent six summers watching this river go by and nine (that I could remember) in northern wilderness. That was a lot of my life. For Luke it would be four of his seven, an even bigger percentage.

It was getting late and we soon called it a day, stacking our tools in a corner of the cabin and trudging down the familiar trail to camp for a dinner of apple sauce and bean burritos spiced with powdered cheese. We found comfort in our simple, familiar routines. A certain blue plastic cup was always used to mix the powdered milk and an old margarine container held leftover oatmeal from the morning. Each person had favorite branches for his socks and a place in the pavilion for rain gear or jacket.

"It's important to know where things are as the season advances," I told my crew as we gathered about our evening fire. "For one thing it's getting dark nights, but also, one of these mornings we'll wake to snow on the ground. If we mislay a tool we may not find it until spring."

Soon conversation turned, as it often did now, to hunting. Dredging up my mother's advice and my own experiences, I shared what I knew of shooting, animal habits and butchering. Tom had hunted squirrels and rabbits as a youth, but Laurie had never fired a gun until she arrived in the Arctic. Tom had set up a target and taught her the basics of each gun in camp, and she proved to be a decent, though hesitant, shot.

"A moose looks big," I told them, "but your actual target isn't. The head is mostly sinus cavities, muscle and bone with a brain the size of an orange. If you aim for the spinal cord in neck or back, you must hit a relatively small area. The middle is all guts. Your best shot is six inches up from the belly, just behind the point of the elbow, where the heart and lungs are. Even so, don't expect him to drop right away. It takes awhile for an animal that size to die.

"Look for a big, fat bull," I went on. "A good animal will give us twice the meat of a poor one. It's surprising how much we'll eat in a year. We may have to take two, but we can decide that after we get the first one. They'll be traveling soon, and if we're out, we'll run into them."

"Do you think we'll get any caribou?" Laurie asked.

"It's hard to tell. We may see the edge of the migration around November, but we can't count on it. And we'll need to get our moose in September. I wish we had a meat house up."

"Are you worried about bears?" she asked me.

I hesitated. "I'd sure hate to have to shoot one," I answered truthfully. "Grizzlies are rare, not here perhaps, but in general. We'll hang the meat high in the trees and hope the bears will be denning soon. I've never had a problem with them, though many people have."

"What about wolves?" Laurie wanted to know.

"No problem unless they find the moose before we get it all hauled home. They're big eaters, but they're shy. The main trick will be to kill our animal upstream and near enough to retrieve easily. Moose are really heavy. And like my mother told me, never shoot one in the water or you'll have to stand there and butcher; you're not going to move it."

"I was just thinking of what it'll be like to eat solid food again," Laurie said. "On our gums."

"Haven't you eaten meat before?" Luke asked.

"Oh, sure. Not moose meat, but I've eaten lots of meat."

"That really gets stuck in your gums," he informed her.

Tom and Laurie were seated together on a bench sharing a bowl of rehydrated apple sauce while I sat near the fire cooking tortillas in the caste iron-skillet. Luke was quietly removing "special" pieces of firewood from the pile and stashing them in his "fort." Shylo watched with keen interest, and as soon as his back was turned, I saw her making off with the prized sticks.

"I miscalculated on the nails," Tom informed us. "I'm going to run short before I get all the floor in."

"I suppose you could dowel it," I suggested.

"I may have to, but it's a lot of work."

"There are a few nails over at the Topo Camp," Laurie offered.

"I was thinking of that. Want to head over after dinner and maybe do a little fishing down at Pike Slough?" he asked her.

"But we're going to play poker tonight!" Luke interjected. He was becom-

ing a fairly good player, but unwilling to bet with candies, so we had switched
to pumpkin seeds. Shylo liked poker because she thought there would be
M&M's, but quickly lost interest with the new stakes.

"We did say that," I agreed.

"Shhh! Shhh!" Tom suddenly froze and we all followed his gaze onto the
delta. A large bear was rolling towards us, wind ruffling his coppery, grizzled
coat. He had appeared as if by magic within forty yards of where we sat. We
held our breaths, delighted, and perhaps a bit apprehensive, to see this beautiful apparition. Within moments he sensed us, and with remarkable speed,
turned and vanished into the willows.

"You see, Luke. There are bears here," I told him as if solidifying my point.
But it wasn't long before I saw him start for the bar to investigate.

After dinner we set large kettles of water over the grill to heat for baths. It
was too cold now to brave the river and we took turns in the galvanized tub.
We had a lovely view and bathing tended to be a more prolonged and enjoy-
able time. There were still bugs and we helped one another by pouring water
over the head and back to keep the bather warm and protected from bites.
Tom usually went first, for he valued clean water. Laurie and I weren't as fussy,
preferring the fuller tub as new water was added. Luke was always last,
remaining immersed with his toys until the bath nearly iced over.

"I think you can stop losing weight now," I told Tom as I washed his back.
He was proud of the fact that he had taken up five notches on his belt, but he
was beginning to look as thin and sinewy as Gandhi, the muscles in his arms
and legs standing out in ropes. It hardly seemed fair that I was still buxom
while my companions had changed dramatically. Laurie belonged on the
cover of a body-building magazine, but I thought Tom looked a bit gaunt and
wild. His long hair and beard were stringy, and without clothes his sun
weathered head seemed a bit large for his white body.

"Look! Geese!" said Laurie softly.

Tom reached for his glasses and we all turned to watch. Into view drifted
a small family, rafting quietly downriver. The young were almost the size of
their parents and all of them were molting and unable to fly. When they spotted us they pulled back, paddling like tiny kayaks into an eddy to confer. It
thrilled me to see their brave little expedition, so much like our own, but
without possessions or home. I couldn't view them as flying drumsticks.
Geese mate for life and may live thirty years. They travel in families and rely

on the wisdom of elders during their migrations. I silently wished them well on their long journey.

Luke stood watching, one hand unconsciously working a loose tooth. "It came out!" he said in dismay. He thrust the tiny pearl at Tom and beamed, showing a new gap in his lower jaw. "Can I put it under my pillow for the Tooth Faerie?"

Tom held out his hand and examined the worn incisor. "Why that's wonderful, Luke! Let's see the hole." Gently he wiggled the neighboring tooth. "Wow, looks like there's another one loose. Want me to try and pull it?"

"No!" Luke answered, backing hastily. "I'm saving it. There's steam coming off your head, Dad. Can you see it? Let me pour more water over you."

I put the tooth in a film can and Luke carefully tucked it under his pillow that evening as he settled in for the night.

"Do you think she'll bring me a quarter?" he asked.

"It's hard to say about faeries," I warned. "They're very capricious. That means unpredictable. And if she brought a quarter, you wouldn't be able to spend it. We'll just have to wait and see. Maybe you'll get moose dropping or something."

He looked appalled. "You really think so?"

"No. I was just kidding. I'm sure it'll be something nice."

"Mama, I am lonely out here," he confided.

"I know." I smoothed the hair back from his eyes.

"I've been making puzzles," he told me. "I smash rocks until they break into pieces, then I try to put them back together again."

"I think it's neat the way you invent things," I said. It was hard for him, I knew, but there was a gift here too. I thought of his little friends who were already miniature Yuppies. They didn't dig holes or nail sticks together. It seemed to me that there was a kind of childhood poverty amid the opulence.

"And I have my dog," he went on. "She's so playful and I really love her. She's like a sister to me. She bites me and hurts me, but she loves me anyway. Don't you Shylo?" He sat up and threw his arms around her furry neck. She endured his embrace as the price exacted for her spot in the tent, but there was no affection in her eyes.

That night we saw the full moon for the first time. It rose late in the evening, pale and big in a southern sky that spread mint green behind black clouds. In the Arctic the moon is up for two weeks and gone for two. During the summer there's only a sliver that one rarely notices in the bright sky. Winters are the time of full moons, and the soft, brilliant light is most welcome when the sun has gone from the land.

We had arisen for a nocturnal visit and stood a long moment watching it. A touch of ice was in the wind and about us the darkening wilderness loomed vast, silent and suddenly unfamiliar. I thought of bears as I shivered in my bare feet and night clothes, and of how dependent I was on vision. I'd grown used to the constant light and now felt vulnerable in this strange, new world.

Luke woke us early with excited cries. The good faerie had left a small toy under his pillow.

We put up the stove that day, a makeshift system out of the wind that now served us better than the fire. Tom was hard at work on the floor. He had fashioned a simple jig for holding short logs while he ripped them using the hand-eye coordination gained through years of cutting glass. Unaware that our chain saw was designed for pruning small branches, and could not (according to the manufacturer) be used for such a purpose, he chewed slowly through them. We hoped it would hold up, for we needed four-hundred-fifty square feet of floor and loft, plus boards for furniture.

Now Tom squatted, planing and fitting his hard-won "boards" onto the joists. Luke was busy with his new toy under the shelter of the loft. Laurie and I were setting the gable logs. Each level was won with great effort now. It had turned colder and a gray drizzle made the icy logs slippery and treacherous. Perched high on the exposed walls, Laurie looked frightened and grim as she drilled the endless holes that would pin the gables in place. These stood alone above the sides, so the twelve foot wall seemed fragile and rocked somewhat with our movements.

"I have to remember to breathe," I said as I balanced to drive in a dowel with the back of my ax. "I think that's why I get so tired."

Laurie managed a weak smile.

"One more pin, Kiddo and we set the last purlin and then the ridgepole." Tom and I had placed the first purlin the day before, each taking an end as we rolled the huge log slowly up the gables. Although I was unable to lift it with my arms, I could brace my knees under the log and use my leg muscles. It was very tricky with nothing to hang on to. Despite her fear of heights, Laurie had climbed ahead of us to film the process.

"I don't think I can get the ridgepole," I confessed.

"The ominous log," Laurie intoned, looking down at it.

"Hey, I almost had Jeanie talked into letting me make it into lumber," Tom called up from his work. He paused to remove his glasses and wipe the sweat from his eyes.

"What talked her out of it?"

By afternoon heavy rain forced us to retreat to the tent. There we sat amid damp folds of down and played poker as evening fell. The temperature was in the thirties and the tent felt clammy in the wet air. Outside a double rainbow spanned our valley arching into the gold and amber of balsam poplars across the river.

The following day we hauled both the final purlin and the massive ridge-pole onto the gables and notched them in place. It was a long awaited mile-stone, much talked of and feared, and it completed the main structure of the cabin. I brought up the purlin with Tom, but Laurie did the big one. It was all she could do to manage it, and I could see her strain to the limit of her strength as she slowly worked her end up the gables. I held my breath watching her lift, muscles quivering and knees shaking as she fought for balance on the eight-pound maul while Laurie and I skinned poles for the roof. Tom was busy with the floor. There was still a great deal to do, and it was difficult to know which way to divide our energy. We needed a couple of hundred poles for the roof and formed expeditions into the wet lands southeast of the cabin to gather small dead trees. Luke was anxious to help and managed to chop through a number of them unassisted.

That evening Tom and Laurie visited Pike Slough via the Topo Camp and returned with six grayling and a can of nails. I helped them clean the fish, but the water was so cold it made my hands burn. Laurie was as happy as a kid on Christmas morning with the windfall of nails she had pulled, and settled on a bench before the fire to straighten them.

Though the peaks remained white, snow soon disappeared from the low country and our world reverted to a patchwork of autumn colors. We celebrated the entire week that Laurie turned twenty-nine, cooking special treats and doing small kindnesses to make her feel loved. We sang "Happy Birthday" and ate poppy seed cake with hard sauce and shared the last of the apricots on pancakes for breakfast. She cried when she opened the surprise present from her mother.

She was doing most of the rafter skinning while I hauled the poles home. My hands were too painful and weak to use the drawknife long and Tom was deep into the floor, needing to permanently set the stove before we put the main roof on. Once she had enough rafters skinned, it only took a few hours to place them over the utility room. The next day we covered them with a plastic tarp and laid a roof of sod. Not wanting to disturb the ground, we cut the sod some distance away, from a bank that was collapsing into the river. Tom fashioned a stretcher of poles and we carried the turves between us.

"Isn't it beautiful!" we said to one another as we stood outside the front door in the blue shadows of evening looking at the new sod roof over our utility room. Crowberry and kinnikinnick sprouted in a colorful quilt, a bit of the ground transported above our heads. A small, solid-looking room had emerged from our log corral. It seemed dark, damp and very quiet, like entering a cave, and I secretly wondered if I would enjoy being so closed in. I found that it depressed as well as exhilarated me to step inside, the first "inside" we had known in two months.

"Now we have a place to get out of the rain," I said aloud. "If we had to, we could live here."

"I don't want to move in until we have most of the interior work done," Tom told us. "We'll just be in our own way. Tomorrow I'll cut the gables to the correct pitch and we can get started on the main cabin roof."

"It's a real work of art," Laurie said, as if she didn't quite believe it.

"It is," Tom agreed.

"Every log is so beautiful, so different," she went on. "And I love what you're doing with the door between the rooms. Who'd have thought to cut it into an arch?"

He grinned. "I didn't want to just slap something up. But I'll be glad to get inside. You know, we've only taken three days off since we started? And we spent those walking."

"I want to acknowledge that this hasn't been easy for Luke," I said, drawing him close. "You're a brave kid. But we're going to have a real home soon. Can you imagine it now?"

"Sort of," he answered doubtfully. "Walls and door. But it doesn't look very cozy." Slits of light showed between the upper logs, and open holes gaped black where the windows and door would be. I had to agree that it looked far from inviting.

"Not yet, but it will," I reassured him. "Wait 'til we finish chinking and Daddy gets the floor in. That'll make it seem a lot lighter inside," I promised, trying to convince myself. "Are you happy to be here?"

"Well, I'm glad to be away from Billy, that big, mean kid at my school."

I laughed. "It'll be more fun once we can take some time off."

"I'm going down to the beach to start taking my time off right now," Luke decided.

"Please don't go out of sight. We'll be working up here a little longer. Maybe you could pick some berries nearby. I'll make a blueberry bread," I promised.

"Ohhh, that sounds good," Laurie added. "Let me put my tools up and I'll go picking with you."

Tom took time from the floor to chisel window sills and make frames for the two south windows in the utility room. Most of our windows would be eighteen by thirty-six inches. Eventually they would be double glazed, but for now, keeping rain out was the main concern.

I worked chinking the utility room and hauling home rafter poles. Laurie was still skinning them, and uncomplaining workhorse that she was, had started to look discouraged. The long grind was beginning to wear us all down. We were weary and seemed to move slowly and ineffectually. Luke whined and was out of sorts, often hurting himself, falling over logs or egging the dog on until she bit him. We were in need of a rest but feeling too pressed for time to take one.

"Getting burned out?" I asked Laurie. It was drizzling again. She had on my black-and-white wool jacket, her hat pulled low, leather gloves cold and soggy.

"Skinner's burn-out," she joked. "Nasty stuff."

"You can trade places with me, if you like."

"What are you up to?"

"I've been digging in the toilet."

"Ah! You really know how to tempt a girl," she said, moving her hands as if weighting two exciting propositions.

"What about lunch then?"

"Better all the time."

We gathered about the stove in the roofless cabin, holding our fingers out to the faint heat. The damper was merely laid on top of the pipe and the stove didn't draw well. Laurie and Luke were singing "Froggy Went a Courtin'." I lifted the lid from the skillet and carefully worked the spatula under the blueberry bread and flipped. "I turned it! Did you see?" I said, triumphantly.

"No, can you do it again?" Laurie asked.

"Yes. Tomorrow."

"Boy, is that crust black," Luke commented.

"I like it that way," I answered. Just then sunlight pierced the clouds and the falling rain became a million diamonds.

"We need a ladder for the loft," Tom observed as I passed around the tin plates. "As soon as we chink these walls, we won't be able to climb them."

A few minutes later the clouds ripped open. Hard rain pelted steadily, and there was nothing to do but retreat to the tent. We remained there for two days while the forest became soggy and the thick moss soaked up water like a sponge. The steady drum of rain on the tarp was accented by the deep growl of the river and creek as they rose and rose in a wild torrent of mud.

At first we slept a good deal, recovering from our days of labor. Within the cold, damp tent we were packed like cordwood, needing to turn over practically in tandem. Tom usually slept on his back, sometimes with a head on each shoulder. He suffered with his arms and a wrist injury so that his hands were often asleep at night. I had back and arm problems and lay on my side, usually with my knees in Tom's ribs. Luke sprawled, arms and legs flopped out and body sometimes turned sideways. Shylo took up the foot space. Only Laurie was a gentle and reasonable bed partner. She fit into a depression known as "Laurie's Hollow," and because of the contours of the ground, was not able to roll far.

As the downpour continued I made quick forays to bring in cold oatmeal, yesterday's apple sauce and leftover corn bread with peanut butter. It was soggy and unpleasant fare and we swallowed it without ceremony, crouched in our small sanctuary. When these ran out, we lived on trail mix and powdered milk. And still the rain fell. I read aloud to Luke from Kipling's *Jungle Books* while the others napped. Then Laurie entertained him from a large volume of Calvin and Hobbes.

It was fairly sophisticated humor, but Luke was captivated. Calvin was destined to become a major hero and Luke learned to recite every line. Soon he was reading it to himself and telling us endless Calvin jokes. It's alarming to have a six-year-old enamored with a role model of this caliber, but I was pleased at his new interest in reading.

The storm lifted just enough the second evening for me to get a fire started and fix a hot supper. It drizzled while we ate, but I managed to cook extra in case we should need it later. We returned to the damp tent as black night and more rain descended.

It's better to get up and face the weather than lie here another day," I said as I shoved the reluctant dog under the tent flap and crawled after her into a quiet rain. "I'm going up to the cabin. I'll call you when the stove is lit." One becomes lethargic and depressed imprisoned in a cold tent eating trail mix. Even if we couldn't work, I knew we'd be better off outside.

The river was at our door, higher than I had ever seen it here. An icy flood of roiling, muddy water buried the whole delta. Big trees hurried past, ripped from banks upstream, and I clearly heard the roar of Luke's Creek; it would be days before we could cross it. So much for moose hunting, I thought. Three of the four quadrants were now closed to us, and in the remaining direction lay dense thickets. We may as well put all our efforts into getting a roof on, I decided. Besides, we needed to handle our lives here before we undertook anything else.

The view from camp was grand and awesome in its power. To the north, Flat Top emerged white and clear above the pearl-gray clouds that spilled like waterfalls over the lower ridges. I stood transfixed, watching the tendrils of fog curl down the slopes and dissolve. Above me clouds scudded, a gray-and-gold river of sky glistening with shafts of sunlight as they melted into one another. Winter was rushing down from the pole to reclaim its land. Across the valley the country lay wet and somber, painted in tones of yellow, brown and olive green.

The stove was full of water and charred wood; the cabin a dismal mess. After I got a fire going, we stood about the smoldering stove, holding stiff fingers to the lukewarm metal in the rain. We breakfasted on cold bread, then Tom and I climbed the slippery logs to nail a tarp over the ridgepole for shelter. Gradually we picked up our work, shaping wet boards and skinning soggy logs. The river was still rising. I kept checking on it and finally pulled our canoe higher into the woods. Luke expressed concern that our camp might be washed away, but I assured him we were safe. As the afternoon wore on, the clouds began to lift, and ragged blue holes appeared in the sky. By evening it was freezing but almost clear.

For the next few days we worked in a fever, skinning and placing the rafters, butting them against a retainer log doweled in place outside of the plate log, then nailing and tying them down with wire. Tom and I balanced on the slanted roof while Laurie handed up poles and bags of moss. I chinked where the rafters crossed the gables and plate logs, making as tight a seal as possible before we covered them with plastic. The roof was high, and the steep front pitch made it difficult to work on. I was afraid the sods would slide off, so I cut two long poles and Tom secured them horizontally over the slippery rafters.

For two days we laid the sod. It drizzled as we cut the muddy squares of turf from the river bank, carried them to the cabin, relayed them up the ladder, and carefully placed them on the roof. Luke was amazingly strong and persistent as he helped. It was an heroic group effort, and finally the main roof was safely covered.

Tom returned to his work on the floor and finished enough to permanently position the stove. Centrally located, it stood on cast-iron legs over the smooth yellow bit of floor, a foot above the icy ground. From its top emerged a short piece of stovepipe and then the lovely sheet metal oven that my sister's fiancé had built. Shaped like a flattened donut, one circle inside another, the oven would use heat from the smoke. The back was covered and on the front was a hinged door and thermometer. Above it the pipe with damper rose to pierce the roof.

"It's fun to make do with what you have," Tom said as he nailed flashing made from an old gas can over the purlin to shield it from the heat of the stovepipe. He was perched on a log wedged between my new ladder and the half-finished loft. He whistled as he happily banged away. He was a good whistler and I enjoyed listening to him. Nearby, Laurie was using the jack plane, smoothing the ripped logs into boards with a rhythmic scraping sound. It was cold inside and Luke was dressed in his wool coat and cap, crouched on the small section of completed floor, building a helicopter from Legos. From the doorway Shylo watched him for a chance to make off with the toys, but he kept a close eye on her.

I was balanced on a crate, packing moss between the upper logs. I felt weary from the long push. The cabin seemed far from inviting with its dark, muddy floor transected with shin-high joists. I was tired of the rain and of cold wet feet. It seemed like weeks since I had taken a bath or put on clean clothes.

"I'm gonna quit early and go hunting," Tom stated, driving home the last nail and swinging to the ground. Meat was still the great unknown in our welfare and we were apprehensive. Now that we could again cross the creek, we went forth day after day.

"It's kind of late," I told him. "If you get one we'll have to stay up all night butchering."

"But at least we'd have it."

"Can I light a fire in the stove now?" I asked. "Maybe dry the place out a bit?" We had discontinued using it to lay the roof.

"Not until tomorrow. I want the putty to set up first."

"I was hoping to take a hot bath. It seems like forever since my feet have been warm. I'm just feeling all in."

"Miss Jeanie," Laurie said kindly, "I'll be happy to build a fire outside and bring up the water for you to have a bath."

"Would you? Oh, that would mean a lot. I'm kind of down right now. I think a bath would do me good, even if I put on the same clothes. My hair is full of dirt from placing the sods."

"Let's all have one," Tom suggested. "It is late for hunting. I'll get the water, Laurie, if you start the fire out front. It's too nasty down on the beach."

"It's gonna be inconvenient hauling water up here," I said.

"Oh, we'll get used to that," Tom told me. "It's seeing the river I'm gonna miss."

We were all silent, thinking of the living river that had flowed through our lives for a summer, as much a part of us as breathing.

"Well," I sighed "we can always move down in the spring." Here we were, I thought, anxious to inhabit our new cabin and already planning to abandon it for a tent.

Tom and Laurie set out hunting at first light the next morning. I could hear the squirrel alarms across the river, marking their progress towards Pike Slough. Laurie was unsure of herself and they traveled together along the dry river channels between the gold avenues of poplar and dark strips of spruce forest. Shylo always stayed close to me and I was not concerned that she would follow them.

Luke and I rose after they had gone. The day was still, the sky clear. Cold sunlight streamed bright across the gliding river. There was heavy frost on the beach and yesterday's tracks were frozen. Luke played near the water as I made breakfast, prying up thin slabs of sandy ice with red fingers and tasting them.

"Yuck," he intoned as he bit into the gritty ice. He handed it to the dog and tried another. "I can hardly wait for it to snow," he told me. "I hope it gets really deep so I can make tunnels."

Arriving at the cabin, I lit the stove, delighted to discover that the oven doubled the usable heat. Despite the gaping door and window holes and dearth of chinking in the upper walls, our home began to warm and dry. I took off my coat for the first time in days. An amber, woody light suffused our new shelter and I looked around contentedly. It had changed dramatically with the addition of a roof. Even Luke could see the potential. The floor was growing daily and four unusually large and straight-grained boards leaned against the wall, destined to be our kitchen counter. But there was still a great deal to do before we could really move in. It was no longer pleasant down by the river. Despite Tom's protests, we had almost abandoned our old kitchen, so life was now complicated with possessions underfoot. Gradually the damp, awkward spaces between the joists had filled with wooden crates, buckets of food, camera equipment and garbage cans of clothing. Not wishing to leave our things unattended, we were slowly transferring the tonnage inside. We still slept in the cold, cramped tent, but with the loft nearing completion, I couldn't imagine doing it much longer.

Humming to myself, I mixed bread and let it rise in a bucket hung from the ridgepole, a surprise lunch for my two hunters who had breakfasted on cold leftovers. I was pleased at the way my new ladder had turned out. Building it had been hard on my wrists, but left me with a feeling of competence. I was reminded of something Laurie had said about the joy of appreciating things. What profit a man if he should gain the whole world and not value it? In part, it was this very austerity that I wanted for my son, and through it, the ability to cherish life.

The following morning, Tom and I set out early. We paddled upstream above the creek mouth, where he let me out before crossing the river to walk the far shore. He wanted to hunt together, feeling perhaps protective of me, but I preferred being alone, my attention on the country. So we compromised, taking separate routes but keeping in touch.

I buttoned my wool jacket, glad to have dry feet for the moment. It had been drizzling at dawn, but the rain seemed to be lifting. Glowing like embers, their undersides afire with sunrise, buttermilk clouds rode the long ridge to the east. Above me the sky was mottled pink and blue like the hand-blown glass I had loved to work with. I caught a glimpse of Tom as I entered the willows.

After the hard frost the fall colors were fading and spruce cones cut by the squirrels had opened. The scarlet of bearberries had turned to rust, and Arctic birch had gone from flame to brown. Everywhere leaves were withering, dropping in a quiet rain of gold. The sharp smell of autumn brought back memories older than thought, as I quietly followed the curve of the beach. Moose were on the move and I could see their deep tracks crisscrossing the damp mud. It was time to hunt: the smells told me so. Before my conscious memory began, my father had carried me on his shoulders through the falling leaves to butcher moose. It was the way of life in this land, the celebration of bounty that secured a family through the coming winter.

The world was so beautiful and different now. Quietly I wandered through the bushes, dark spruce to the left, the open river on my right, fading leaves like yesterday's flowers spilling about my waist. Soon my legs were soaked from the dripping foliage. I carried my mother's old .30-06 comfortably on a leather strap over one shoulder, my knife on my belt, matches and repellent in my pocket, and a chunk of cold muffin in one hand, which I chewed as I stepped along. The rifle had open sites, easier to keep in alignment than a scope, and I had walked hundreds of miles with it. It felt somehow like an old friend in this benign position.

I was thinking about the hunting ceremonies of people who lived on the land that affirmed their place in the cycle. "The wolves and the caribou are one," the Eskimos had said. It seemed important that I, too, purify myself in some way before partaking in this great mystery of life and death. For me to intrude in the ageless dance of moose, wolf and forest, I needed to approach it with humility. Inwardly I blessed the great moose and thanked him for the gift of his life as I prepared myself for a violence I disliked.

I wondered at my place in Creation. As a girl on the Mackenzie River I had wished to become a part of Nature. But, we can no longer live a totally "natural" existence. Aside from our great numbers, our bodies are embarrassingly fragile. Nearly devoid of protective fur, we are subject to cold, sunburn and abrasions, and have neither the teeth nor digestive systems to live on food in its unprocessed state.

Somehow, in raising our celebrated cerebral powers, we had become separated from the rest of life, shut off, as it were, from the Garden perhaps as much by our knowledge of good and evil as our physiques. Certainly man has reached a stage of moral responsibility and the freedom to learn how to use it. We cannot go back the way we have come. The only path is forward, through wisdom. Thus do we stumble about in the dark, seeking a return to the Garden, not as innocent children, but as Gardeners.

The river bar ended in a cutbank at the bend and the going soon became more difficult. Tom kept pace with me on the far shore and I lifted a hand to him whenever he appeared, small and dark between the trees. Near John's Stone I surprised a large animal and it made off rapidly through the brush. I didn't get a good look but thought it was a bear. The evidence of fresh digging in the area seemed to confirm this. Tom had scaled the high bluff and I waved at him before cutting inland to check Horseshoe Lake. These lakes are common in the north, remnants of the river left behind by her changing moods.

As I emerged from the trees into open marsh land, I could see a large cow moose, water to her belly, feeding in the middle of the long, shallow lake. The reeds around the edge had turned gold and a faint mist clung to the water. I stalked her, keeping two dwarf spruce between us as I worked my way over the boggy ground and through the brush. Every time she put her head under, I hurried forward. When she raised it, water dripping from the bell under her chin, I froze. The ground was wet and very cold as I crawled the last few feet.

She was a beautiful animal. Bereft of a calf, she had used her summer to pack away a thick pad of fat. I lay there in the wet sedges for most of an hour, listening to the voices in my head: My mother's, "Never shoot a moose in the water . . ."; Tom's voice, "It's too far to haul a moose from that lake when the river is low . . ."; and the background of my concern, "What if we don't get another chance?"

The cow was a picture of health and serenity as she browsed undeterred by the freezing water, and I cringed at the thought of piercing her sleek body with my bullet. She was broadside to me and so close I could hear her breathing. Her big ears remained above the surface, scanning the exposed shore like radar as she listened for danger, while about her milled half a dozen ducks. They didn't appear to be feeding and seemed to simply enjoy her company.

My joints were beginning to ache and I was starting to shiver. With a smile at the moose, I rose. She jumped and started across the lake, taking great, splashing strides directly away from me. Within moments, she was gone and the marsh was empty. We think of the moose as "awkward" and "clumsy," and may fail to see the animal through our opinion of it. A giant member of the deer family, moose are beautiful, perfectly adapted to the moods of this difficult land, and amazingly graceful in crossing it. Like timid ghosts, they melt into the forest and disappear before your eyes. I defy anyone to follow a moose over this boggy, pitted ground and not come to respect them.

My clothes were wet and I was cold, but I felt suddenly happy as I turned for home. My life had been brushed by magic. Just as I reached the river, I heard Tom shoot, clear and far away. I held my breath and counted shots. One, two, three. God, I hope he got it! My worse fear is to wound an animal and have it escape.

It was a long walk home and I arrived tired and hungry. Tom was waiting by the canoe, impatient to get back to his moose. I checked the load for pack frames, rope, buckets, skillet and lunch items before we paddled across the river. Then Tom lead the way about seven hundred yards inland through stands of yellow poplar. There a modest bull lay, shot through the head and neck. It was a good location, the ground was dry and fairly level. I thanked my stars I had resisted the cow. Better a hundred shots not taken than one done poorly.

"I'm so excited," Luke said, extracting his little, red pocket knife. "I can hardly wait to start skinning."

"Let's take a moment to thank the moose," Tom told him, kneeling beside the animal and putting an arm around his son's shoulders. "This is not like ordering a hamburger. Somebody else had to kill that animal. We had to kill this one."

For a few moments we gathered quietly around the big, dead creature, patting his smooth, brown fur and silently acknowledging his life. "Thank you moose," we each said in turn and smiled shyly at one another, knowing that something great had been given to us and something beautiful had been taken away.

The day had turned warm and the host of insects that traveled with the moose now alighted upon us. I built a fire and Tom fastened his tag around the antler, though no one would ever see it. It took all of us to maneuver the heavy carcass onto its back, chest as high as my hips, a position it was too thin to maintain. We pulled the antlers back and planted them under the great head, then I tied the top front leg to them with a piece of parachute cord and took out my old knife to make the first incision. The skin was tough and my technique less than perfect, as I slowly worked up the belly.

"We need to peel the hide back before I slit the abdomen," I told them. I was the only one who had ever butchered anything larger than a rabbit, but the others were eager to help, each whittling away at some part of the great animal. Already the guts were beginning to bloat, distending the abdominal wall so that care was needed as I ran my blade through the sheaths of connective tissue and released the soft, hot billows of intestines.

"Now let's roll him sideways and try to paw the guts out." I wiped strands of hair from my eyes with a bloody hand. "They're fastened along the spine and you have to get in there and cut them free without puncturing anything or we'll have a mess."

"Nothin' up my sleeves," Laurie retorted, as she felt around in the entrails. She grinned at me and wiggled her eyebrows. "I can cook too!"

Luke was tugging away at the thick hide, working his knife ineffectually but with determination. "Don't try this at home, kids!" he chimed in for an invisible audience.

"This makes me feel like I'm part of a clan," Laurie told us. "There's something very ancient about all of us butchering together. We'll have meat tonight and the drums will play. Something like that."

Butchering a moose is always hard, gory work and I had forgotten much in twenty years. The appendages and organs are well fastened together and not intended for easy dismantling. As I leaned into the cavernous chest, my back ached and my hands were fatigued from pulling against the heavy hide. Luke soon tired of skinning and wandered about while we called him back again and again. A strong, meaty smell hung on the air and I kept an eye out for bears. Strangely, one had recently died here and we could see the bones, still pink, scattered in the brush. It hadn't been killed or even scavenged by larger animals, for the skeleton was mostly intact, and we speculated on the cause of death.

The Arctic is a hard place to live. It's a land of great contrast where the plant growth, which feeds all life, is almost tropical for a few weeks then falls to nothing. Migratory and seasonally dormant animals exploit this brief abundance, but the rest must have strategies to survive the other nine months. Niches are limited and the number of resident species is small. Life often exists here at the edge of its requirements. This creates a natural instability, and when one species crashes, it may pull several others with it.

It was late afternoon when I stopped to fry up a meal of liver, kidney fat, and pieces of meat haggled from the pelvis. There was no water for washing and our hands were crusted with blood. It was the first fresh meat we had eaten all summer and tasted wonderful.

"Doesn't Shylo look wild?" I commented as we squatted around the fire eating with our knives. She had been gobbling morsels snatched from the gut pile and her face was streaked with blood. She now circled us warily, wolfish eyes alert.

"Shylo?" Laurie laughed. "You ought to see yourself!"

I grinned. "Tom, ya done good. Shall I cook up some more?"

"Not for me," he answered. "It's almost too rich." He wiped his hunting knife on the leaves and reached into a bucket for the stone to sharpen it. "Laurie, did I tell you the history of this knife?"

Most of our knives had a story, but the strangest was this one. My cousin Ralph had longed to win the Congressional Medal of Honor and volunteered for one tour after another in Vietnam. It was secret work, deep behind the enemy lines, and through all those years he'd carried a folding Buck knife and this hunting knife. He had been wounded physically and psychologically by the brutality of those years, but had never won the medal. Once he came close, but all his men were killed and there were no American witnesses.

When Ralph heard we were going to the Arctic, he called and asked if we'd take his knives. "They mean a lot to me," he told us. "I once cut my way out of a downed helicopter with the Buck. Took me forever to get a good edge on it again. And the hunting knife . . . well, all I want to say is that I think it's time I let go. It needs to skin a moose."

I looked over at the knife. Several ominous notches were cut in the handle. I wasn't sure I wanted to know about them. "Here's to cousin Ralph," I said, quietly raising my mug of tea. "And to releasing that which no longer serves us."

I thought of the people and situations that had molded me. The pack frame I had inherited from Mother leaned in the bushes, carrying patches from Australia and Tasmania. After she died I remembered cleaning the mud from it and unraveling the odd array of knotted strings. In her sixties, my Mother, the helpless explorer, had still been doggedly hiking the Pacific Crest Trail, one section a summer, from Canada to Mexico, usually alone. Yet her gear had been held together with old shoelaces and rusted safety pins. In half an hour I had refurbished the pack, smiling as I set it right. Phil had taught me this. From him I learned that one can repair and design equipment. He, who had never built a log cabin or butchered a moose before we came to the Arctic, had taught me how and I was now passing this gift along.

Evening approached as we worked and storms ranged across the valley. It seemed inevitable that we would be caught in one. Black clouds rolled down the peaks leaving them dusted with snow, as sunbeams, like great search-lights, played over the foothills and river. We were all exhausted by the time the woodland giant had been reduced to a slippery pile of cold meat. He had become merely a head with antlers, a neck, a pelvis, two sets of ribs (one with spine attached), four legs (cut off at the knee), a hundred pounds of hide and several buckets of organs and gut fat.

Strapping awkward, hundred-pound quarters of meat to our pack frames, we slogged back to the canoe. I dropped onto the cold rocks, staying with Luke while Tom and Laurie returned for another load.

"It'll be dark soon," I told Luke, "and I'm afraid it's going to storm. How would you feel about staying alone in the tent? We have to get this meat home, but it probably won't take too long."

"I don't want to be alone," he answered, seating himself on my knee as if I were a chair. Our clothes were splotched with gore.

"I don't like it either," I agreed, "but at least you'd be under shelter."

"Well, okay . . ." he said bravely. "But can Shylo stay with me?"

"That's a good idea. It'll keep her out of mischief. But you can't control her in the tent. I'm afraid she'd just tear right through. So I'll tie her nearby."

When the others appeared out of the twilight, we splashed over the rocks with the heavy pieces and muscled them into the canoe. The four of us set off across the darkening river. When we reached shore I tied Shylo to a tree and hurriedly settled Luke in the tent with Oliver and the beloved Calvin book, while Tom and Laurie grappled the meat ashore onto a tarp. Within minutes we were skimming back across the river in a race with the fading light and the weather.

As we grounded on the far side, Shylo began to wail loudly; she's calling every bear within miles, I thought angrily. Stumbling with fatigue, I made one fast trip for meat and then asked Tom to paddle me back across. Moose or no moose, I couldn't leave my child alone. I was almost useless anyway. I would make a warm dinner for the family, I decided. The supportive role was important, too, and if I was no longer a prime mover, there were other things I could do.

Laurie and Tom finished the job, bringing out the meat and paddling back in growing darkness. Together they hauled it up the bank and put it into the pavilion. The stars were out, cold and bright in a clearing sky as we washed the blood from our arms and retired to the tent for the night.

I awoke late, feeling tired and sore. It had turned unseasonably warm. A few blowflies were buzzing around the meat. Bright sunlight bathed our camp and it seemed a far cry from winter, but I knew it wouldn't last. I rose quietly, compelled by a feeling of urgency at the passing days, and left the others asleep.

I have always enjoyed the mornings alone. It's my special time and from it I gain the balance needed for the rest of my day. I lit a fire and started cutting up the fat we had salvaged from around the guts and organs, slicing it on a split log held over my knees, and rendering the tallow in a big kettle on the fire. I would save the crackling for dog food. In this land it was never wise to waste anything.

"A moose comes with a lot of spare parts," I said as Tom emerged from the tent about an hour later. "We'll have to handle them right away or they'll spoil. Hope you're in the mood for more liver."

"We carried off most of the animal," he agreed as he put on his wet boots and tied the laces. His fingers were cracked and mangled from the hard life. He had packed most of the meat but had less blood on his clothes than I did. "Still, something is lost in the killing," he continued thoughtfully. "It's a relief to have the food, but you can't equate a living moose with a pile of meat."

"Well, yes," I agreed. "But all life, except plants, feeds on other life. Even a vegetarian can't get out of that cycle." In some ways, being forced to confront killing leads to a deeper acknowledgement of life. You might not feel kinship with a hamburger, but it was hard to deny your participation when you killed the animal.

"I'm sorry to say, I believe we need to get another," I added.

He nodded. "I was thinking that too."

"He's not as big I had hoped for . . . and a good deal leaner than he might be. Perhaps we can shoot an old fellow who has lived a good life. Anyway, no hunting for awhile until we handle this."

"Shall I put on my bloody clothes?" Laurie called from the tent.

"Yeah. No point cleaning up. We're gonna hang the meat today. It'll keep back in the shade, but it's too warm in the pavilion. Besides, we don't want to attract bears into camp with us."

"So what happened to winter?" she inquired.

"It'll be here within two weeks," I predicted. "Get up, lazy bones. Half the day is gone." We had agreed on a day of rest, but there were things that needed to be done.

"Coffee?" Tom asked, raising his eyebrows plaintively toward the pot on the grill.

I smiled. "Yes, it's coffee and it's hot. Go ahead and pour yourself a cup while I finish cutting up this fat."

"I hope someone sends me a real coffee cup in our November flight," he grumbled. "It just doesn't taste the same out of these enamel things."

We were listless and grouchy with fatigue. Only Laurie seemed her usual steady self. Utilizing the warm weather, she hauled buckets of water and washed the accumulated laundry, while Tom and I built a high meat rack back in the woods out of reach of the bears. We constructed it of two strong poles roped to either side of a pair of trees, about fourteen feet in the air. Tom climbed onto them and balanced as he slowly pulled the hide up, nailing it on the south side to protect the meat from sun. Throwing a rope over the other log, Laurie and I struggled to raise the quarters, while Tom tied them by short pieces of parachute cord.

The remaining meat Tom and Laurie hauled up to the cabin and hung from a rack on the north wall under the roof. Not wanting to leave it unguarded, we moved our bedding up for our first night inside. As darkness came on, Tom filled and lit the kerosene lamp. Its unaccustomed glow drove back the shadows and lent a cozy ambience to our log walls against which the open door and window holes stood out black and ominous, filled with night.

Luke and I put on night clothes and ascended the ladder to the new bed. It felt good to remove my contact lenses, sleeping without them for the first time since we arrived. The bed was well padded and covered with blankets, our sleeping bags spread open as quilts. The loft stretched the length of the cabin, was seven feet deep and high enough to sit comfortably at its lowest point near the outside wall. The bed was nine feet wide, ending at a break where the ladder descended. A further section of the loft (yet to be completed) would be used for storage.

After the cold, lumpy ground our bed felt very flat and warm. I lay contentedly on my back and watched the lamp light dance over the rafters above my head. Below us Tom centered an empty crate over the joists and dealt Laurie a game of cribbage. She was his only worthy opponent in cards and we could hear their happy banter as the plays fell out.

When they came to bed dark filled the cabin. It was strange sleeping within the close blackness. Accustomed to hearing the wind and river, I felt cut off from my senses. The extra space was strange as well, and although I enjoyed the freedom of curling up without sticking my knees in Tom's ribs, I found myself reaching out to make sure everyone was okay. Close physical contact had come to feel natural, communicating safety and affection. I was afraid Luke would scoot forward and fall over the edge, and at one point I remember waking everyone as I groped about in some confused dream, calling for him.

There was no longer any concern about tent zipper or bugs, but since we needed to crawl over the sleeping group to get to the ladder, we continued our custom of nightly forays. There was comfort in facing the dark together. We felt our way across the pitted clutter of our unfinished floor and out into the starry night to the designated spot. The woods about us loomed mysterious and alien, black silhouettes against the sky. Overhead, a curtain of green fire waved across the heavens, dwarfing us with its majesty. In sweat suits and slippers we bunched together, faces raised in awed silence, watching the aurora borealis ripple and curl in great streamers through the vastness of starry night.

Our third night in the cabin, I woke before dawn to the sound of wind in the stove pipe. It was very quiet inside, but the gentle tremble of logs beneath me spoke of the storm that thundered down the exposed river. I could imagine the flapping of our lonely tent and feel, more than hear, the vast tide of Arctic winter rolling indomitably southward over the sleeping land. I lay awake and watched the slow, gray birth of a new day. Snow was still falling, quietly erasing the last of summer, when I roused the others. It was only September ninth. Winter had come early.

Our attention turned to consolidating belongings so that we wouldn't lose them under the snow. Laurie, Luke and I spent the day dismantling camp and finding space for it within the crowded cabin. We took down the old pavilion, folding it into tarps as we said good-bye to a way of life that was no longer friendly. Tom wanted to store the majority of our supplies outside until he finished the floor, but I was anxious about their safety and so piled them in the cabin.

I tacked a piece of plastic over the open door hole to keep in the warmth. I was still grappling with odd moose parts, cooking meals of tongue, steak-and-kidney pie, and jellied nose as I tried to organize and move our supplies. I felt discouraged at the amount of work still ahead of us. The cabin seemed so dreary and cluttered as I thought of the coming winter, remembering the effort it took to handle life at cold temperatures: hauling water, cutting frozen meat, gathering firewood in deep snow, washing clothes.

Our world had changed overnight. It had only snowed a couple of inches and would have melted off if the temperature had risen, but it hovered in the teens. Withered grass protruded through the crystals giving the land a faded, drab appearance. The autumn colors were gone and a clean, cold wind rocked the spruce, causing them to creak and moan. Back in the thickets, bare willows rattled like so many cold bones where the occasional dry leaf tapped. We dug out felt-lined shoepack boots and put away our summer footgear. The muskegs froze, making travel easier, and snow crunched and squealed underfoot. Our creek was still flowing strongly, the same thirty-four degrees it held all summer, and presented a challenge for crossing, but on the delta it built cascading layers of slippery ice, honeycombed with noisy water.

Hunting again consumed a good portion of our efforts and day after day we tramped the thickets and bars. Some days were clear, but many were ghostly and unreal, seen through the whisper of falling snow. It was easy to lose one's sense of direction in the obscure light and often the peaks would be hidden from view. The moose were still moving, as the great activity of tracks attested, but harder to approach in the noisy snow. Tom did bag four spruce chickens which we cached away for Thanksgiving dinner. Our local birds had become quite tame, often strutting through the yard like hens, and these we left alone. Tom always accompanied us hunting, quietly supportive while Laurie or I combed the land. He became even thinner and more wiry as miles stretched out behind him, his ragged, bearded face looking like an old prospector. My feet were very sore and tired from trying to keep up with him, but they were warm inside my shoepacks.

The river was beautifully clear now, a deep blue ribbon laced between the growing shelves of shore-fast ice. Large pans of slush moved in a stately procession down the narrowing center, scraping over shoals with a hissing sound. It was difficult to cross, for one needed to propel the canoe over several yards of ice, paddle through the relentless rafts of slush, then heave out like a walrus onto the far shelf and slide to shore. No longer a sunny stream, its temperament changed by the hour and we were afraid of being stranded on the far side. Nevertheless we did cross, scouting the willow thickets day after day.

"If we got a moose now we'd have to pack it home," I reminded Tom as we stood gazing from the bluff above Lake Eugene. Although Horseshoe Lake was frozen hard enough to walk on, Eugene was still open, windy and blue-black. To my surprise a few fish ducks dove in its uninviting depths.

"We need to go wherever they are," he answered. "Perhaps we could cache the meat and haul it home, a little at a time."

"Yes. I suppose miles of packing beats not getting it at all. And every day they get thinner. But just remember how heavy a moose is."

"I enjoy seeing this country," he answered. His head was high and his eyes far away. "It seemed like all we did last summer was work on the cabin and it's good to get out."

Gradually the mossing was completed and the cabin began to look enclosed. Little by little Tom chiseled out sills and installed our windows. He built a kitchen counter along the front wall and fashioned shelves for our treasured library. Laurie kept planing floor boards. I finished the toilet hole and built a sturdy seat over it, then erected another meat rack in preparation for a moose.

I was learning to cook with the stove, and meat added greatly to our diet and the enjoyment of meals. The morning that Tom hung the door was a turning point for me. Light and fragile as it was, it somehow closed out winter and turned our cabin into a home. I celebrated by making sourdough donuts dipped in lemon icing for breakfast, while Tom cleaned the guns and Laurie taught Luke the fine points of chess.

After breakfast, Tom and Laurie set out hunting. It had been two weeks since we killed the first moose and the season was quickly passing. I was tired and needed time to recover from the long miles I had put in with Tom the day before, but he covered the same country again while I worked in the cabin. I wondered if he wasn't running himself too hard. They were out most of the day, arriving home around sunset, their faces windburned and tired from the long hike. I had a meal of baked ribs and fresh rye bread waiting.

"I'm taking a spin around the block," I said, indicating the loop up Luke's Trail and back down the creek.

I picked up my rifle and stepped through the new door, leaving the family warmth for a different world. It was stark and beautiful out, but no longer friendly. One sensed that foolish mistakes would not be easily forgiven.

Quietly I followed the trail Luke and I had cleared so long ago, curving along the bench west to the creek. The snowy woods were already in deep shadow and a pastel sky of tangerine washed into yellow over the jagged peaks of King Mountain ahead. The temperature would drop below zero tonight and there was little moon. The creek was a faerieland of ice, water rushing black through fanciful caves and lattices of lacy white, but open and swift in the middle. My boots were waterproof halfway to the knee, but I took my time crossing the slippery stones, then turned downstream into the wind.

The fading light was to my back, setting the country before me aglow with sunset. The shore rose in a sandy, four-foot cutbank clothed in the short, bare stems of bushes. I could easily skirt the creek on this side and arrive at the delta to cross again. From my raised position there was a clear view of the stream in both directions, and with the light behind me, I almost felt I stood before a stage on which a play was about to begin.

Somehow I knew the moose would be waiting. It came as no surprise when the big antlers emerged from a tall thicket across the creek about ninety yards away. The moose backed and drove into the willows, shaking his antlers in challenge before stepping into the open.

My heart was pounding with what I had to do as I knelt, then finally sat, in the snow to steady my rifle over one knee. It was hard to see through the open site in the failing light, but the moose stood forth as if painted. I allowed myself a moment of compassion, acknowledging the splendor of the great animal, then took a deep breath and pulled the trigger. At the first shot the bull leapt forward, splashing across the creek unaware of where his peril lay.

The second round struck his neck, and as he turned sideways, I caught him a third time through the shoulder and upper ribs, taking him down. He lay panting on the frozen gravel perhaps fifty yards from me, steam rising into the cold evening.

I froze, awaiting his death, afraid he would get up and run if I moved. His throat and legs were towards me and I could see his eyes rolling. Every now and then he would raise his head. I hated to witness his fear and pain, and prayed for a quick death. I blinked away the tears and fired a fourth shot, trying for the brain from this odd angle. He jerked mightily but still did not die. Unwilling to prolong this macabre play, I stood up and walked along the bank. The moose watched me as I steadied my rifle and placed the final shot through his brain.

It was over and I felt numb and sad as I approached to make my peace with him. When I was sure that he was dead, I pulled driftwood free from the sand and started a fire. The blaze climbed, rosy and cheerful in the purple light, gusting in the breeze that flowed up the creek. It would be dark soon and there was not a minute to waste. As I started for home Tom appeared from the twilight, rifle in hand, and crossed the creek. We returned to the moose and together worked him onto his back. He was a bit larger than the other but just as thin. His legs were wet from the stream. His stomach was shrunken (for bulls do not eat at this season) and a strong smell of rut hung about him.

"I'm sorry to make you work when you're so tired," I said. "I think if we just skin his legs and get the guts out we can do the rest in the morning. I'm headed back for the tent and butchering equipment."

"I'll get started," he answered. His face looked gray in the fading light. "Don't tarry."

The trail was already becoming indistinct as I hurried along. The cabin seemed dark as a cave inside despite the feeble kerosene lamp.

"We heard your shots. Did you get one?!" Laurie squealed as I opened the door.

"Another bull."

"Luke, we've got lots to eat this winter!" She grabbed his hands and danced him around.

"Tom and I are staying out tonight," I told her. "I need to pack. Can you carry the butchering equipment? It's just downstream from the crossing."

"You bet. Is there anything else I can do?" she asked.

"Just take care of the boy. And have a nice breakfast for us tomorrow. You'll be okay by yourselves?"

"Oh, we'll have a fine night. But I don't envy you out there."

"I want to help, too," Luke interjected.

"You can help Laurie with the buckets," I told him. "Hurry or you'll have a hard time finding your way back home in the dark. You take good care of her tonight."

"I will," he promised.

They set off before me, and had cleared the sand of snow and put up my little yellow tent by the time I arrived. I had bought the tent after my divorce, and although it was old and leaky, it had finally made it to Alaska.

Hugging us good-bye, they scurried for home. I could hear their happy chatter as Laurie piggybacked Luke across the icy stream and into the black woods. On the open bar Tom and I stood beneath a hemisphere of velvet blue sky, fading to orange at the horizon. The first bright stars were out and the northern lights played coldly overhead, illuminating snowy peaks and reflecting off the black water. A chill breeze drifted up the little valley carrying the song of the stream.

We butchered by firelight late into the night. Luckily there was a good supply of driftwood frozen into the gravel and we didn't need to search far. The waxing moon rose late, dancing with the aurora in the creek. Blood froze to our clothes and we stopped often to warm our hands. By midnight the moose legs were mostly skinned and severed at the knees. I was proud that I had managed to get the digestive track disconnected at both ends and the organs removed without breaking the bladder or bowels as I groped around in the dark. Tom propped open the great rib cage with a stick and we called it a night.

We cleaned our hands by rubbing them with snow as dry as sandpaper and melting them over the embers. Then we crawled into our sleeping bags and curled up in a tight knot together for the remainder of the night.

We awoke in the gray dawn to the task of butchering the partly frozen moose and carrying the awkward pieces home. By lunch I had given out. I packed up the camp gear and retreated to our cabin with Luke, who was miserable and whining in the cold, leaving Tom and Laurie to complete the dreary task. The sun had set by the time they hauled the last pieces safely into our yard. Over the next few days we would need to hang the meat, handle the organs, and wash the blood from our clothes, but after three months of constant effort we were finally safe from winter.

➥ JEAN ASPEN is the author of *Arctic Son* and *Arctic Daughter*, both epic tales of survival and adventure in Alaska. The child of a famous female explorer, she has followed in her mother's footsteps to seek out challenges in the wilderness and, more importantly, writes beautifully about her experiences so that we can all share in them.

Excerpt from *Good-Bye, Boise . . .*
Hello, Alaska: The True Story of a Family's Move
to a Remote Alaskan Island Ranch

CORA HOLMES

The crackle of radio static woke me to a pitch-black morning.

"You got this on, Milt?" The voice floated above our heads and I felt Milt stir beside me.

"This is Mike Lynch on the *Silver Clipper*. I'm coming in to get pots."

Our feet hit the icy floor on opposite sides of the bed at the same time. A match flared and I saw the plume of steam from Milt's breath curl up around the kerosene lamp. In the soft light, we pulled clothes on over our long johns. The clock said 6 a.m.; the sun wouldn't be up for another 4 hours.

While Milt felt his way into the radio room, I lit my lamp and hurried to the kitchen, thankful I'd taken time to rake down the coals and lay a fresh fire the night before. I dreaded getting up in the dark to a cold house.

All I had to do in the frigid pre-dawn was put a match to it. Some mornings I snuggled back under the covers for another half hour of cozy warmth before the fire was hot enough to cook breakfast, but not today. I already knew we'd be busy.

Milt wanted to butcher three of the steers Chuck and I had brought in. From the sound of his conversation on the radio, we'd add several hours of crab pot hauling to that job. Mike Lynch was one of our best customers and a good friend. He and his sons owned two crab boats, the *Silver Clipper* and the *Tanya Rose*, which fished the Bering Sea.

They lived in Seattle, and when they brought their boats out to the Aleutians, they'd always carry up our supplies—grain one year, groceries the next. One of the animals we'd butcher today was for them.

I heard Milt sign off before I stepped outside to get bacon and milk from the storeroom. Even before my feet slipped on the frozen walk, I knew the weather had changed. The wind was still, hardly enough to sway the steam from my breath, but the temperature had plummeted to 20°.

Back inside, the roar of the coal fire and the lamp's rosy glow enclosed us in a cocoon of comfort. I fixed breakfast before I woke the boys. They were tired from 2 days of hard riding and I had to shake them both awake. Like me, they didn't enjoy getting up in the dark and cold, but they were a little more vocal about it.

"It's the middle of the night," Chuck protested as I lit the lamp beside his bed and left it shining mercilessly in his face.

"Go away, Mom," Randall groaned, grabbing at the covers I pulled into a heap at the bottom of his bed with callous disregard for the goose bumps I caused. "I hate school." He hid his head under his pillow.

"No school today," I announced. "We have to butcher and haul crab pots for Mike."

Randall jumped up and dashed into the kitchen with his clothes. During breakfast, he kept up a steady stream of questions. "Did Mike bring the mail?" He swallowed two slices of bacon in one gulp and washed it down with a whole glass of milk.

"I don't know," I answered from the stove where I was cooking the last of the pancakes. "He didn't say."

"Can I drive the boat, Milt?"

"Not in the dark. Maybe on the way home," Milt answered, sandwiching fried eggs between sourdough pancakes and pouring maple syrup liberally over them.

"But you can drive the Bobcat from the slaughterhouse to the dock for me when we start hauling pots." He slid bacon onto the rim of his plate and handed the dish to Chuck, who sat quietly in the shadows of the lamp.

"Super!" Randall shouted, spooning up the last of his oatmeal and reaching for the pancake platter. "Can I get on Mike's boat and watch TV?"

"You'll have to ask your mom about that."

"We'll see," I said, pouring a second cup of coffee and taking it to the sink with an armful of dirty dishes.

The water sputtering from the tap never fails to amaze me. With only the help of gravity, coils circulating through the fire-box and Milt's ingenuity, I always have hot water at my fingertips. Filling the sink with steaming soapy water, I called out, "Bring your dishes when you finish."

"Hey," Randall exclaimed as Chuck came into the lamplight with his dishes. "How come you're all dressed up?"

I glanced around, still mildly surprised to find myself looking up at this youth whose eyes had been level with mine a few short months ago.

It was true. Besides the clean shirt, Chuck had taken pains with his hair. Instead of the hit-or-miss treatment he usually gave the long, dark mass, it was neatly combed and secured with a bandanna around his forehead.

Chuck glared at Randall. "I'm not dressed up!" he hissed. "Just because I put on a clean shirt doesn't mean I'm dressed up."

"Hah," Randall smirked. "You think there'll be girls from the processors walking on the beach today." He danced out of Chuck's reach, splashing his dishes into the sink as a reason to get closer to me. "Well, I'm going to tell them you're only sixteen."

"Who cares?" Chuck shrugged his shoulders. "They'll never believe you. You're just a kid." With a supercilious smile, he turned on his heel and followed Milt outside.

"It isn't fair," Randall complained after they'd gone. "All the girls from the boats think Chuck is nineteen. They're always hanging around him." Randall rubbed his face with a dejected sigh. "I wish I had a mustache—that's what makes Chuck look so old." He pushed out his upper lip. "When will I get one?"

I stared at him in astonishment. He really was serious. "You're only 12, son," I finally said. "Chuck didn't get one until he was 14, and there's no guarantee you'll be like him. You're adopted, remember. You don't have the same genes."

Randall had always known the circumstances of his birth, that he had been adopted when he was three days old. As far as I could tell, it had never bothered him. Now he just sighed again and nodded. "I can't wait two whole years," he said. "I need something now."

I groped for something to say that would cheer him up. "Those girls are much older than you are, Randall. All of them are over eighteen—most are in their twenties and thirties."

I wiped down the counters as he rinsed the last dishes and set them in the drainer. "Why do you want them to notice you?" I asked. Was he that lonesome out here?

"If Chuck can get girls, then I want girls, too," he said with a stubborn set to his chin. He dried his hands on his jeans and hurried after Milt and Chuck.

I added a bucket of coal to the fire, knowing it would never last until we came home, but hoped the water would still be warm in the tank and the house not entirely frigid. Then I pulled another sweatshirt over the one I already wore, poured the rest of the coffee into a thermos and blew out the lamp. Feeling my way out the door, I followed the others into the dark.

So that was it! I should have known. The competition between the boys was fierce, for my attention, for Milt's . . . and now for girls!

As I closed the horse pasture gate leading to the beach, I heard the marine ways engine start. I quickened my steps. The engine pulled our 21-foot, double-ended dory into and out of the water on miniature railroad tracks that extended into the bay about 25 feet, far enough to clear our 4-foot tide change. If I missed getting into the boat before it was lowered, I'd have to walk out to it on the slippery tracks.

I needn't have worried. When I got there, Milt and Chuck were prying with crowbars on the dolly wheels, which were frozen fast to the metal tracks.

"Help Randall," Chuck panted to me.

I boosted myself over the bow and rolled into the boat. Inside, Randall was rocking back and forth, so I added my weight to his. Between us we provided enough motion to jar the dolly beneath the boat and break the wheels free from the frozen tracks. With a screeching lurch, the dolly started down the tracks toward the black still water. At the first motion, Milt dashed into the winch house to monitor the cable coming off the spool.

Randall and I toppled backward and collapsed onto the first wooden seat while Chuck vaulted over the bow. "Is the plug in?" he yelled.

Without waiting for an answer, I launched myself toward the stern, clambered over the second seat and motor well, my hands feverishly searching for the bolt that fit into the drainage hole in the bottom of the boat.

"I already put it in," Randall called out, just as the boat entered the water with a gentle slap and my fingers touched the familiar ring. I gave it another couple twists just to be sure.

When we felt the boat float off the dolly, Chuck signaled Milt with a flash-light and the winch motor stopped. Then, while Chuck and Randall untied the mooring lines, I held the flashlight on the tracks so Milt could see. With a ten-foot aluminum pike held like a tightrope walker's pole, he balanced on the slippery frozen track and inched toward the boat.

For the last fifteen feet, the track had treacherous footing, covered with water and slick with dead seaweed. I kept the beam in front of Milt, biting the inside of my lip, releasing a pent-up breath when he stepped out of the freez-ing water into the boat.

As soon as he had the 25-horsepower outboard started, the boys let go of the mooring lines and we moved out into the smooth black water. By this time, my eyes were accustomed to the dark and I could see the outline of the headland rearing up ahead of us.

Without any wind to ruffle the bay's flat surface, the boat plowed through the water like a knife, leaving a wide V-wake behind. The boys sat quietly on the seat in front of me, the outboard noise discouraging conversation.

I looked at their straight backs and wondered again if I'd made the right decision. Was I cheating them out of a normal childhood by isolating them from friends and classmates? And what about their education? Was it fair to take them out of public school, where they had the benefit of up-to-date teachers, facilities and resources to stimulate their minds?

I thought back to the summer two years before when Chuck had gradu-ated from eighth grade. I remembered the police car pulling up outside our house with him and a friend inside, their fishing poles beside them on the seat. The guilty yet defiant look on his face when the officer explained to me he had caught them throwing rocks at mailboxes hadn't disturbed me as much as his offhand rationalization, "Everybody does it".

Randall, meanwhile, was displaying disruptive behavior in the classroom and fighting on the playground. By the fourth grade, he still could not read.

Shoved into special classes, tagged as "different" by his classmates, defeated scholastically before his tenth birthday, he'd retreated into a fantasy world of television characters and video games.

As our boat rounded the headland and started through the channel into the inner harbor, I watched the boys' faces in the lights from the big crab processors we passed. Randall grabbed Chuck's arm and pointed. His eyes shone with excitement.

No, I told myself again. I'd made the right decision and . . .

Thud! The boat suddenly shuddered and swerved in the darkness.

"Ice!" Randall shouted, peering over the side. The boat shook again and I heard the sound from the engine change. "Look!" he yelled. "It's everywhere!"

We were surrounded by great jagged chunks of slow-moving ice. They banged into us, shaking the boat, looking huge and menacing in the reflection from our running lights. I turned panicky eyes to Milt. His calm face didn't reassure me.

"What's happening?" I yelled.

"Don't worry!" he shouted back. "It's freshwater ice from the head of the bay." He stood up and swung the boat into an opening.

"Navigate for me, Chuck!"

The boat tipped crazily as Chuck lurched to the bow just as another solid chunk nudged us. Randall clambered over the seat beside me. The boat slowed to a standstill.

"This is neat!" he exclaimed. "We're iced in."

"Sit down!" I screamed. It took all my willpower to stay calm. My heart was bouncing inside my chest like a handball. I clung to the wooden plank seat. The sound of ice grinding against the boat's hull terrified me. When Milt's hand tapped my shoulder, I gasped.

"Don't worry." He spoke close to my ear. "I want you to rock." He made swaying motions with his body. "It helps." Randall's eyes lit up still more.

"All right!" he shouted. "Come on, Mom!" He lunged against the side of the boat making it tip sluggishly. "Rock!"

I nudged my body gingerly against the railing, sucking in my breath as the boat dipped, bringing the black water closer to my face.

"More!" Randall shrieked. "Like this." He slid across the seat and into me, pushing both of us against the side of the boat. The black water rushed toward us, so close I could count the individual ice crystals. Would they find our bodies? I wondered. When Chuck felt the motion of the boat, he added his own weight to our rocking. Since he couldn't shout loud enough for Milt to hear over the motor, he pointed the direction he wanted him to take; his arms flailed like a windmill.

The boat zigzagged as it rocked, and still the chunks rammed into us, crunched along our sides, swirling into our wake, hitting the propeller shaft with solid, sickening *thunks*. Behind me, Milt tightened his grip on the outboard's tiller.

Darkness enveloped us again as we crept away from the anchored crab boat's lights. I felt small and alone and far from shore. The *Titanic* came to mind.

Then, as suddenly as it had appeared, it was gone. A channel widened in front of us and we reached open water. The boat picked up speed. Behind, I looked at the floating mass of ice—the twinkling boat lights reflected off it in a million sparkling glitters. I wish I could say I appreciated the adventure and beauty of an incident most people never get to experience, but all I could think about was going back through that ice to get home.

The boys loved it. As soon as the chunks thinned out, Randall stopped rocking and scrambled to the bow where he and Chuck searched the water for ice floes.

"Look at the size of that one!" Chuck yelled.

Randall aimed his imaginary gun. "I wish we had polar bears."

In the still, cold dawn, I envied their excitement, untinged by any concept of mortality, admonishing myself for my own fears. Just then Milt squeezed my shoulder. "All clear," his husky voice whispered behind my ear.

Oh yes, I had made the right decision.

We docked near the slaughterhouse safely, but as Chuck and I unloaded the boat in the semi-darkness, we had a mishap . . . I hit him right in the face with one of his tennis shoes.

Since I didn't want the shoe to land in the water, I had thrown it hard, then heard the solid *whack* as it connected with his cheek.

"Sorry," I mumbled, but couldn't muffle a chuckle when I saw the look of disbelief as he pulled off his glove and rubbed his jaw. After a moment, he grinned, too. "Good shot, Mom."

Soon, we were both laughing like idiots . . . after our ordeal in the ice, I needed some silliness.

"Heads up!" I sang out between chuckles, sailing his other shoe to shore.

Chuck had a thing about shoes—he was always striving for the perfect foot gear. After nearly freezing his feet on a ride with Milt after some bulls, he sent away for a pair of "bunny boots." He loved them because they kept his feet warm on the coldest days. But they weighed seven pounds apiece, so he brought tennis shoes to wear when he got tired of walking in such heavy boots. The rest of us wore gum boots and two pair of socks.

By the time we staggered up the rocky trail with our supplies, Milt and

Randall had the slaughterhouse open and the generator started. While Milt checked the compressors and cool rooms, Chuck and Randall moved the steers from the outside corral to the holding pen and I started the fires, one to heat water for the meat-cutting rooms and one in our living quarters.

Inside, we all had our jobs. Milt did the actual cutting, while the boys and I skinned. When a carcass was quartered, I washed it down and rolled it into the cool room on an overhead rail. But I wasn't big enough to wrestle the heaviest pieces of meat.

I kept the fires stoked, brought hot drinks from the bunk room, and, under the pretext of checking on the boat, dashed outside every thirty minutes to monitor the water, hoping against hope that the ice would move out before we finished.

As Milt cut, the boys watched.

"Yuck!" Randall screwed up his face at the sight of a beef tongue. "I can't believe people eat that."

I scrubbed its pebbled surface. "After I boil this with pickling spices and slice it paper thin, you'll gobble it up," I teased, knowing he'd be suspicious of everything I cooked for the next few days.

"Not me!" he snorted.

"Hey, lots of people eat this stuff," Chuck said, pointing to a beef heart. "Don't they, Mom?"

"Sure," I agreed. "Big-city delicatessens call heart, liver, brains, tongue, even kidneys 'variety meats', and use them in specialty sandwiches."

"Kidneys?" Even Chuck's eyebrows shot up.

"Well, maybe not for sandwiches," Milt broke in. "But the English make steak and kidney pie. My mother fixed it for me when I was a kid."

"I don't care," Randall insisted. "I won't eat it . . . and I'll be able to tell, so don't try to sneak it on my plate."

Milt grinned. "My mom couldn't fool me, either."

I made my rounds while they finished up, adding coal to the fires and checking the boat. Because our butchering facilities took up only one small area in a cavernous warehouse left by U.S. soldiers after World War II, it took a minute to walk to our bunk room near the entrance.

Outside, the sky was gray as flint and the water reflected back the somber color. It lapped against the beach, making soft sloshing sounds as it moved around the boat. I looked to the horizon and saw another boat's lights appear around Observatory Point a mile away, gliding toward the dock on the opposite side of Mutton Cove.

I knew Mike was already anchored up in the head of the bay and he was the only one scheduled, so this boat was a surprise. I couldn't make out the name, but the sleek white shape looked familiar. I hurried back to tell the others. They were already working on the third animal. "The *Intrepid* just tied up at the pot dock," I announced.

Chuck's head jerked up. "Oh, no, not Sigmund! Are you sure?" He dropped his knife and bolted for the door.

I took his place, glancing across at Randall and Milt, who were both smiling. "Why is Chuck so upset?" I asked.

Milt shrugged. "You know Sigmund. He doesn't think Chuck is careful enough with his pots."

I really didn't know Sigmund. Like most of the fishermen who stored their crab pots with us, he was simply a voice on the radio, one of several with strong Norwegian accents. I'd never met him in person. He kept Milt supplied with some dreadful Norwegian goat cheese, which I'm sure was a great delicacy and hard to part with as far away from home as Sigmund was.

He also gave us crab, still alive and kicking from his tanks. With a king crab fetching as much as $15, it was a generous gift and one we loved getting. Ranch work kept us too busy to fish for ourselves, and we didn't have a big enough boat or any of the expensive equipment it took. I didn't blame Sigmund for worrying about how his equipment was handled. I hoped Chuck gave those pots all his attention.

The heavy door behind us burst open. "It's him, all right!" Chuck's face was a mixture of consternation and despair. He jammed his hands into his pockets and rocked back and forth on his heels.

"Vhat you doon, boy?" He mimicked the voice I'd heard on the radio with surprising accuracy. "You vatch out, vhat you do. Don't rip da veb on my pots vith dat backhoe fork."

Chuck jerked his hands free and locked them together. "If he says one thing to me—*Pow*, right in the kisser!"

"You know, Chuck," Milt said, turning on the electric hoist and lifting a carcass off a cart, "all you have to do is be careful with the man's pots and he won't yell at you."

"I *am* careful," Chuck defended, retrieving his knife and nudging me out of his way. "Accidents can happen to anyone."

"What did you do?" I asked.

"I turned and two of his pots fell off the trailer. When I put them back on, the prongs got caught in the webbing. It didn't tear, just stretched it a little . . . of course, Sigmund had to see me do it."

"I know he gets pretty excited, Chuck," Milt said, "but he's a good customer and we want to do our best for him."

"I suppose," Chuck grumbled, "but does he have to call me 'Boy'?"

"You're lucky," Milt chuckled. "You should hear what he calls his crew."

Chuck held a carcass steady as Milt sawed it in half. "Shall I go see what he wants?" Chuck asked after the noise of the saw died away.

"He'll want the rest of his pots," Milt said. "The season isn't finished yet. You might as well go on over with the backhoe and get started on them." Milt looked around at the six quarters still waiting to be washed. "I'll come as soon as I can."

Chuck struggled out of his butchering gear, pulling it down over the bunny boots, then clomped away in those balloon-sized shoes.

"You go, too," I told Milt. "I can finish here."

"You're sure?"

I nodded. He didn't need any persuading. Crab pot storage was important to us.

"Yippee!" Randall yelled. "You promised I could drive the Bobcat!"

"That's right," Milt said. "I'll take the boat." Milt pulled off his butchering gear. "Let's go."

As their engine sounds faded, I started washing down the quarters. They were so big, each one weighing more than I did, and clumsy for me to move, even when hanging on rollers.

Before long, the entire room was wreathed in steam from the hot water I was spraying. The swaying carcasses looked like ghostly sentinels emerging from the fog misting up around my face as I worked.

When I finished washing, I took a sharp knife and started trimming. I was working on the last quarter when two men walked into the room. One was George Grunholt, skipper of the *Akutan*, a processor anchored in the harbor. With him was a dark young man who stared at me with wide eyes.

I must have looked strange to him, with knives and meat trimmings strewn everywhere and the ghostly steam floating all around me, like something out of a bad horror movie. I laid down my knife and gave them my best smile. "Hi."

George, whom I had met briefly before, answered. "I'm looking for the water Milt told me I could get at the valve down on the dock. Our water maker is on the fritz."

"It's turned off right now," I answered. "I need all the water pressure I can get in here." I opened the cool room door and started pushing the unwieldy quarters along the rail toward it. The young man jumped hastily back. "I'm almost done," I said. "Then I'll show you where to turn it back on."

"Can I help?" George asked.

"Sure," I pointed through the door, not wanting them to touch the freshly washed meat I was handling with gloved hands. "Go pour us all some coffee." I gave him directions to the bunk room. "Make yourselves at home; I'll come as soon as I finish."

The bunk room, with its sawhorse table and rusty iron beds, exuded a friendly warmth after the chilly atmosphere of the butchering rooms. We huddled around the potbellied stove and warmed our hands with mugs of thick boiled coffee.

George was part Aleut, a native of Sand Point, Alaska. He was about 60 years old and had been Milt's friend for many years. I first met George when he brought the *Akutan* into the harbor in November to buy crab from fishermen and process it on the ship.

His crew was mainly young people from the Seattle area, a lot of them college kids earning money for school. Some were Asian immigrants new to America and still groping with the language—like the young man beside George at the moment. I didn't catch the man's name when George introduced us, only that he was from Vietnam.

When I extended my hand, he pumped it enthusiastically while an excited volley burst from his lips. I smiled and nodded without understanding: I thought he was thanking me for the coffee.

After I showed the men where the outside water valve was, I walked out on the dock. A cold northwest breeze touched my face. Good, I thought, it will blow the ice out of the channel. Tiny riffles scudded across the water, and beneath my feet I heard the gentle splash of waves washing around the pilings.

Directly across the bay to the south, I could see Cutter Point jutting into the water. The sight of it always gave me comfort—only a mile distant and protected from the north wind, it was the nearest landing on the headquarters side of the harbor.

It was a good mile and a half away from the house, but if the wind ever got too bad while we crossed the harbor, we could duck behind Cutter Point, leave the boat and walk home. I started back down the dock, thinking about the mess I still had to clean up.

"Mom! Mom!" Randall yelled, dashing around the side of the slaughter-house. His head was bare, his gloves were gone and his open coat flapped behind him with each piston stroke of his legs.

"What's the matter?" I sprinted the remaining yards.

"There's another boat at the dock," he gasped, his brown eyes alive with excitement. "The *Teacher's Pet.*"

"You ran a whole mile to tell me that?" I pulled his coat together and managed the top button before he jerked away. "What's so special about it?"

"Miss Universe is on it!" He stopped to catch his breath. "No, not Miss Universe . . . Miss Iceland . . . or something like that."

"Now, Randall," I chided, knowing his penchant for exaggeration. "Are you sure?" His enthusiasm sometimes distorted the facts, but his stories always contained an element of truth. I probed. "Who told you that?"

"Helga."

I raised my eyebrows.

"That's her name," he insisted. "She don't talk English too good, but she's real pretty and about 10 feet tall." He stretched his arm above his head. "And she asked to meet you; she wants some sheep heads."

His words tumbled over one another. "They eat them! Can you believe that?" He made a gagging sound. "I might eat tongue if I was starving to death, but never a sheep head!"

This had gone far enough. "Randall, what kind of dumb joke is this? Nobody eats sheep heads." I walked into the long warehouse to the meat cut-ting rooms. He followed me.

"It's the truth!" he declared. "Honest. Come see for yourself."

"Okay," I told him. "But first we have to clean up this mess."

For once he didn't complain. While I washed the equipment, he hosed the floor, then together we wrestled the heavy wheelbarrow of scraps outside. The eagles and foxes would make short work of them.

Before we left, I found him some gloves and made him put on his stock-ing cap. As we walked, the wind was in our faces, brisker now and very cold. I noticed the erratic tire tracks made by the front end loader. "Did you have any trouble with the Bobcat?" I asked.

"Nah." He turned and faced me walking backward into the wind. "Milt said I did good."

"Did Sigmund say how many pots he wanted?" I asked Randall. Milton and Chuck could move forty-eight pots an hour, and I hoped they would finish by dark. The increasing wind brought with it a niggling unease. The bay could become a furious caldron of smoking water within minutes if this rising wind were part of a storm front. I hadn't listened to Peggy Dyson's 8 a.m. weather on the marine band radio before we left home because I was too busy. Now I wished I had taken the time.

"I don't know how many pots they're loading," Randall said, then grinned sheepishly. "I watched TV while they talked. The cook gave me some ice cream."

"It doesn't matter," I said. "I'll ask Milt when we get there."

We walked as fast as the frozen ruts would allow, and as we got closer, I saw Chuck pulling a loaded trailer along the beach road from the gravel point where we stored the pots. That meant Milt had the Bobcat on the point another half mile away.

When we reached the dock, Randall grabbed my arm and pointed. "See, just like I said, the *Teacher's Pet*."

A white boat, beautifully painted, with the name etched prominently on the bow, was tied up next to the *Intrepid*. "Come on, Mom." Randall tugged my sleeve.

"I want to talk to Milt first," I told him. "You go ahead."

Randall dropped my arm and scampered across the plank bridging the boat and dock. In a moment, he disappeared from sight.

Chuck was waiting for the boat crew to transfer the pots from his trailer to their deck when I passed. Instead of speaking like I had planned, I just waved. He acknowledged me with a slight nod and turned back to the three young women clustered around him. I guess Randall hadn't had time to pass the word about Chuck's age.

I found Milt stacking pots with the Bobcat onto our second trailer. He jumped out of the cab when he saw me. "How much longer?" I asked.

"A couple hours," he said. "We'll have to come back tomorrow. I still have Mike to do." He rubbed his hands together. "I'll have to chill down the cool room again, too."

I unzipped my coat and put his hands inside. "Man, it's cold," he muttered. "This wind must be blowing off a glacier in Russia."

Chuck clattered up behind us with an empty trailer. Milt pulled his gloves on and went to unhitch it. I watched for a minute as they jockeyed the vehicles around, exchanging the loaded trailer for the empty one. When they finished, I jumped on the trailer and rode back to the dock, wondering again where Randall had gotten his story and what to expect when I met his "Helga".

The three women who'd been talking to Chuck, little more than girls, sat on an overturned fuel drum. I waved as I passed them on my way to the *Teacher's Pet*. "Hi," one called. "Are you going to see Miss Iceland?"

I gave them a surprised nod and hurried on. So it was true. What in the world was Miss Iceland doing on a fishing boat in the Bering Sea?

I got my answer soon enough. When I crawled over the rail on the boat's back deck, a huge blond man ducked out the galley door. When he straightened up, he towered above me. "Ja?" he asked in a soft voice I could not believe came from that massive chest.

"I'm looking for Helga," I faltered.

A wide smile split his face. He motioned me through the door. Three steps down and I came face-to-face with one of the most beautiful women I'd ever seen.

While not quite ten feet as Randall had described, she was indeed tall. Tall, willowy and exquisite. She was bent over the minuscule galley sink, peeling potatoes, her silvery blonde hair carelessly pulled back with a rubber band.

"My vife, Helga," the man behind me said. "Miss Iceland and second runner-up for Miss Universe 1972." The pride in his soft voice spoke louder than a shout.

The woman lifted her head. "Gunnar." Her clear blue eyes pleaded. Then she looked at me and smiled. "He embarrass me." Wiping her hand on her sleeve, she held it out. "You verk on boat?"

"No," I shook my head. "I'm Mrs. Milt . . ." My words were cut off as I was enveloped in a bone-crushing hug.

"Milt's new vife!" Gunnar said as he lifted me off my feet and kissed me on both cheeks. "Ja, gut!" He dumped me onto a galley bench and sat beside me. "From da sheep ranch," he said to his wife. "Dey haf sheep heads."

Helga's eyes lit up. "Randall?"

"My son," I nodded. "He said you wanted sheep heads."

"Ja." She set the potatoes on the stove. "Gut vith spuds."

"I'm sure," I said lamely. "How do you fix them?"

With a great deal of relish and stumbling broken English, she explained in detail how to cook a sheep's head . . . she even patted her stomach.

"We're butchering sheep soon," I told her. "I'll ask Milt to save the heads."

"Tanks." She brought coffee to the table, sliding into the galley seat opposite us. "Randall haf horse?"

"Yes," I said, wondering what that had to do with sheep heads. "George."

"Ja, George." Helga beamed. "He say he take me ride on George." She pantomimed pulling back on the reins. "I luf horses. I rode all time in Iceland." A wistful tone crept into her voice.

"Do you miss Iceland?" I asked.

She shrugged, "Ja, sometimes." She stared out the porthole at the brown grass-covered hills. "But I like here; no trees—just like home, only little booshes."

"Why did you leave Iceland?"

She looked at the fair giant sitting beside me. "My husband is fisherman," she replied softly. "So I live on boat."

I sipped my coffee and looked at her. Later I learned she had modeled for *Cosmopolitan* and was a ballerina with the Reykjavik Ballet for 10 years. But for that moment, she—tall and beautiful in bib overalls, with wind-roughened cheeks and chapped lips—and I—short and plain, with dried blood on my face and under my fingernails—were just two women who had followed their hearts.

We smiled at each other.

➻ CORA HOLMES followed her heart to Alaska. A nurse in the Pacific Northwest, she met and married a man who owned a ranch on a remote Alaskan island. Moving out of the civilized world to join him, along with her two sons, was the adventure of her lifetime, and changed them all forever.

ALASKAN VOICES

IN ALL OF the writings about Alaska, the voices of the people who discovered and settled it first—the native Alaskans—can be hard to find. In the early 1980s, the Yukon-Koyukuk School district decided to do something about that. They sent out their students and teachers into the wilderness to talk to some of the elders who remembered what life had been like in the old days. The oral histories that these talks generated became a series of books published by the school district. What follows here are selections from four of those volumes, tales in the voices of native Alaskans.

Editors' Note: The school district would love to continue the project, but costs are high. Just hiring a bush pilot to take the kids out into the field runs into the thousands of dollars. If you are interested in supporting this project, or would like to buy some of the many oral histories assembled by the school district, their address is Yukon-Koyukuk School District, 4762 Old Airport Way, Fairbanks, Alaska 99709, phone number (907) 474-9400.

Kaltag

SERUM RUN

I guess you know about the Iditarod Dog Race being started on account of
the Serum Run. I don't know why 'cause it doesn't even follow the real serum
trail. Mr. Redington, Sr., he's the one that started it. Nobody said it would
take but it sure has. We see all the racers going through here at Kaltag. Last
winter they were everywhere in town here. They stop all over you know.

ABC from the "Wide World of Sports" was here too. They interviewed me
here and in Anchorage. They took movies, too. I guess on account of the
Serum Run. To find out more about it. During the original run there was only
two people got notoriety out of it, right in the beginning. That was Leonard
Seppala and Gunner Kasten. I guess because they were the last two teams on
the run. The rest of us they didn't know anything about. It was a relay so the
rest of the sixteen teams didn't make it to Nome.

There were eighteen teams all together. Mr. Bob Bartlett put it in the *Congressional Record*. Only one team they left out. Said they didn't know who it
was. That's the team that I gave the serum to, Dan Green. I gave it to him in
Hot Springs.

If you don't know about the Serum Run there's a book written on it by
Ungermann. You see, it was a diphtheria epidemic in Nome. They needed
serum. There was no way to get it in there outside of dog team because it was

too cold. Fifty and sixty below. Horse teams was tied up on account of the weather. Airplanes couldn't fly. They was all open cockpit. So they organized the dog teams.

Governor Bone got things rolling here in Alaska. The NC Company was one of the biggest instigators of the bunch because they had mail contracts and mail teams, all the way from Nenana to Ruby.

I happened to be working for the NC as an extra driver. I'd been hauling the auditor around from Tanana to Hot Springs, up to Nenana, all the way over to Circle, Fort Yukon, then retraced to Tanana. I didn't know anything about this Serum Run. I was just playing around.

I was in Tanana on account of the cold weather. John Palm in charge of the dog team and horse team mail for NC Company, said to me, "I want you to hook your dogs up tomorrow morning and make the horse team runs between here and Nenana." The next morning I was at the post office before eight. Tied my dogs. Load my sled up. Took off.

I travel twenty-five miles a day. I got into Hot Springs, went up river to Tolovana and was at Minto Roadhouse. At that time it was thirty-two more miles to Nenana. I figured, well, tomorrow I'll be in the big city. Tomorrow never came.

About five o'clock in the evening, I was laying down in the bunk, just got through feeding the dogs. The telephone rang in the roadhouse. Johnny Campbell answers, says, "Ed, that's for you."

It was T. A. Parsons, NC Agent at Nenana. He says, "I want you to go back to Tolovana."

I said, "Gee, I just left there. I'll be tomorrow in Nenana. I don't want to go back tonight. It's after five." I didn't know anything about what's going on.

"Well," he said, "there's a diphtheria epidemic in Nome. The train will be in here with the serum about five o'clock tonight. They're running a special non-stop train from Seward to Nenana. We'll have relay teams running the serum to Nome. Bill Shannon is going to leave here as soon as the train gets in. I want you to meet him in Tolovanna."

"What'll I do with the mail?"

He says, "Put the mail in the roadhouse."

"Fine." So I went and had something to eat. Then I hooked up the dogs and headed back. Pretty near sixty below. Beautiful moonlit night. I got to Tolovana about ten thirty or eleven o'clock. Harry Martin and another man was there. They helped me unhook the dogs, put them away, and fed them. I went in and Mrs. Martin had supper ready again for me. I watered dogs and went to bed.

Shannon came in next day about eleven o'clock. I took the serum and headed for Hot Springs. I got there about four o'clock in the afternoon. They warmed the serum up a little bit. Dan Green hooked up his dogs and took off for Fish Lake.

I had something to eat and took care of my dogs. He hadn't gotten to Fish Lake when I went to bed. That was twenty-five miles. But when I got up next morning, why, the serum was already on it's way to Ruby from Tanana.

I just took my time, hooked up and headed back to Tanana. Then we all listened to where the serum was by telephone. It was the old abandoned Army telegraph line that people took care of between Tanana and Ruby. It took five days from Nenana to Nome traveling night and day. That's over six hundred miles and more than that by dog team. They were really moving.

Between Nenana and Tanana is 132 miles. From Ruby to Kaltag is little over 120. It's 80 to 90 miles across the portage from Kaltag to Unalakleet. But those teams picked up momentum as they were going along. They all think, well, I'm going to beat the other fellow's time. They had lighter sleds and made good time.

We each got a citation from Governor Bone. I lost mine in the fire. And H. K. Mulford Company who developed the serum also gave us a gold medal worth twenty dollars at the time. Eighteen of us. I misplaced that one. I took it out of my pocketbook, said, "Well, I'm going to leave it home from now on. I'm liable to lose it." I guess I should have kept it in my pocketbook. Because I haven't seen it since.

That first run was about the second week in January, 1925. They had another run pretty near the last week in February. That second run was just bringing more serum to spread to different places along the line, 100 pounds in that one. First run had nineteen pounds.

I carried it that time between Nine Mile Point and Kokrines. I made that thirty-two mile run in three hours and a half going down. I'm scared to say how long it took coming back. You want to know when driving dogs is lots of fun? It took two full days to come back the same distance from Kokrines to Nine Mile Point. Twenty-six dogs and two men. Me and Mike Nickoli.

You see, we just had snow. They must have opened up the basket up there in the sky and just dropped it. When it quit snowing we had three and a half feet of snow where our trail was. I'd walk ahead ten minutes breaking trail.

Then Mike would catch me with the dogs. I'd get off the snowshoes and he'd get ready and break trail. I'd wait for him for ten minutes and catch up. Oh, it was wonderful. Every step we made we'd go down over our knees. If those dogs got off our trail, they were lost. I'll tell you that was tough.

That's not the only time it was tough. It's been tough after that too. But I never even thought of giving up dogs. I liked them. They knew what I was going to do. They were good.

TRAPPING

I treat all my dogs the same. I had dog teams that wouldn't run away from me. I played with them all the time. That's one reason. I turn them loose and I play with them. And when I go away and come back and they're waiting for me, I pet them all right away. I wouldn't just pet one and go on. I pet the whole bunch. Anytime I got up amongst them, they were all right around me.

I had no necklines on my dogs, which gives them more freedom. They could lay down anyway they want to lay down when I walked away from the sled. There was none of this, straighten out, and never laying down this way or that. They curl up anyway they want to. And no, they didn't fight. It's all according to the way you treat dogs. You treat them good and they're right back to you like that.

I trapped with those dogs I raised. Raised some good ones too. The only dog we couldn't make a leader out of was Gypsy. He was a wheel dog and wouldn't go anywhere else. And Rover, he was my leader only. Nobody else could drive him, only me. Well, my daughter, Anna, could drive him anywhere in town when she was nine or ten years old. Soon as she went down the bank he'd turn around and want to come back. He wouldn't take her out of the village. Period. I could drive him anywhere.

Rover was one of my six leaders out of seven dog teams. He was the last dog I ever put in lead. Somewhere in the '50's. I never had no other leader that I wanted. I walk away from the sled, that was it. Nobody could move him. And if he didn't move to go, the other dogs wouldn't go. I could walk away from the sleigh and when I come back two hours later the whole team was still there. All glad to see me.

That was when I was trapping between here and Old Woman, about forty miles from here. I didn't trap the full distance because there was people trapping from town here to about twenty miles out. I trapped from Twenty Mile on out. Two of us. Elia Stanley and I. Missouri Stanley's older brother. Trapped for mink mostly. There was no marten then. Maybe one in ten miles.

My family was in town here at that time. Anna had to go to school. I'd go out three, four, five days. Sometimes a week. Once I was out pretty near two weeks but I had plenty of wood home.

There was hardly anything out there. I was lucky to get five or six mink before Christmas. But after our daughter married George Madros we trapped beaver together out there. We did well on beaver. I took him under my wing, and kind of showed him how to set traps. I made sure the trap was set okay. When we got through that first year, we both had forty beaver each. We hadn't broken any rules because we each had two limits. I had twenty for myself and twenty for my wife. We both took our wives out to spend the night out there. We had our tent on top of three logs high, fixed up real nice and warm. It was fun.

That winter we had to trade beaver skins for fish. I was too busy working on the boats in the summer to fish for dog feed. Right there I says, "George, I'll make a deal. You fish for the dog teams and I'll make sure we've got flour, sugar, milk and the rest of our food." That's the way it's been all the way through.

When we got beaver meat we'd feed them beaver meat with fish. Believe me, that beaver meat makes them feel good too. You bet. And you can call dogs dumb if you want to, but I know different. We give them each a fish and a half a day while we was trapping. They'd eat it. Then if we was going to feed them beaver meat, we'd give them only one fish. You know, them rascals wouldn't eat their fish. No. They'd sit there and wait. So George and I we went in tent and let them wait. They still waited. So we went back out and fed them the beaver meat. They ate that first.

After that first year we averaged around thirty-five beaver every year and we didn't try to kill our country. We caught beaver right up to about five years ago. Then George went to Anchorage one winter. He came back the next year. In the meantime, a couple of men went out there and just cleaned it out. Young babies and all. Killed all the houses. It's beginning to build up again now. That land belongs to Anna and George now. Nobody can trap there but them. They have a tent frame there.

I enjoyed trapping beaver more than anything else. It's harder work and all that, but I liked it. You've only got one place to set your traps and you're right there. And you're outdoors and your own boss. Period. In town, why, you really got nothing to do. Out there you've got something to do every day. We had our radio with us. Listen to the news, nighttime. We enjoyed it.

After trapping we'd go up to Koyukuk and sell most of furs to Dominic. Spend three or four days up there with him and had a good time. Marten wasn't much back then. Maybe eight or nine dollars. Big beaver blankets was running about thirty dollars.

I gave up trapping bout '58. I had a bum knee and couldn't walk on it very good. I didn't want to throw all the work on my partner. It's got to be fifty-fifty in the work when I'm out trapping. So I just quit.

Then I had surgery on my knee and that was the end of having dogs. You had to be able to walk with dogs. Because if there's lots of new snow, you have to put on snowshoes and walk ahead of the dogs for long hours. When you get on snowshoes it means lots of work. I got my first sno-go in 1961 and that was the end of it. It was the first Ski-Doo in Kaltag. I got it mostly to haul wood.

NULATO

SPRING MUSKRATS

We used to go out in the spring you know. On the crust. Most of the time we used to walk. My adopted sister Janet and I used to start three or four o'clock in the morning. Walking two or three hours ahead of my uncle and aunt. We used to enjoy running across the river and running and walking all the way on the Kaiyuh Trail. They catch us up around Dinner Camp. That's about halfway between here and Kaiyuh. After they caught us up, there was no place for us to ride on the sled. So we had to run and walk trying to keep up with them. All the way to Kaiyuh. Maybe fifteen to twenty miles. We didn't think nothing of it.

We used to stay up there for three weeks. Altogether get maybe two, three hundred muskrat. Most the time we come out the last week of May. Come out by boats, by Kaiyuh Slough. Used to be quite a sight, four, five, six families coming out in six, seven boats maybe, and only one inboard pushing it all. We would have to tie up to them cause we had only a rowboat. People pay in those days, about ten, fifteen dollars for towing you out.

It used to be a lot of fun. Most of the time we travel night and day. It would take two days and a night. The men relieve each other steering. Only one person had to steer the boat and another person would be way out in the other boat where you couldn't make the real quick bends. He'd have to hit it with a paddle. And we'd stop once or twice during the trip to make tea. Everybody eat. But a lot of times you just keep going and people eat in the boat.

Sometimes there would be other groups of boats. We used to wait at Two Mile till all the boats caught up with each other. Then we all come right behind each other coming to town. Soon as we leave Two Mile we start shooting shotgun and rifle. All the people that are in town, they answer us. It sound good.

I remember one of the Sisters, her first year here, during the Second World War. She didn't know what was going on every spring when the people come out of the Kaiyuh. Early one morning around four o'clock she start hearing a lot of shooting. She got scared. Ran to the next room to wake the other Sisters, telling them the Japs are coming. Here it was Kaiyuh people, coming out.

Sometimes we used to have to make camp at the mouth of Kaiyuh Slough when the river was rough. But when you're coming out of Kaiyuh Slough and it's not too rough, even if you're hungry you don't want to stop there. You want to keep on going. You want to get to this side of the river before the wind comes up. You want to get home as soon as you could. While it's calm.

When everyone get home from Kaiyuh, you pack up all your spring outfit, clean up your houses and dance. Mostly dancing and drinking. In the older days I think they used to gamble a lot with muskrats, traps, bullets and matches. But not very often in my time. After all the dancing they get ready for fishing.

FISHING

I remember a story my grandpa, Charlie Mountain, used to tell about my dad and Daniel Sipary, when they were young. They just got married, maybe two or three years. They used to really like each other. Brother-in-laws, he never saw any brother-in-law like that. They really thought a lot of each other.

One time they moved to camp. There was nothing at the camp. They pitched up the tent and started to work. They bet each other, to see who was going to last the longest without sleep. They just started to work. They started to make wheel first. They finished the wheel, built the smokehouse, and the fish racks. By that time they had set the wheel and everything. It was time to cut fish. They had worked three days and three nights. Around the clock without sleeping. The third day around noon, they started cutting fish.

My grandpa and grandma were telling me. They go to bed at night, you know, my grandpa and grandma. The next morning when they get up my dad and Uncle Dan is still working. So this third day, Grandpa say it's just like he don't see my uncle around. Grandpa looked under the fish rack and here he saw him passed out right on the rocks. The slime from the fish was just dripping down in his face. Three days and three nights without sleeping.

My Uncle Dan was the best friend I ever had. Remember when I talk about going back and forth between the two families. I didn't mind it. First, I want my mom. After I got used to it, it didn't bother me. I didn't want to leave my uncle. I remember how I cried when he died of cancer around '58 or '59.

My uncle wasn't a hunter, so I more or less had to learn by myself and from other people. My uncle was a fisherman. And I think it's better. I wish I had his skills. Because now to fish year round, you'll never get hungry. But with the hunting, a lot of times you'll come home skunked. Especially when you have to feed a family. He used to work a fishwheel. Fishtrap. Fresh fish all year around. Not one kind, you know, grayling, lush, trout, sheefish, and a little greasy whitefish.

I should tell you how we used to get them. In the fall, September, we put in fish trap across the Nulato River. All the way across. Now it's against the law and we could put the fishtrap only halfway. We cannot block the whole river. In those days we used to block the whole river.

The trap was small wire, maybe five or six feet long and a little funnel in the front. We used to face it upriver right in the riffles. Put in pegs all the way and willows against it. Then the fish would be facing upriver, just like swimming but they're drifting down. They go into the fishtrap tail first. We catch them *sil yee lookk'a'* in White man way we call them little skinny whitefishes. Then we used to catch trout, grayling and lush. We have Indian name for them too, but it would take me time to remember them. So, that's falltime.

Then, later on in the winter, around February, we put in fishtrap out in the Yukon. A bigger one. We used to catch lush, sheefish, whitefish and little whitefish. Not the same kind of little whitefish in the Nulato River. These ones are about the same size, but they're fatter and they're greasy. What we call them in Indian is just on my tongue now, *dilmiga*.

To put in a fishtrap is a lot of work out in the river. In Nulato River it's easy, but out in the Yukon, no. First you got to go out in the woods and find a big tree that'll split easy. Into little sticks. I used to see him working way late at night. Midnight, two o'clock sometimes. Sitting down on the floor splitting these things. Lot of patience. That's the only thing I think that would get me stuck to put in fishtrap. I think about it a lot of times. I'm sure I could put one in. Because after I got a little older my uncle used to just like let me direct the operations. I used to be the eye-man.

There's certain way you have to put down those poles for the trap to go between. It has to be perfect or you'll have trouble all the time. The fence is nothing, you can put your poles in any old way. But putting in fishtrap takes a lot of work, a lot of time and a lot of patience.

During the winter most of the fish was for food. We never used it for dogs. My uncle used to sell a lot of fish cheap. Sometimes he'd sell only to certain people even if there was lots of fish. He wouldn't sell to people who feed fresh fish and bones leftovers to the dogs. You'd have to wait because next time there'd be no fish if you feed fresh fish to dogs. There was a pilot used to come in here. He put in order and haul them back to Fairbanks. I guess he resold them. I don't know. Whitefish and sheefish but not too much lush. So we ate a lot of fish when I was growing up. I didn't mind because it was all different and fresh. It's not like going to your freezer right now. It doesn't taste the same.

Nobody use trap in winter now. A few people put in fishnet and get whitefish and sheefish in the Yukon. In the fall, we put in hooks out on the ice. Last fall we did and caught a few lush. Put in big bait hook with a piece of fish on it. Maybe ten hooks on a line and string a line under the ice. Lot of people did that last fall. I'm going to do that again this year.

Then in summer, we'd have fishwheel. We catch whitefish, dog salmon, king salmon. Not very much king salmon. Mostly silvers and chinook salmons. My uncle never used fishnet. Only fishtraps and fishwheel.

All our lives, up until a few years before uncle died, we never had no inboard or outboard. We used to walk, pulling the boat two and a half miles upriver. Every morning. Hot sun. Two people. One in the boat and one walking, pulling. I was the younger, so I used to walk. I let my uncle steer.

I got to where I used to hate that walk two and a half miles, pulling a rowboat. Then we put 500 fish in the boat and row back down. All arm power.

For a while we had couple dogs that were pretty good. They were pulling us, like pulling a sled. They walk along the beach with harness on them. You sit in the boat and have a free ride. Dog has to be really good for that. Then when you get to the fishwheel, you have to row real hard around it. The current was strong. Now all you got to do is get in the boat and pull the kicker. Take off. Sometimes I enjoy walking with boat but sometimes I used to say to myself, I'm going to buy kicker first chance I get. I did. Around 1960, after I got married.

KALTAG

FATHER

My father was from downriver. He said before my time there were lots of caribou around there. The Native name is *Sislaakkaakk'at*, like you're saying bear, so in English they call it Bear Creek. There was no village, just maybe a couple families stayed there. Old-timers never looked for a village like Kaltag to live in. There were no jobs. Only income in Kaltag then would be the postmaster and teacher. Postmaster owned the store and only one single teacher. That would be the only income. So these people didn't have a village down at Bear Creek. They just stop there because it was a good area for fish or caribou.

No tents then, either, or log cabins. They used to have real mud houses. I think that was the best kind of warm house there was. Warmer than the log cabins we have now. They call them *naahalooyah*. About average size was 10' by 10'. They had a fire right in the middle. No stove just a hole in the roof. All the smoke would draw up there. I was never in one, but when I was 15 or 16 I saw some that were already caving in. That's the kind our parents were living in.

Before Kaltag moved up from the old town a few miles below here my dad got pretty sick. He couldn't do nothing for his family. I wasn't born yet. My brother-in-law who is married to my cousin brought the family up to Nulato to the Mission. Sisters, brothers and a priest in Nulato. And they had a clinic. That's the closest place they could go by dog team so my brother-in-law brought my dad and my mother and the family up. They stayed by the mission for several years. All the time after that he had to go to church. Even if he had to crawl he wouldn't miss Easter Mass.

Christmas was the same way. All those Catholic holidays he wouldn't go out and split wood. But he didn't like Independence Day, Fourth of July or St. Patrick's Day. He said because that's just a time for people to be happy. To make one another happy and drink. Well, my dad was quite a drinker, too, but he was like me. He think about his family more than drink. He never refused a drink from anybody. But he wouldn't overdo himself with the drink. When we used to go out trapping he used to have a bottle of whiskey with him all the time. Every night after getting through work, he used to take one drink and then go to bed.

He had a fish trap sixteen miles down here on the island. He used to catch trout, grayling, lush, sheefish, and whitefish. All different kinds of fish in that trap. It was really good, but I never learned how to put one in. Wintertime under the ice, I mean. Eddie Hildebrand in Nulato has one.

My dad made his trap all out of spruce and willows. He used to say anytime you put iron in the water, the fish don't like it. He was quite a bit superstitious about fishing, because fish in the water, like bears hibernating, don't make tracks. When he brought up the first fish he wouldn't pass it around until the next day. It had to stay overnight in the cache first. Later when you bring fish up from the trap, if somebody buy it before you bring it inside your house or cache, that's fine. But the rest, if you keep it or put it away, it has to be there overnight.

He was the same way about black bear. He said there's some girls don't eat black bear because they could give you bad luck. You wouldn't find a bear again easy. It's hard to catch black bear anyway in the fall because there's no snow. They hibernate early in the fall and that's all. You walk around just like you lost something in the woods looking for bear den. Pretty soon you don't even catch anything. You don't even see a sign of it. You can spend days and days out hunting, looking around for black bear in the dens and you'll never catch it. So he was right.

Sometimes he did get a black bear in the fall. The fat was about couple inches thick on the back. We always put that away for special time like New Year's canvas toss. People come around shaking a canvas in front of your door and you throw in some food. Then they take it all to the community center and potlatch it out to people. They cut the bear fat into strips because it was very valuable. That's just about the richest food there was for falltime.

MOTHER

My mother was from out Unalakleet way. They call it Reindeer Station in English but in Native it is *K'inaakkoy Nʉggʉt*. My mother was raised there so she is part Eskimo. The rest is Indian. I don't know her parents' names. She didn't know herself. She said she was pretty small when her father died, but big when her mother died.

There was a trail through *K'inaakkoy Nʉggʉt* between Kaltag and Unalakleet. The only place there was store before the one here came up was in St. Michael and Unalakleet. N.C. Co. had big outfits in those places. Lot of people from the Yukon used to go over there to get groceries. Five dogs was the most people had. Some just with three or four and some pulling their toboggan on foot.

Kaltag is not a really old village. It's people from all the surrounding areas. Some came from Innoko River. Some came from seventy miles down the Yukon at *Sislaakkaakk'at* and from down further. Some came from near by and some from *K'inaakkoy Nʉggʉt*. Slim Rubin, John Chiroskey and Old Man Stanley all came from Reindeer Station.

When I was about 8 or 9 they used to bring a herd of reindeer over. Practically all the Unalakleet people had a herd of their own. Hardly any moose or caribou so when the trader here wanted some reindeer they just herded them over. They camped about a mile back from town. They corralled them, kill them off, and butcher them right there. I've seen it. They sell the meat to the store or traders in Nulato. Then they would give us all the extras like the head or hoofs or skin. Whatever they can't sell they give to the Natives.

BORN

I was born here at Kaltag December 21, 1920. That was about the year people moved the village up from the Old Village. A trader came and built a store here so people wanted to be closer to it. Jim Addison was the first store owner. Adolf Miller was the next one. He was married to Edgar Kalland's mother's sister. Along with the store Adolf had a pool table. After he died people say his spirit still rolled the balls around with no one else there. He is buried on the bank by the old church.

Then another guy came and bought the store. He was a mail carrier. They used to have a mail run on the Yukon by dog team. And the same time the main line for mail service to Anchorage and Fairbanks was through the portage here to Unalakleet. No airplanes in those days. During the summer they packed the mail on foot. Each man could carry only seventy-five pounds. Over to Unalakleet there are six creeks about as big as the Kaltag River, some much bigger. They had bridges across all of them for summer packing, spring when there's hardly any snow left on the ground, and fall before the ice freezes good. Since they're used mostly for walking I call them footbridges.

Ninety miles from here to Unalakleet and the trail was good. Not growed in like now. They had mail cabins at 22 Mile, forty miles out, what they used to call 10 Mile, one at Old Woman, fifty miles out and one more at Whaleback named after a crippled man, twenty-three miles out of Unalakleet. At all those cabins they had a telephone. No satellite phone like we have now. It was a wire running all the way from St. Michael to Tanana and beyond.

John Sommers, a White guy, had the mail contract here. His house was just about where my place is now. He used to hire some Natives to pack mail for him. And those days there used to be a lot of mail. Summertime you carry only first class mail, but just about the end of the season after they buy fur in April you used to carry hundreds of pounds of mail by dogteam.

I was a little boy when I used to go with my dad. He carried mail from Nulato to 40 Mile out here. His dogs were too rough to handle alone in the beginning of the season, falltime, so he used to take me out of school to hold the brake for him. He had to hold the gee-pole at the bow of the sleigh and stand on skis. That's the only way he could keep the sleigh on the trail because the load was so heavy. We'd have eight or nine hundred pounds of mail on every trip. He couldn't handle that much load from the handlebar. And whenever there were any rabbits or ptarmigans on the road, he'd have a tough time holding the dogs back.

One trip I'll never forget. When my oldest sister got married to Clement Esmailka I went to live with them in the fall. We stayed out in Kaiyuh. Then my dad sent word up that he needed me to come back to hold the brake for him on his mail team. The dogs were too rough to hold especially if there was a light load coming back. We took a heavy load out then we turned around at 10 Mile, that's forty miles from here. And only had ten pounds of mail to bring back in. That's not much load for thirteen dogs. Especially since we had one dog that liked to bark and jolly up the dogs. He'd get them to run and gallop.

That morning my brother left ahead of us with his team. He was trapping out that way. Boy, those dogs could smell the fresh trail of his team ahead. They really got going. My dad had a four inch by eight inch brake and I stood on that brake almost the whole way. Well, that's why I went with him. It's not level, either, some places are pretty steep.

Ten miles out from here we stopped at a creek. The creek was frozen over so we weren't going to use the bridge but the bank was eight foot and steep. He told me to hold the brake so he can get off the gee-pole and put the skis in the sled. He wanted to ride the runners and let me carry the skis across the creek. I got off the sled. Just as he got on the handlebar the dogs started barking. They took off. He held the brake all the way down into the creek, up the bank, and into the woods. By the time I got up the bank he was gone. I couldn't see him anymore. Only fresh snow where he was holding the brake into the trail. I stop and listen. I could hear him hollering quite a ways up ahead. I was just only a little boy. I got scared and started crying, but I never stopped running.

I ran about a mile and came out in an open flat. That flat was about a mile long but I still couldn't see him. Running, running. I could see places where he caught onto old stumps with the snubbing line. Old stumps where guys cut wood long time ago by the trail. Too old I guess. He pulled them right out. I keep running and keep holding onto those skis. Four miles I chase after him.

Finally at 6 Mile I found him. He rammed his sleigh down in the creek into the willows. He was standing in front of the leader with his ax trying to keep those dogs quiet. Threaten them. Try to scare them and keep them from jerking. "Okay, my son," he said, "get in the sleigh. We're going to make those dogs *go* next six miles!"

I sat in the sleigh while he broke off some little willows to scare the dogs. He make those dogs gallop all the way in for six miles. He was mad. "Gee, those dogs are pretty rough," he said. That was the first time I was alone in the woods.

The next day he went to Nulato and came back with three or four hundred pounds. He said, "You don't have to come with me son." So I went back to school. That's why I didn't have much schooling. I was the only other boy left at home. I had six brothers but they were all out trapping. I had to go with my dad when he needed me. Out of nine months of school I only went about four months. And I went only as far as fourth grade.

In those days you could go up to sixth grade, then you were done with school. There was not a high school that you could go to. Mt. Edgecumbe school wasn't open yet. Later on it started to get a little bit better. After I quit school. Well, after you're 16 then you're done with school, too.

Sometimes here there would be only four students from September on. All the parents would go out in September and stay out till December. Come back. Then January we're all out in our camps again. In those days you had to stay out and live off the country. There was no mail plane. No fresh food like eggs we're getting right now. Only time we get our fresh food is in the beginning of the spring in June and the last boat in September. Twice a year, that's all we used to get some eggs or some fresh food. All the rest of the time we just had to live off the land. When we want to get something fresh then we had to go out and kill it.

My family had five boys and three girls when I was growing up. We all stayed in one building. I remember Dad used to get fifty pounds of flour pretty near about twice a week. That's the sweetest thing we could get. And my brother used to bake bread. Eight loaves and that bread would only last one day. Next day he'd have to bake some more.

My parents were really busy. My mother was out every day trying to catch something for us. Out snaring rabbits, or ptarmigans or go to fishnet. If Dad was out trapping he might be on the trapline for thirty days. During that time we had no extra dogs so we had to haul wood out by our neck or pack it out. At least wood was close at that time. Right now you have to go quite a ways back to get wood because it's all chopped out. Things were way different in those days.

My parents didn't know much English. My mother didn't speak English at all. They didn't see many White people around here. In fact, we used to be scared of White people when we were kids. If some White guy come down, some miner come down in a boat, we'd be scared of him. We wouldn't even talk with him. Maybe we'd be about thirty or forty feet away from him watching. Now these days, some stranger comes into town, you see a little boy or little girl go up and start talking with him. "Where you come from? What you're doing?" And all those questions. My days we never used to do that because there was only one White man here, the guy that's buried on the bank, Adolf Miller. Plus the school teacher would come in the falltime.

After the school teacher came there used to be a curfew. They ring the bell every night and you got to go in. If they catch you out your parents have a fine, like fifty cents or twenty-five cents. They thought it was good for us for the beginning of our schooling. My parents didn't really go for it. They didn't want me to learn. They didn't want me to go to school. They said that was just wasting time. They wanted me to learn out in the woods. I was the youngest boy in the family and my dad was trying to spoil me I guess. Tried to make a pet out of me. But my brothers Burke and Benjamin went to school at Holy Cross. My oldest brother stayed there nine full years. Never came home on vacation. Nine full years at the mission.

GALENA

FIRST ONE BORN

I was born just the way they deliver babies, I guess. I must have been just about the first person born in Galena. A lot of people moved there from Old Louden about that same time. But I don't know much about how that town got started. My dad, Edgar Nollner, is living there now and he could tell a lot of things about why people moved there.

My grandfather, John Antoski, ran a roadhouse for the mail teams. He and his wife, Agnes, were the first people in Galena. I was born February 1, 1922, in grandfather's house, I suppose. I never talked to my mother about it and that house is gone over the bank now. It caved in a lot, you know, so it's not there anymore. I was the first grandchild so I was something special. They used to pack me on their back, Eskimo style, all the time. They say I got spoiled by it. I just want to be packed all the time. And I have two grand-mothers to do it.

My dad was a trapper in those days. His parents, Al and Cecelia Nollner ran a store in Old Louden. Later they moved it to Galena. Al Nollner was a German. Tall, blue-eyed guy. We used to go to the store and he used to give us peanuts. I still like peanuts. Grandmother Cecelia was an Indian. I can't tell you how many kids they had, but it was a big family. Not that many on my mother's side. They just died off as they were born, I guess. My mother is the only one that survived. They adopted Lincoln Antoski so she had one brother until he died in his thirties from TB.

I don't know why they lost so many children. At least twelve and my mother is the only one that survived. In my family we had sixteen and there's still a lot of us living; Gabriel Nollner, Paddy Nollner, Alfred Nollner, Cecelia Burgett, Jean Cooper, Angela Grasso, and Mary Carlo.

Both of my grandmothers died when I was only about three or four so I don't really know too much about them. It seems like my parents never had too much time to sit and talk to us about my grandparents and things. Parents then had to work hard to make a living.

Springtime we have to go to spring camp to hunt muskrats, ducks, and beaver. And fish. Then we have to take care of it. Cut fish and take care of meat. Pluck all the ducks, dry it, and salt some in rock salt. And, boy, skinning muskrats is work! But after a while you get to be expert even though you are young. When I think about it there was nothing else for us to do anyway. For me, anyway. Just help my folks.

From the time I was 11 years old, seems like I was taking care of my little brothers and sisters. When we stay in Galena, Mom and Dad used to go way back in the mountains and stay out ten days at least. My uncle, Lincoln Antoski, stayed with us to take care of us, but it's up to me to get the other kids up and feed them. When Mom and Dad get back they're tired.

I never know a time when my parents ever talk with me like I do with my children now. If my kids feel like talking we get to talk. If they don't feel like talking, okay, but I wish they could talk with me more. I think it's a good thing for them and for me, too.

After muskrat hunting we get back to Galena and get ready to go fishing. We had two camps. The first one was at Old Louden. We stayed there from June till August. Then we go to our other camp just above Galena on the south bank.

For some reason the kings that run on the north bank are much richer than those on the south bank. So most people try to fish on the north side for the kings. Then in the fall we switch to the south side because dog salmon run so much heavier there. My father still has his camp there to this day.

I don't know when we had our schooling. Short time we're in town, I guess, because after fishing we went to fall camp. We used to cut steamboat wood and pile it on the bank. After they cut as much as they want, we go back to Galena.

In the fall when the ice is not too thick we put our net under the ice for whitefish. We take a stick about twenty feet long and tie a rope to one end. Then we chop holes about fifteen feet apart and push the stick under the ice from hole to hole. Four or five holes anyway. That way we get the line stretched fifty or sixty feet. When we put the net in we have to hang it kind of low so it wouldn't freeze to the ice.

It's really good to see all the whitefish coming out of the net. Fresh fish. Falltime is good because we get fish eggs too. Lush especially is good. That's the only kind my sister Angela likes.

Lush really go for blackfish on hooks. My sister sent me some blackfish from Galena so I could get lush here. I had them in a jar from spring till October, but it got too cold so I let them loose in the lake up the road.

Those blackfish are amazing. You don't feed it nothing. Just change the water and it lives. You don't feed it at all. We used to catch them on a lake. Scoop them up with a frying pan when they come up for air. We either freeze them in the snow or put them in a rabbit skin if we want to save them. Bring them home in a rabbit skin and put them in a dishpan. Keep it alive. You could hear them at night make little noise. Then we put the hook through the tail and let it swim in the river water. Never miss for lush and pike, too.

There was plenty to do in fall camp. I set rabbit snares and hunt willow grouse besides helping my mother. Short days but we get it done. Dad is making a living so the kids cut all the house wood, get ice, water, whatever.

Wherever we went, my father always make a cabin. I don't know how many he made. A couple below Old Louden and at our fall camp. But maybe not where they go back in the mountains to trap because they always took a tent with them then.

MY OLD HOME TOWN

Koyukuk was way bigger than Galena. They had a store and a post office so they felt they had something over us. Even the steamboats never used to stop in Galena. They just slow down and throw the mail up the bank. Yeah, that's my old home town.

There were thirteen or fourteen families there. George Jimmy and his family, his brother, Little Jimmy, Ambrose Abraham and his mother, Mrs. Abraham. We just call them old women like Mrs. Abraham, "Grandma." We don't even ask what their name was those days. Then there was Eenyas Paul and his family and the Nollners, that's us. My uncle, Walter Nollner and his family, Sam Stannish and his family, Old Wholecheese and his family. And my grandfather, John Antoski, Bessie Wholecheese and her husband. She was married to my uncle first, but he drowned so she remarried. And other old names, like Ayluk Dayton, kind of odd name. I don't even know how you would write it.

We were all one big family. Real close knit. When somebody catch a moose everybody shared. Nobody went without meat, I guess because it was so small. Men used to get together in the evening and tell stories about how they got moose. We'd be there listening, if we're not playing. Like if it gets too dark or too cold to play outdoors.

Mostly we'd play post office. We girls would write letters to each other in the other houses because we can't be going out running all over the place. So we always had some boys being postmaster running from house to house delivering letters.

We play paper dolls a lot too. I don't know how we knew there was paper dolls, but we used to make our own out of hard cardboard. Summertime we used to pull out long grass by the roots and use that for the hair. We must have had a lot of fun. We'd find big leaves and cut them like fish and hang them on a fish rack. That's how we used to play. I don't see kids do that nowadays. They have all kinds of toys but they're not satisfied. We made our own things to do. I guess we just didn't know any different. I was lucky.

DON'T LAUGH...IT'S NOT FUNNY

JUST BECAUSE ALASKA is full of life and death confrontations and soaring vistas of incredible beauty doesn't mean that you can't laugh at the place. Alaskans, perhaps in defense against the long winters and the perils of their chosen home, have fabulous senses of humor. Here are a couple of pieces that poke fun at the sheer silliness of life up north. The first piece, Jack London's description of housekeeping standards among the gold rush miners, will make you laugh out loud and run for the Lysol. The second, an ode by *Alaska Magazine*'s Bruce Woods to the biting insects of spring, will make you pray for deliverance from a similar plague, even as you laugh until you cry.

JACK LONDON

Housekeeping in the Klondike

Housekeeping in the Klondike—that's bad! And by *men*—worse. Reverse the proposition, if you will, yet you will fail to mitigate, even by a hair's-breadth, the woe of it. It is bad, unutterably bad, for a man to keep house, and it is equally bad to keep house in the Klondike. That's the sum and substance of it. Of course men will be men, and especially is this true of the kind who wander off to the frozen rim of the world. The glitter of gold is in their eyes, they are borne along by uplifting ambition, and in their hearts is a great disdain for everything in the culinary department save "grub." "Just so long as it's grub," they say, coming in off trail, gaunt and ravenous, "grub, and piping hot." Nor do they manifest the slightest regard for the genesis of the same; they prefer to begin at "revelations."

Yes, it would seem a pleasant task to cook for such men; but just let them lie around cabin to rest up for a week, and see with what celerity they grow high-stomached and make sarcastic comments on the way you fry the bacon or boil the coffee. And behold how each will spring his own strange and marvelous theory as to how sour-dough bread should be mixed and baked. Each has his own recipe (formulated, mark you, from personal experience only), and to him it is an idol of brass, like unto no other man's, and he'll fight for it—ay, down to the last wee pinch of soda—and if need be, die for it. If you should happen to catch him on trail, completely exhausted, you may blacken his character, his flag, and his ancestral tree with impunity; but breathe the slightest whisper against his sour-dough bread, and he will turn upon and rend you.

From this it may be gathered what an unstable thing sour dough is. Never was coquette so fickle. You cannot depend upon it. Still, it is the simplest thing in the world. Make a batter and place it near the stove (that it may not freeze) till it ferments or sours. Then mix the dough with it, and sweeten with soda to taste—of course replenishing the batter for next time. There it is. Was there ever anything simpler? But, oh, the tribulations of the cook! It is never twice the same. If the batter could only be placed away in an equable temperature, all well and good. If one's comrades did not interfere, much vexation of spirit might be avoided. But this cannot be; for Tom fires up the stove till the cabin is become like the hot-room of a Turkish bath; Dick forgets all about the fire till the place is a refrigerator; then along comes Harry and shoves the sour-dough bucket right against the stove to make way for the drying of his mittens. Now heat is a most potent factor in accelerating the fermentation of flour and water, and hence the unfortunate cook is constantly in disgrace with Tom, Dick, and Harry. Last week his bread was yellow from a plethora of soda; this week it is sour from a prudent lack of the same; and next week—ah, who can tell save the god of the fire-box?

Some cooks aver they have so cultivated their olfactory organs that they can tell to the fraction of a degree just how sour the batter is. Nevertheless they have never been known to bake two batches of bread which were at all alike. But this fact casts not the slightest shadow upon the infallibility of their theory. One and all, they take advantage of circumstances, and meanly crawl out by laying the blame upon the soda, which was dampened "the time the canoe overturned," or upon the flour, which they got in trade from "that half-breed fellow with the dogs."

The pride of the Klondike cook in his bread is something which passes understanding. The highest commendatory degree which can be passed upon a man in that country, and the one which distinguishes him from the tenderfoot, is that of being a "sour-dough boy." Never was a college graduate prouder of his "sheepskin" than the old-timer of this appellation. There is a certain distinction about it, from which the newcomer is invidiously excluded. A tenderfoot with his baking-powder is an inferior creature, a freshman; but a "sour-dough boy" is a man of stability, a post-graduate in that art of arts—bread-making.

Next to bread a Klondike cook strives to achieve distinction by his doughnuts. This may appear frivolous at first glance, and at second, considering the
materials with which he works, an impossible feat. But doughnuts are all-
important to the man who goes on trail for a journey of any length. Bread
freezes easily, and there is less grease and sugar, and hence less heat in it, than
in doughnuts. The latter do not solidify except at extremely low temperatures, and they are very handy to carry in the pockets of a Mackinaw jacket
and munch as one travels along. They are made much after the manner of
their brethren in warmer climes, with the exception that they are cooked in
bacon grease—the more grease, the better they are. Sugar is the cook's chief
stumbling-block; if it is very scarce, why, add more grease. The men never
mind—on trail. In the cabin?—well, that's another matter; besides, bread is
good enough for them then.

The cold, the silence, and the darkness somehow seem to be considered
the chief woes of the Klondiker. But this is all wrong. There is one woe which
overshadows all others—the lack of sugar. Every party which goes north sig-
nifies a manly intention to do without sugar, and after it gets there bemoans
itself upon its lack of foresight. Man can endure hardship and horror with
equanimity, but take from him his sugar, and he raises his lamentations to the
stars. And the worst of it is that it all falls back upon the long-suffering cook.
Naturally, coffee, and mush, and dried fruit, and rice, eaten without sugar, do
not taste exactly as they should. A certain appeal to the palate is missing.
Then the cook is blamed for his vile concoctions. Yet, if he be a man of wisdom, he may judiciously escape the major part of this injustice. When he
places a pot of mush upon the table, let him see to it that it is accompanied by
a pot of stewed dried apples or peaches. This propinquity will suggest the
combination to the men, and the flatness of the one will be neutralized by the
sharpness of the other. In the distress of a sugar famine, if he be a cook of
parts, he will boil rice and fruit together in one pot; and if he cook a dish of
rice and prunes properly, of a verity he will cheer up the most melancholy
member of the party, and extract from him great gratitude.

Such a cook must indeed be a man of resources. Should his comrades cry
out that vinegar be placed upon the beans, and there is no vinegar, he must
know how to make it out of water, dried apples, and brown paper. He obtains
the last from the bacon-wrappings, and it is usually saturated with grease. But
that does not matter. He will early learn that in a land of low temperatures it
is impossible for bacon grease to spoil anything. It is to the white man what

blubber and seal oil are to the Eskimo. Soul-winning gravies may be made from it by the addition of water and browned flour over the fire. Some cooks base far-reaching fame solely upon their gravy, and their names come to be on the lips of men wherever they forgather at the feast. When the candles give out, the cook fills a sardine-can with bacon grease, manufactures a wick out of the carpenter's sail-twine, and behold! the slush-lamp stands complete. It goes by another and less complimentary name in the vernacular, and, next to sour-dough bread, is responsible for more men's souls than any other single cause of degeneracy in the Klondike.

The ideal cook should also possess a Semitic incline to his soul. Initiative in his art is not the only requisite; he must keep an eye upon the variety of his larder. He must "swap" grub with the gentile understandingly; and woe unto him should the balance of trade be against him. His comrades will thrust it into his teeth every time the bacon is done over the turn, and they will even rouse him from his sleep to remind him of it. For instance, previous to the men going out for a trip on trail, he cooks several gallons of beans in the company of numerous chunks of salt pork and much bacon grease. This mess he then molds into blocks of convenient size and places on the roof, where it freezes into bricks in a couple of hours. Thus the men, after a weary day's travel, have but to chop off chunks with an axe and thaw out in the frying-pan. Now the chances preponderate against more than one party in ten having chili-peppers in their outfits. But the cook, supposing him to be fitted for his position, will ferret out that one party, discover some particular shortage in its grub-supply of which he has plenty, and swap the same for chili-peppers. These in turn he will incorporate in the mess aforementioned, and behond a dish which even the hungry arctic gods may envy. Variety in the grub is as welcome to the men as nuggets. When, after eating dried peaches for months, the cook trades a few cupfuls of the same for apricots, the future at once takes on a more roseate hue. Even a change in the brand of bacon will revivify blasted faith in the country.

It is no sinecure, being cook in the Klondike. Often he must do his work in a cabin measuring ten by twelve on the inside, and occupied by three other men besides himself. When it is considered that these men eat, sleep, lounge, smoke, play cards, and entertain visitors there, and also in that small space house the bulk of their possessions, the size of the cook's orbit may be readily computed. In the morning he sits up in bed, reaches out and strikes the fire, then proceeds to dress. After that the centre of his orbit is the front of the stove, the diameter the length of his arms. Even then his comrades are continually encroaching upon his domain, and he is at constant warfare to prevent territorial grabs. If the men are working hard on the claim, the cook is also expected to find his own wood and water. The former he chops up and sleds into camp, the latter he brings home in a sack—unless he is unusually diligent, in which case he has a ton or so of water piled up before the door. Whenever he is not cooking, he is thawing out ice, and between whiles running out and hoisting on the windlass for his comrades in the shaft. The care of the dogs also devolves upon him, and he carries his life and a long club in his hand every time he feeds them.

But there is one thing the cook does not have to do, nor any man in the Klondike—and that is, make another man's bed. In fact, the beds are never made except when the blankets become unfolded, or when the pine needles have all fallen off the boughs which form the mattress. When the cabin has a dirt floor and the men do their carpenter-work inside, the cook never sweeps it. It is much warmer to let the chips and shavings remain. Whenever he kindles a fire he uses a couple of handfuls of the floor. However, when the deposit becomes so deep that his head is knocking against the roof, he seizes a shovel and removes a foot or so of it.

Nor does he have any windows to wash; but if the carpenter is busy he must make his own windows. This is simple. He saws a hole out of the side of the cabin, inserts a home-made sash, and for panes falls back upon the treasured writing-tablet. A sheet of this paper, rubbed thoroughly with bacon grease, becomes transparent, sheds water when it thaws, and keeps the cold out and the heat in. In cold weather the ice will form upon the inside of it to the thickness of sometimes two or three inches. When the bulb of the mercurial thermometer has frozen solid, the cook turns to his window, and by the thickness of the icy coating infallibly gauges the outer cold within a couple of degrees.

A certain knowledge of astronomy is required of the Klondike cook, for another task of his is to keep track of the time. Before going to bed he wanders outside and studies the heavens. Having located the Pole Star by means of the Great Bear, he inserts two slender wands in the snow, a couple of yards apart and in line with the North Star. The next day, when the sun on the southern horizon casts the shadows of the wands to the northward and in line, he knows it to be twelve o'clock, noon, and sets his watch and those of his partners accordingly. As stray dogs are constantly knocking his wands out of line with the North Star, it becomes his habit to verify them regularly every night, and thus another burden is laid upon him.

But, after all, while the woes of the man who keeps house and cooks food in the northland are innumerable, there is one redeeming feature in his lot which does not fall to the women housewives of other lands. When things come to a pass with his feminine prototype, she throws her apron over her head and has a good cry. Not so with him, being a man and a Klondiker. He merely cooks a little more atrociously, raises a storm of grumbling, and resigns. After that he takes up his free out-door life again, and exerts himself mightily in making life miserable for the unlucky comrade who takes his place in the management of the household destinies.

Excerpt from *Alaska* magazine, August 2000

BRUCE WOODS

STILL A FEW BUGS
IN THE SYSTEM

The conventional wisdom, repeated in brochures, vacation guides and even occasionally in the pages of *Alaska* magazine, has it that one of the advantages of visiting Alaska in the late summer is the relative absence of biting insects. In May and June, you might well have heard or read, these pests can reach the proportions of a Pharaoh's plague; but come July (and certainly by August), their populations will have dropped, leaving the backcountry more hospitable to human travelers.

I try to keep that thought in mind as I huddle behind the thin skin of a tent that has gone dark with a satanic bouillabaisse of no-see-ums, mosquitoes and white-socks. The bugs are seething over every inch of the tight nylon in a maddened eagerness to get at my poor pink flesh. It has been like this for two days now, in our light camp on the bank of an anonymous stream in the southwestern Alaska tundra. Not willing to risk eating in the tents and leaving a bear-bait of food odors there, fellow sufferer Dave Petersen and I have crept out of our shelters at the slightest breeze to fumble with the camp stove and bolt down half-cooked food. Even then, our eating (and cooking) has been done on the run, with hungry clouds rising around us if we dare to pause. When a freak wind does spring up strongly enough to put the pests down, we have only to squat on our heels in doomed complacency and they will take advantage of the windbreaks of our bodies to rise behind us and attack anew.

A man armed with a botanist's fine-weave sweep net would never starve in this country. One swing, we surmise, would bag him at least a pound of food: a gray, grapefruit-sized clot of maniacally churning living protein. Then again, I suspect that his situation might resemble that in the apocryphal tale of the Shelby Cobra with its engine left running at the filling station: I fear our imaginary botanist would be hard pressed to take in fuel fast enough to keep up with the withdrawals.

We are not eager to test that theory. Coffee is usually one of the real joys of backcountry camping, but we've forgone even this simple pleasure so far, not wanting to deal with the potentially awkward aftereffects of imbibing too much of the juice of the bean. Over the course of two long days, however, nature will eventually have her say.

The groan from the other tent is thick with despair; the kind of sound you'd expect to follow the loss of a lover or the death of a particularly good dog.

"Dave . . . ," I call tentatively across the space separating our two shelters. The boiling skin of insects seems to quicken at the sound of my words. "You OK?"

His voice is a monotone, a condemned man's pole-axed drone, but I can make out his meaning well enough, and, I shudder.

"What are you going to *do*?" I whisper.

There's a long pause, filled only by the moan and whine of the seething world around us.

When he speaks again it is with a grim determination.

"I don't know," Dave says, "but I'll crap in my hand and hold it till tomorrow before I drop my pants out there."

I roll over atop my mummy bag, closing my eyes to the still, hot air and the insane richness of life just beyond the walls of my tent, desperately seeking an unlikely sleep.

After all, there are some things it's simply better to not know . . .